I0446523

Data Structures
&
Program Design In
C
A Complete Reference

B. BOSE

To

Mother

<u>*My Sincere Thanks to:*</u>

Ms. Sumana Giri (*Sr. Developer IBM*)

Mr. Diganta Bhatacharyya (*M. Tech (EC), Asst. Prof. PhD Aspirant*)

Mr. Nakshatra Ghosh (*Pursuing (M. S. in Bio-Maths) University of St Andrews,*

Scotland, M. Sc (Maths) NIT, Guest Lecturer, PhD Aspirant)

<u>*References:*</u>

Blog :   www.open-sesames.blogspot.com
**   https://www.wikipedia.org**
**   Data structures using C - by Tenenbaum, Aaron M**

About The Book

This book stems from my observations of the challenges students encounter during their undergraduate and postgraduate studies, particularly in mastering data structures. *Data Structures & Program Design in C, A Complete Reference* focuses entirely on data structures, covering topics from arrays to graph theory. It delves into searching, sorting, linked lists, queues, stacks, trees, binary search trees, B-trees, balanced trees, and graph algorithms such as greedy methods, dynamic programming, backtracking, and branch & bound. Additionally, it includes nearly fifty programs with algorithms, complemented by concise theoretical explanations.

TABLE OF CONTENTS

Programs Index:

Introduction

Algorithms and data structures rank among the most crucial components in computer science. Data organisation and storage are made possible by data structures, and data processing is made possible by algorithms. Developing knowledge of data structures and algorithms will make you a better programmer. Humans use data structures in their day-to-day existence. We employ a data structure, a type of arranging strategy, in the field of computing to organise everything from our contact list to our book piles, organisational structures, and to-do lists. Data structures are the best means of organising information in the digital age.

What is Data Structures?

A data structure is an efficient way of storing a pool of data in computer memory, so it can be organised for various purposes, such as Sorting and Searching. Some examples of data structures are: Arrays, Linked Lists, Stacks, Queues, Trees, Graphs, and Hash Tables etc. Data structures are always needed for any program or software development.

Types of Data Structures

Linear Data Structure: A **non-linear data structure** is a type of data structure where elements are not arranged sequentially or in a linear fashion. In these structures, each element can be connected to multiple elements, creating a more complex hierarchy or relationship between them. Common examples of non-linear data structures include:

1. **Trees** – A hierarchical structure with a root node and child nodes (e.g., binary trees, AVL trees, etc.).
2. **Graphs** – A collection of nodes (vertices) and edges that connect pairs of nodes, representing more complex relationships (e.g., directed graphs, undirected graphs).

These structures are useful for representing more complex relationships and allow for efficient searching, traversal, and manipulation of data that cannot be easily represented by linear structures like arrays or linked lists.

Topics to be Covered

Linear Data Structure	
Array	**Linked List**
Sorting	Single Linked List
Searching	Double Linked List
Stack	Circular Linked List
Queue	Queue
1. Priority Queue	Stack
2. Circular Queue	
3. Double Ended Queue	

Non-Linear Data Structure	
Tree	**Graph**
Binary Tree	Directed Graph
Binary search Tree	Un-Directed Graph
Threaded Binary Tree	Adjacency list
AVL Tree	Adjacency matrix
Red-Black Tree	BFS & DFS
B tree	**Shortest Path Algorithm**
B+ Tree	Dijkstra's Algorithm
M-way Tree	Bellman Ford algorithm
	Minimum Spanning Tree (MST)
	Kruskal & Prims Algorithm

In the case of hash table implementation, the execution often requires the use of either linear or non-linear data structures. When collisions increase, the data may be stored in alternative non-linear structures, such as a Binary Tree, to handle these collisions effectively.

Before diving into various data structure-related programs, it's helpful to revisit some fundamental concepts that are essential for studying data structures:

1. Array.
2. Pointers.
3. Structure

Array

An array is a collection of elements of the same data type that are stored in a contiguous memory location. In computer programmes, an array is primarily used to organise data so that it may be searched or ordered as a collection.

There was always something that needed to be looked for or organised in order for that data to be stored properly. In a string array, for instance, a list of names can be organised alphabetically, descendingly, or ascendingly.

Memory occupied by an array mainly depends on the type of array and also the type of system being used, because the amount of memory that can be accessed will depend on the system used to execute the program. On a 32-bit system, it is 2^{32}. Arrays can be declared statically or dynamically. Statically, arrays can be declared globally or locally, but dynamic allocation is possible only inside the methods.

Example 1

int Arr[5];   // An array of integer types is declared statically.

int Arr[5]={ 7, 5, 9, 3, 2}; // Initializing an array with the values at the time of declaration.

An integer-type array named Arr[] for storing five user-defined numbers in the collection. If a set of numbers are stored in the same array, such as 7, 5, 9, 3, 2, it will look like.

Arr[5] ➜

Index	0	1	2	3	4
Data	7	5	9	3	2

Once an array is declared, the size of the array cannot be changed. Even if the declared array size turns out to be inadequate. To solve this problem, arrays can be declared dynamically or at runtime, and for dynamic declaration, we need pointers.

Single Dimensional Array

In a programming language, a single-dimensional array is an array with the collections of values assigned to a single index. A single-dimensional array only has one column and multiple rows, or vice-versa.

Double Dimensional Array

A double-dimensional array can be measured as a matrix. 2-D arrays can have multiple rows as well as multiple columns.

Arr[3][4] ➔ A Double Dimension Array with 3 rows and 4 columns.

Index	Data	Index	Data	Index	Data	Index	Data
[0][0]	1	[0][1]	2	[0][2]	3	[0][3]	4
[1][0]	5	[1][1]	6	[1][2]	7	[1][3]	8
[2][0]	9	[2][1]	10	[2][2]	11	[2][3]	12

Pointers

What is a Pointer?

The variables declared in a program are allocated some memory locations, and the size of the memory assigned to the variables depends on the variable type. The pointers in 'C' programming are also variables but used to store the memory addresses of other variables. The memory location where the data is stored is known as the address of that variable. The ampersand ('&') is known as the address operator. To know the exact address of a variable, one can either print the variable with an address operator or use the pointer itself. The use of pointers is much more frequent in C than in any other language, and because use of pointers has made C such a popular language.

Pointer Address-of Operator (Ampersand (&))

The ampersand is the **address-of operator**. It is used to get the memory address of a variable. When a variable is declared, an amount of memory is assigned to it at a specific location in the memory. To know the exact location of the variable, we use & operator.

Example 2

```
int n=10,*p;
p = &n;
```

Dereference operator (*)

A variable which stores the reference of another variable is called a pointer. Pointer variables should be declared using a dereference operator.

Example 3

```
int n,*p=10;
n = *p;
```

Example 4

Using an ampersand or address operator, one can print or access the address of a variable.

```
#include <stdio.h>
int main()
{
    int num = 23;
    printf("Value Stored : %d\n", num);
    printf("Address of num : Hexadecimal %p Decimal Numbers %u ", &num,&num);
    return 0;
}
```

Output

> Value Stored: 23
> Address of variable num: Hexadecimal 000000000062FE1C Decimal Numbers 6487580

Example 5

```
// Note that variable and the pointer data type should be same
#include <stdio.h>
int main()
{
    int num = 20;
    int *ptr; // pointer declaration
    ptr = &num; //Storing address of num in ptr
    printf("Value stored in num = %d \n",num);
    printf("Value at pointer using defrences operator *ptr = %d \n", *ptr);
```

```
    printf("Address of num stored in ptr = %p \n",ptr);
}
```

Output:

```
        Value stored in num = 20
        Value at pointer using deference operator *ptr = 20
        Address of num stored in ptr = 000000000062FE14
```

Example 6

```
#include<stdio.h>
int main()
  {
      int a,*a1,b;
      a=20;
      b=a;
      a1=&a;
      printf("\n Address & the Values\n");
      printf(" a = %d  &a = %p  a1  = %p *a1 = %d  b = %d \n",a,&a,a1,*a1,b);
      a=a+5;
      printf("\nPointer updated with new value\n");
      printf(" a = %d  &p = %u  a1  = %p  *a1 = %d  b = %d ",a,&a,a1,*a1,b);
  }
```

Output

```
        Address & the Values
         a = 20   &a = 000000000062FE0C  a1  = 000000000062FE0C *a1 = 20  b =
        20
        Pointer updated with new value
         a = 25   &p = 6487564  a1  = 000000000062FE0C  *a1 = 25  b = 20
```

NULL Pointers

If the pointer variable is not assigned with an address, a NULL value can
be assigned to it. Also, the pointer without any address is necessarily
assigned with NULL before being sent to a function as an argument.
NULL pointers also help in error handling.

Example 7

```
#include <stdio.h>
int main ()
  {
    int  *ptr = NULL;
```

```
    printf("The ptr valie is = %p\n", ptr );
    return 0;
}
```

Output:

The ptr value is = 0000000000000000

Arrays of Pointer

Arrays of pointers in C are arrays where each element is a pointer that can store the address of a variable, rather than the variable's value itself. This allows you to create an array of pointers that can point to different data types or locations in memory. **Eg.** datatype *arrayName[size];

Dynamic Memory Allocation

Allocation is a way to allocate memory blocks to a pointer and it is done during the execution of a program using malloc() or calloc(). Dynamic memory allocation is not regarded as a language feature because it relies on library routines.

malloc() : The malloc() function dynamically allocates memory on the heap and returns a pointer. It initializes each block with a default garbage value. The free() function can be used to free the memory blocks. malloc(s) returns a pointer with enough storage for an object of s bytes.

Return Value:

malloc() returns a pointer to the newly allocated block of memory if the operation is successful. If failed (not enough space is available for the new block), malloc() returns null.

calloc(): calloc provides access to the C memory heap, which is available for dynamic allocation of variable-sized blocks of memory. calloc() allocates a block (nitems * size) bytes and clears it to 0. To allocate a block larger than 64K, use farcalloc.

calloc(m, n) is essentially equivalent to p = malloc(m*n). It does not provide useful null pointer values or floating-point zero values since it initializes all of its bits to zero. The memory allotted by malloc or calloc can be released using the free() function..

realloc() : The realloc function is used to resize a block of memory that was previously allocated.

free(): The free() function frees the memory space allocated to a pointer, which have been returned by a malloc(), calloc() or realloc().

Example 8

int *ptr;

ptr = (int*) malloc(n * sizeof(int *));

ptr = (int*) calloc(n, sizeof(int));

free(ptr);

ptr = realloc(ptr, n);

Here, pointer is reallocated with the size of 'n' .

Difference Between malloc() and calloc()

calloc	malloc
1. calloc() requires two arguments, the number of variables for which memory should be allocated and the size of a single variable in bytes. Calloc calculates the product using two arguments.	1. Malloc() takes a single argument and allocates bytes of memory as per the argument taken during its invocation.
2. calloc() initializes the allocated memory to ZERO.	2. malloc() doesn't clear and initialize the allocated memory.
3. Whereas, calloc(n,s); returns a pointer for enough contiguous storage for *n* objects, each of *s* bytes. The storage is all initialized to zero's.	3. malloc(s); returns a pointer for enough storage for an object of s bytes.
4. Comparatively slow.	4. malloc() is fast.
p=(int *)calloc(40, sizeof(int))	p=(int *)malloc(40* sizeof(int *));

Example 9

int *p, n=10,i

p=(int *)malloc(n*sizeof(int *)); // pointer to array

```
for(i=0;i<10;i++)
  scanf("%d",&p[i]);
p=(int *)calloc( n, sizeof(int))
```

Pointer Arithmetic

An address of a variable that is stored in a pointer is a numeric value, so performing arithmetic operations on a pointer address is possible. However, a pointer is definitely NOT an integer. A pointer can be used with the arithmetic operators ++, --, +, and -. When incremented, it increases the pointer by one block of memory. So for a character pointer ++ch, ptr adds 1 byte to the address. For an integer, ++p adds 2 or 4 bytes depending on the compiler, whereas ++p adds 4 bytes to the address for floats.

Example 10

```
#include<stdio.h>
  int main()
   {
      int a[5]={12,23,34,43,21},*p,i=0;
      p=&a[0];  // array to pointer
      printf("\nPrinting array elements using Pointer\n");
      while(*p)
       {
         printf(" %d ",*p++);
       }
   }
```

Output

```
        Printing array elements using Pointer
        12  23  34  43  21
```

Function Pointer

Function Pointers are also pointer-type variables that store the address of the function and invoke the function whenever required.

Example 11

```
#include<stdio.h>
int Add (int a, int b)
  {
```

```
    return a+b;
  }
int main()
  {
    int a=15,b=25;
    int (*p) (int, int)=Add;
    int Sum = p(a, b); //function called using a function pointer
    printf("The Sum of %d and %d using Function Pointer: %d",a,b,Sum);
    return 0;
  }
```

Output

The Sum of 15 and 25 using Function Pointer: 40

Pointers pointing to another Pointer

If a pointer holds the address of another pointer, then the pointer is known as a **pointer-to-pointer, also known as a double pointer.** This has several indirections. A pointer to a pointer is a form of multiple indirection, or a chain of pointers.

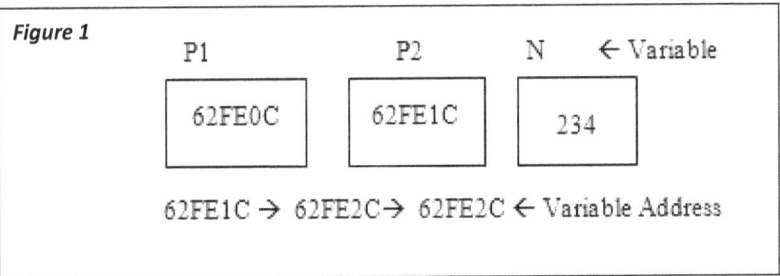

Structures & Union

Structures

Structures are a form of container, like arrays. The difference between an array and a structure is that an array can store only the same type of data, whereas a structure is a container of different data types. Structure is used to store and keep records such as, for example, an employee's details, employee name, employee number, address, salary, etc. It is possible to store all these sets of data under a single variable name as "EMPLOYEE" and it is possible to access all these parameters under one name as well, "EMPLOYEE." A structure is a group of one or more variables; usually various types of data are identified by a single name.

Structure Declaration

To declare a structure, one has to first define the contents of the structure. The same will then be applied as a template for declaring variables for that particular structure. (Example 12)

Example 12

struct EMPLOYEE

{ char emp_name[20] ;

   int age,salary; } EMP, *PTR;

Here, EMPLOYEE is the name of the structure, also known as the structure tag, and the declaration of the tag is optional. Unless a structure variable is declared, no memory is allocated for the structure elements. To allocate the memory to the structure, one has to declare a structure variable. Here, EMP and *PTR are the structure variables, also known as structure labels. Without dynamic allocation of memory, building complex data structures is not possible, and dynamic allocation is also possible for a structure if the structure is represented by a pointer.

Using Structure Elements

1. Dot operator or structure member access operator (•).
2. The structure using a pointer accessible by an arrow operator (→) is used (a hyphen – and a greater than symbol >).

Example 13

EMP.emp-name, EMP.age

          or

PTR->emp_name, PTR->age.

Nested Structures

Structures can contain other structures as their members. It is known as a nested structure.

Example 14

struct date_of_birth {

     int dd,mm,yy; };

```
struct personal {
    char name[20],address[30];
    struct date_of_birth  dob;  };
```

Array of structures

In C, arrays of structures are just as permissible as arrays of fundamental types like integers and floats. An array of structures is declared in the usual way:

Example 15

struct student

{ char name[20] ;

  int roll, eng, science, maths;} stud[5];

Union

Unions are declared in the same fashion as structures, but in the case of unions, the memory is shared. Unions have a major difference, only one item within the union can be used at any time because the memory allocated for each item inside the union is in a shared memory location. (Example 16)

Example 16

union student

 { char name[20] ;

  int roll,eng,science,maths; } stud;

Different Between Array and Structure

Array	Structure
1. In an array, all elements are of the same data type, or an array is a collection of the same type of data. 2. In an array, the components are identified by an index, like Arr[3], where 3 is the index. 3. Accessing elements in an array takes less time than structures.	1. A structure is also a container but can have different data types, or a structure is a collection of heterogeneous types of data. 2. Structure elements are access using operator (dot operator•). 3. Accessing structure elements takes more time than Arrays.

Different Between Structure and Union

Structure	Union
1. A structure is a mixture of various elements that can be predefined data types or some other predefined structures. The total size of the structure is the sum of the sizes of each element. 2. A structure allocates memory equal to the total memory required by the members. 3. In a structure, each member has their own memory space.	1. A union is also a combination of various elements. It can be predefined data types or any other predefined union. But, the size/length of unions is the maximum of internal elements. 2. The union allocates memory equal to the maximum memory required by the members of the union. 3. In a union, one block is used by all the members of the union.

typedef

A typedef is a keyword in C and C++ that is used to define an additional name for a data type. It does not create a new type, but it can be used to define an alias type for a structure label (variable) or other primitive data type too.

Dynamic Allocation Using a Pointer

PTR=(struct EMPLOYEE)malloc(sizeof(struct EMPLOYEE));

Additional Structure label can be created later by using structure name, struct EMPLOYEE EMP1;

Example 17

typedef struct

{ char name[20] ;

  int roll,eng,science,maths; } student;

student stud;

Structure Example

Example 18

```
#include <stdio.h>
#include <math.h>
//length of a line segment
int main()
    {
        float Lseg;
        struct Point
        {  int x, y;  } p1,p2;
            p1.x=8;
            p1.y=1;
            p2.x=2;
            p2.y=5;
            Lseg=pow((p2.x-p1.x),2)+pow((p2.y-p1.y),2);
            Lseg=sqrt(Lseg);
            printf("\nDistance of X1: %d X2: %d Y1: %d Y2: %d is :
%f8.2",p1.x,p2.x,p1.y,p2.y,Lseg);
    }
```

Output

Distance of X1: 8 X2: 2 Y1: 1 Y2: 5 is : 7.2111028.2

In Example 16, the structure struct Point has two elements of integer type and they are both accessed by two structure variables, p1 and p2. So in this structure, memory is shared. Ambiguity is more prevalent in union.

Union Example

Example 19

```
#include <stdio.h>
int main()
    {
        union books
        {
            char bname[20];
            int price;
        } book;
```

```
printf("\nEnter Book Name... ");
gets(book.bname);
printf("\nEnter Price... " );
scanf("%d",&book.price);
printf("\nName : %s ",book.bname);
 printf("\nPrice : %d\n",book.price);   }
```

Output

Enter Book Name... Romeo Juliet
Enter Price... 500

Name : ⌈☺
Price : 500

Example 19, In union data is not shared as the block used to store book names. It is overwritten by the price unless data is copied into another variable.

Before proceeding with the program using data structures, here are some example programs using single-dimension arrays, double-dimension arrays, structures, and pointeres.

Array Example Program

Prog-1. Maximum and Minimum in an aray.

```
#include <stdio.h>
//Maximum and Minimum
 int main()
   {
     int Arr[20],i,n,max,min;
     printf("\n\tEnter Array Size below 20 : ");
     scanf("%d",&n);
     printf("\n\tEnter %d Array Element at  : ",n);
     for(i=0;i<n;i++)
       {
          scanf("%d",&Arr[i]);
       }
     max=min=Arr[0];
     printf("\n\tNumbers in Array : ");
     for(i=0;i<n;i++)
       {
```

```
            printf("\t%d",Arr[i]);
            if(Arr[i]>max)
               {
                   max=Arr[i];
               }
            if(Arr[i]<min)
               {
                   min=Arr[i];
               }
         }
      printf("\tMaximum : %d   Minimum : %d",max,min);
      return 0;
   }
```

Output

```
            Enter Array Size below 20 : 5
            Enter 5 Array Element at  : 4 3 -1 77 45
            Numbers in Array :  4    3    -1   77   45  Maximum : 77  Minimum : -1
```

Prog-2. Intersection, union and difference.

```
#include <stdio.h>
#include <conio.h>
// Union, Intersection, Minus.
void input(int x[],int n)
   {
  int i,j;
  for(i=0;i<n;i++)
   {
     printf("\t\t");scanf("%d",&x[i]);
     for(j=i-1;j>=0;j--)
    {
      if(x[i]==x[j])
        {
        printf("\n\t\t**** Duplicate Entry, Enter again ****");
        i--;
        }
    }
   }
   }

   void print(int x[],int n)
```

```c
{
int i;
for(i=0;i<n;i++)
 {
    printf("\t%d ",x[i]);

 }
printf("\n");
 }

int inter(int x[],int y[],int z[],int n)
 {
int i,j,k=0,f;
for(i=0;i<n;i++)
 {
    f=0;
    for(j=0;j<n;j++)
    {
      if(x[i]==y[j])
        {
        f=1;
        }
    }
    if(f==1)
    z[k++]=x[i];
 }
 return k;
 }

int unions(int x[],int y[],int z[],int n)
 {
int i,j,k=0,f;
for(i=0;i<n;i++)
 {
    z[i]=x[i];
 }
k=n;
for(i=0;i<n;i++)
 {
    f=0;
    for(j=0;j<n;j++)
    {
      if(z[i]==y[j])
```

```c
      {
        f=1;
        }
    }
      if(f==0)
    z[k++]=y[i];
 }
 return k;
}

int min(int x[],int y[],int z[],int n)
{
int i,j,k=0,f;
for(i=0;i<n;i++)
 {
    f=0;
    for(j=0;j<n;j++)
  {
      if(x[i]==y[j])
        {
        f=1;
        }
    }
      if(f==0)
    z[k++]=x[i];
 }
 return k;
}

int main()
{
    int arr[10],arr1[10],un[20],intr[10],mins[10];
    int n,c;
    printf("\n\tEnter Nos. of input (Below 10 ) ");
    scanf("%d",&n);
    printf("\n\tFirst Array \n");
    input(arr,n);
    printf("\n\tSecond Array \n");
    input(arr1,n);
    printf("\n\tFirst Array : ");
    print(arr,n);
    printf("\n\tSecond Array : ");
    print(arr1,n);
```

```
        c=unions(arr,arr1,un,n);
        printf("\n\tAfter Union : ");
        print(un,c);
        printf("\n\tAfter Intersection : ");
        c=inter(arr,arr1,intr,n);
        print(intr,c);
        printf("\n\tAfter A-B  Minus : ");
        c=min(arr,arr1,mins,n);
        print(mins,c);
        printf("\n\tAfter B-A  Minus ");
        c=min(arr1,arr,mins,n);
        print(mins,c);
        return 0;
}
```

Output

```
        Enter Nos. of input (Below 10 ) 5
        First Array
            9 1 4 6 7
        Second Array
            8 2 4 5 2

            **** Duplicate Entry, Enter again ****    1
        First Array   : 9   1   4   6   7
        Second Array : 8   2   4   5   1
        After Union  : 9   1   4   6   7   8   5   1
        After Intersection :   1   4
        After A-B  Minus :   9   6   7
        After B-A  Minus    8   2   5
```

Prog-3. Array Operation

Once declared, the size of an array can't be extended or reduced. It is not possible to delete an element; instead, it is overwritten by the next item, and the number of elements remains constant. Also, if there is a valid index position given within the size, then only inserting an element is possible.

```
//Array Operation : Append, Remove, Delete and Insert in an Array
#include <stdio.h>
#include<stdlib.h>
//Add, Remove, Append and Delete in an Array
 int arr[20],c,n;
 void view(int);
```

```c
int append(int);
int del(int);
int inst(int);
int main()
  {
     int ch=0,i=0;char x;
     c=0;
     printf("\n\t\t\tHow many no. (Below 20)? : ");
     scanf("%d",&n);
     printf("\n\t\t\tEnter %d Nos : ",n);
     for(i=0;i<n;i++)
       {
          scanf("%d",&arr[i]);
       }
     c=n;
     while(ch!=5)
       {
          printf("\n\t1. Append");
          printf("\n\t2. Delete");
          printf("\n\t3. Insert");
          printf("\n\t4. View");
          printf("\n\t5. Exit\n");
          printf("\n\t\tEnter Your Choice : ");
          scanf("%d",&ch);
          switch(ch)
            {
               case 1:  c=append(c);break;
               case 2:  c=del(c);break;
               case 3:  c=inst(c);break;
               case 4:  view(c);break;
               case 5:  printf("\n\n\tQuit...");exit(0);
               default: printf("\n\tInvalid Option ");
            }
       }
        return 0;
  }
void view(int c)
  {
     int i=0;
     printf("\n\t\t\tChoice 4. View : Nos. is in Array : ");
     for(i=0;i<c;i++)
       {
```

```c
            printf("%d ",arr[i]);
        }
    }
int append(int c)
    {
        if(c>=n)
            {
                printf("\n\t\t\tChoice 1. Append : Array is Full ");
            }
        else
            {
                printf("\n\t\t\tChoice 1. Append : Enter No. to Add at the End : ");
                scanf("%d",&arr[c]);
                c++;
            }
        return c;
    }
int del(int c)
    {
        int p,i;
        printf("\n\t\t\tChoice 2. Delete : Enter Position : ");
        scanf("%d",&p);
        for(i=p;i<c;i++)
            {
                arr[i]=arr[i+1];
            }
        c--;
        return c;
    }
int inst(int c)
    {
        int p,i;
        if(c>=n)
            {
                printf("\n\t\t\tChoice 3. Insert : Array is Full ");
            }
        else
            {
                printf("\n\t\t\tChoice 3. Insert : Enter Position : ");
                scanf("%d",&p);
                for(i=c;i>=p;i--)
                    {
                        arr[i+1]=arr[i];
```

```
        }
        printf("\n\t\tEnter the no: ");
        scanf("%d",&arr[p]);
        c++;
    }
    return c;
}
```

```
                How many no. (Below 20)? : 4
                Enter 4 Nos : 1 2 3 4
        1. Append
        2. Delete
        3. Insert
        4. View
        5. Exit
            Enter Your Choice : 4
                Choice 4. View : Nos. is in Array : 1 2 3 4
            Enter Your Choice : 1
                Choice 1. Append : Array is Full
            Enter Your Choice : 2
                Choice 2. Delete : Enter Position : 2
            Enter Your Choice : 4
                Choice 4. View : Nos. is in Array : 1 2 4
            Enter Your Choice : 3
                Choice 3. Insert : Enter Position : 2
                        Enter the no: 45
            Enter Your Choice : 4
                Choice 4. View : Nos. is in Array : 1 2 45 4
            Enter Your Choice : 5
        Quit...
```

2-D Array

Prog-4. Sum of Rows, Columns and Diagonals of 2-D Array

```c
#include <stdio.h>
/*Input a 3/3 Matrix, Print the sum of rows, Columns, Left Diagonal and Rigth
Diagonal*/
  int main()
    {
        int ar[3][3];
        int i,j,c,sr=0,sc=0,sld=0,srd=0,sum=0;
        printf("\n\tEnter 9 Element for 3/3 Matrix ");
```

```c
for(i=0;i<3;i++)
    {
        for(j=0;j<3;j=j+1)
            {
                scanf("%d",&ar[i][j]);
            }
    }
//sum of row, column, left diagonal, right diagonal
printf("\n\n");
for(i=0;i<3;i=i+1)
    {
        sr=sc=0;
        for(j=0;j<3;j=j+1)
            {
                sum+=ar[i][j];
printf("%3d",ar[i][j]);
                sr+=ar[i][j]; //row sum;
                sc+=ar[j][i]; //column sum
                if(i==j)
                    {
                        sld+=ar[i][j];//left diagonal
                    }
                if(i+j==2) // 2 means n-1 right diagonal
                    {
                        srd+=ar[i][j];
                    }
            }
        printf("\tSum of row %d  Sum of column %d\n",sr,sc);
    }
    printf("\n\n\tSum of Matrix: %d Left Diagonal: %d Right Diagonal: %d\n
",sum,sld,srd);
    }
```

Output

Enter 9 Element for 3/3 Matrix 1 2 3 4 5 6 7 8 9
1 2 3   Sum of row 6 Sum of column 12
4 5 6   Sum of row 15 Sum of column 15
7 8 9   Sum of row 24 Sum of column 18
        Sum of Matrix: 45 Left Diagonal: 15 Right Diagonal: 15

** All tasks are possible because it is a square matrix, otherwise for columns, one has to switch the row loop and the column loop. Of-course diagonal sum only possible with square matrix.

Prog-5. Matrix Addition

```c
#include <stdio.h>
#define MAX 5
/* Matrix Addition*/
 void disp(int x[][MAX],int y[][MAX],int z[][MAX],int r,int c)
   {
      int i,j;
      for(i=0;i<r;i++)
        {
           printf("\t");
           for(j=0;j<c;j++)
             {
                printf("%3d ",x[i][j]);
             }
           printf(" + \t");
           for(j=0;j<c;j++)
             {
                printf("%3d ",y[i][j]);
             }
    printf(" =\t");
           for(j=0;j<c;j++)
             {
                printf("%3d ",z[i][j]);
             }
           printf("\n");
        }
   }
 void input(int x[][MAX],int r,int c)
   {
      int i,j;
      for(i=0;i<r;i++)
        {
           for(j=0;j<c;j++)
             {
                scanf("%d",&x[i][j]);
             }
        }
   }
 int main()
   {
      int a[MAX][MAX],b[MAX][MAX],c[MAX][MAX],n,m,i,j;
      printf("\n\tRow and Column Size of matrix[Below 5] : ");
```

```
scanf("%d%d",&n,&m);
printf("\n\tFirst Matrix [%d] Element: ",n*m);
input(a,n,m);
printf("\n\tSecond Matrix [%d] Element: ",n*m);
input(b,n,m);
printf("\n\tThe Matric's : \n");
for(i=0;i<n;i++)
  {
      for(j=0;j<m;j++)
          {
              c[i][j]=a[i][j]+b[i][j];
          }
  }
disp(a,b,c,n,m);
}
```

Output

Row and Column Size of matrix [Below 5] : 2 2
First Matrix [4] Element: 1 2 3 4
Second Matrix [4] Element: 4 3 2 1
The Matric's :
1 2 +   4 3 =   5 5
3 4 +   2 1 =   5 5

** Taking into consideration that both matrices are the same size, the addition was not possible, so if one is taking different sizes, then it should be checked for equality.

Prog-6. Matrix Multiplication Using pointers

Rule : c[] []= b[ ][] * c[][], with dimension of a[][]=r1 x c1 and for b[][]=r2 x c2. According to the multiplication rule the c1 and r2 should be equal. Where resultant matrix dimension will be r3=r1, c3= c2 or r1 x c2.

```
#include <conio.h>
#include <stdio.h>
#include <stdlib.h>
// Matrix Multiplication

void disp(int **Arr,int r,int c)
  {
      int i,j;
```

```c
        for(i=0;i<r;i++)
          {
              printf("\t");
              for(j=0;j<c;j++)
                 {
                     printf("%3d ",Arr[i][j]);
                 }
              printf("\n");
          }
    }
void input(int **Arr,int r,int c)
    {
        int i,j;

        for(i=0;i<r;i++)
          {
              for(j=0;j<c;j++)
                 {
                     scanf("%d",&Arr[i][j]);
                 }
          }
    }
void mmult(int **Arr1,int **Arr2,int **Arr3,int r,int c,int r1,int c1)
    {
        int i,j,k,s;
        for(i=0;i<r;i++)
          {
              for(j=0;j<c1;j++)
                 {
                     s=0;
                     for(k=0;k<r1;k++)
                       {
                           s=s+Arr1[i][k]*Arr2[k][j];
                       }
                     Arr3[i][j]=s;
                 }
          }
    }
void main()
  {
      int **M1,**M2,**M3,n,m,n1,m1,i;
       printf("\n\tEnter Row and Column of First Matrix : ");
      scanf("%d%d",&n,&m);
```

```
    printf("\n\tEnter Row and Column of Second Matrix : ");
    scanf("%d%d",&n1,&m1);
if(m!=n1)
 {
   printf("\n\tInvalid Matric's Size");
  exit(0);
 }
M1=(int **)malloc(n*sizeof(int *));
 for(i=0;i<n ;i++)
   {
      M1[i]=(int *)malloc(m*sizeof(int *));
 }
 M2=(int **)malloc(n1*sizeof(int *));
  for(i=0;i<n1 ;i++)
   {
      M2[i]=(int *)malloc(m1*sizeof(int *));
 }
 M3=(int **)malloc(n1*sizeof(int *));
  for(i=0;i<n ;i++)
   {
      M3[i]=(int *)malloc(m1*sizeof(int *));
 }
   printf("\n\tFirst Matrix [%d] Elements : ",n*m);
   input(M1,n,m);
   printf("\n\tSecond Matrix [%d] Elements : ",n1*m1);
   input(M2,n1,m1);
   mmult(M1,M2,M3,n,m,n1,m1);
   printf("\n\tFirst Matrix : \n");
   disp(M1,n,m);
   printf("\n\tSecond Matrix : \n");
  disp(M2,n1,m1);
   printf("\n\tResultant Matrix :\n ");
  disp(M3,n,m1);
 }
```

Output

```
        Enter Row and Column of First Matrix : 3 2
        Enter Row and Column of Second Matrix : 2 3
            First Matrix [6] Elements : 1 2 3 4 5 6
            Second Matrix [6] Elements : 1 2 3 4 5 6
            First Matrix :
            1  2
            3  4
```

```
        5  6
    Second Matrix :
     1  2  3
     4  5  6
    Resultant Matrix :
     9 12 15
    19 26 33
    29 40 51
```

Structure

Prog-7. Structure – Example Program

```c
// Example of Nested Structure with Array
#include <stdio.h>
#include <stdlib.h>
int main()
    {
        struct date
          {
              int dd,mm,yy;
          };
        struct emp
          {
              int ecode;
              char name[20];
              struct date jd;
              float sal;
          }*em;
        int i,n;
        float s;
        printf("\n\tEnter Nos. of Employee  : ");
        scanf("%d",&n);
        em=(struct emp *)malloc(sizeof(struct emp));
        for(i=0;i<n;i++)
          {
              printf("\n\tEnter Employee Code : ");
              scanf("%d",&em[i].ecode);
              printf("\n\tEnter Employee Name : ");
              fflush(stdin);
              gets(em[i].name);
              fflush(stdin);
              printf("\n\tEnter Employee Date of Birth : ");
              printf("\n\t\tEnter Day : ");
              scanf("%d",&em[i].jd.dd);
```

```
            printf("\n\t\tEnter Month : ");
            scanf("%d",&em[i].jd.mm);
            printf("\n\t\tEnter Year : ");
            scanf("%d",&em[i].jd.yy);
            printf("\n\tEnter Employee Salary : ");
            scanf("%f",&s);
            em[i].sal=s;
        }
    printf("\n\n\t The data \n");
    printf("\n-----------------------------------------------------------");
    printf("\n Code   Name                 Date of Join    Salary");
    printf("\n-----------------------------------------------------------");
    for(i=0;i<n;i++)
        {
    printf("\n %d\t %-20s",em[i].ecode,em[i].name);
    printf("\t%2d-%2d-%4d",em[i].jd.dd,em[i].jd.mm,em[i].jd.yy);
    printf("\t%8.2f",em[i].sal);
        }
    printf("\n-----------------------------------------------------");
    return 0;
}
```

Output

```
            Enter Nos. of Employee  : 1
            Enter Employee Code : 111
            Enter Employee Name : Anik Saha
            Enter Employee Date of Birth :
                    Enter Day : 12
                    Enter Month : 05
                    Enter Year : 1984
            Enter Employee Salary : 35000
            ----------------------------------------------------------
            Code   Name           Date of Join    Salary
            ----------------------------------------------------------
            111    Anik Saha      12- 5-1984    35000.00
            ----------------------------------------------------------
```

Recursion

Recursion is a process in which a function calls itself, typically with a termination condition. It achieves the same outcomes as an iterative statement. Any function that calls itself is referred to as a recursive function. All recursive functions must include a base case to ensure the recursion terminates at some point. Recursive functions are generally slower than non-recursive functions because they rely on the stack for their execution.

Tail and Head Recursion.

In tail recursion, the last operation of a function is the recursive call, making it similar to how traditional loops operate. In contrast, in head recursion, the recursive call occurs before any processing within the function. In head recursion, the recursive call is typically the first statement in the function, and the processing happens afterward.

The Advantages and Dis-advantages of Recursive Function.

1. Programs written using recursive techniques are shorter and simpler to write. 2. Recursion is widely used in recursive data structures such as the Binary Tree, Graph Theory, and Tower of Hanoi, among others.	1. Recursive functions are generally slower than non-recursive functions. 2. It may require a lot of memory space to hold the overhead Data on the stacks. 3. It is relatively difficult to understand the code. 4. Neither space nor time complexity is good. 5. With an improper Base-Case the program may run out of memory as it uses stacks.

Program on Recursion

Prog-8. Factorial, Using Recursive Function

```
#include<stdio.h>
long fact(int n)
 {
  if (n == 0)
   return 1;
  else
   return(n * fact(n-1));
 }
int main()
 {
  int n;
  printf("Enter a No: ");
  scanf("%d", &n);
  printf("Factorial of %d is %ld\n", n, fact(n));   }
```

Another example of Recursion – Tower of Hanoi

The Tower of Hanoi consists of three pegs (or towers) and n disks of different sizes. The disks are initially stacked in ascending order, with smaller disks placed on top of larger ones. The objective of the puzzle is to move the entire stack to another peg while following these rules:

1. Only one disk can be moved at a time.
2. A larger disk cannot be placed on top of a smaller dis.

Illustration of the Hanoi Tower using three pegs, A, B, and C, and three disks, 1, 2, and .

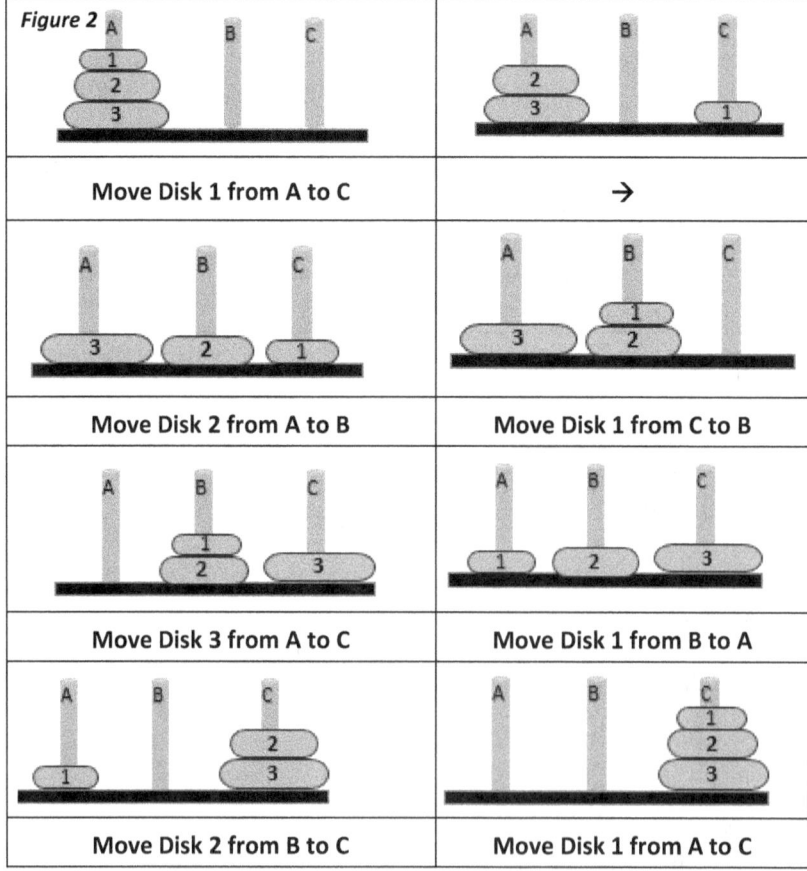

Move Disk 1 from A to C	→
Move Disk 2 from A to B	Move Disk 1 from C to B
Move Disk 3 from A to C	Move Disk 1 from B to A
Move Disk 2 from B to C	Move Disk 1 from A to C

Prog-9. Tower of Hanoi.(Recursion)

```c
#include <stdio.h>
//Tower of Hanoi
void TOH(int np, char fromP, char auxP, char toP)
{
   if(np==1)
    {
     printf("\n\tMove Disk 1 from %c to %c",fromP,toP);
     return;
    }
   else
    {
     TOH(np-1,fromP,toP,auxP);
     printf("\n\tMove disk %d from %c to %c",np,fromP,toP);
     TOH(np-1,auxP,fromP,toP);
    }
  }
int main()
{
   int n;
   printf("\nEnter number of disk : ");
   scanf("%d",&n);
   TOH(n,'A','B','C');
}
```

Output

```
Enter number of disk : 3
        Move Disk 1 from A to C
        Move disk 2 from A to B
        Move Disk 1 from C to B
        Move disk 3 from A to C
        Move Disk 1 from B to A
        Move Disk 2 from B to C
        Move Disk 1 from A to C
```

Computational Complexity Theory

Computational complexity is a broad topic that cannot be explained in just a few words. However, it is essential to provide a brief explanation, as it is impossible to discuss various data structure topics without addressing complexity.

What is Complexity?

Complexity is used to measure the amount of time and space required by an algorithm for specific input.

There are 2 types of complexity –

1. **Time complexity** – The total amount of time an algorithm takes to complete its execution.

2. **Space complexity** – Space complexity is the total amount of memory space used in an algorithm. Spaces required by instruction are known as Instruction space and spaces occupied by the data are known as Data Space. However, spaces can be reused during the duration of an algorithm's completion.

Space Complexity

Space Complexity = Auxiliary Space + Input space

Auxiliary Space = Temporary space allocated to solve a problem.

Assume that an integer needs 4 byte of memory then :

```
int a=10, b=20;
return a+b;
```

Total space required: 4 bytes each for variable **a** and **b**, as well as 4 bytes for the return statement. The total space = 12.

Time Complexity

Time complexity depends on various things, such as:

1. Processor in use for specific (32 or 64 bit) tasks.
2. Data types.
3. Compiler.
4. Implementation of the program or the programming skills of a programmer.
5. Complexity of primary algorithm.
6. Size of the input.

The Big O notation is the most common scale for calculating time complexity. The constant factors are omitted, and the running time is valued at **N**.

O(1): For a single line statement, the time Complexity will be **Constant or O(1).**

```
int a=1;
```

O(N): Linear time complexity. The running time of the loop is dependent on N, O(N).

```
for(i=1; i<=n; i++)
    {          Some Statements;          }
```

O(N²): The **Quadratic** time complexity, the following code will be **Quadratic**. Nested loop is proportional, running for N*N times. So it is O(N*N) or O(N²).

```
for(i=1; i<=n;i++)
    {
    for(j=1;j<=n;j++)
        {                    Some Statements;    }
    }
```

O(log N): Logarithmic Time is faster than O(N). Logarithmic Time uses breaking the problem into smaller sub-problems of the same size. Example: binary search.

```
while(start <= end)
    {
        mid = (start + end) / 2;
            if(val==Arr[mid])
                flag=1;
                break;
            if (val < Arr[mid])
            end = mid - 1;
            else
            start = mid + 1;  }
```

O(N log N): Linearithmic time complexity, a bit slower than a linear time complexity but quicker than a quadratic time complexity. Example: MergeSort, QuickSort.

Some other time Complexities are:

O(N³): Cubic Time, almost same as O(N²).

O(2^n) : Exponential Time is slower because of large input.

O(N!): Factorial Time is slowest of all.

Notations for Time Complexity

Asymptotic Notation:

Describes the run time of any algorithm. The time an algorithm takes with input 'N'. Time required by an algorithm can be categorized as:

1. Best Case: Execution time is minimum in best case. "more than or Equal" (Big Omega)
2. Average Case: Execution time is average. "Equal" (Big Theta)
3. Worst Case: Execution time is Maximum. "Less than or Equal" (Big Oh)
4. Little Oh denotes: "Less than" <expr> iterations.
5. Little Omega denotes: "more than" <expr> iterations.

O(expr): O stands for "order of magnitude." It measures the time taken to run a function when input grows. It gives the worst case of an algorithm's time complexity.

Big Oh O(n): This notation is the proper mode to express the upper bound of an algorithm's running time.

Omega(expr): The Big Ω notation is used to describe the best case running time for a given algorithm.

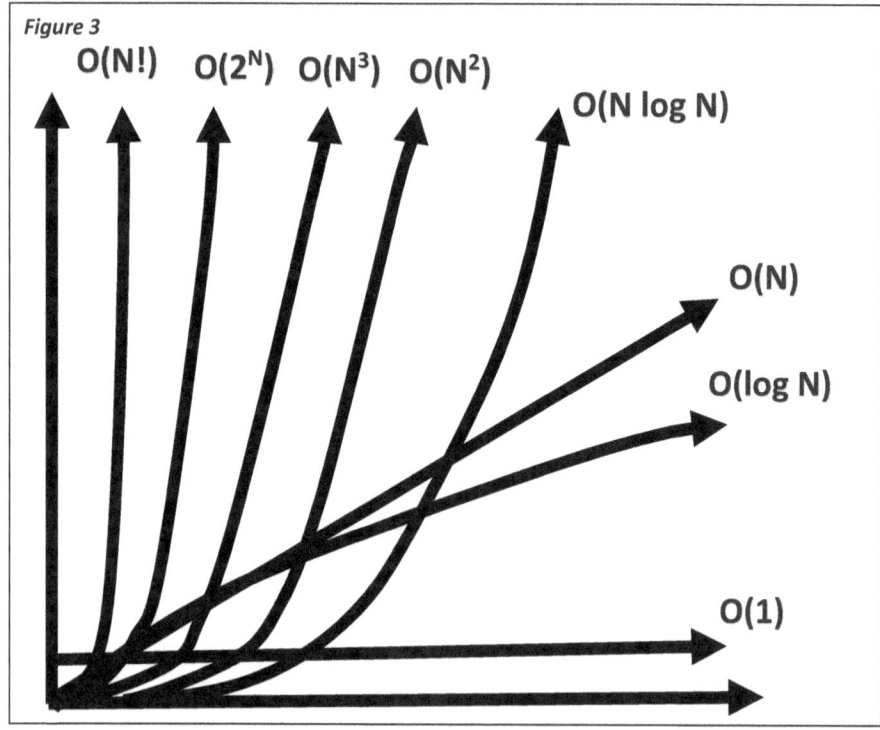

Figure 3

Theta(expr): θ consist of all the functions that lie in both Big O(expr) and Ω(expr). It specifies the average bound of an algorithm.

In other words, Big O is the upper bound in time complexity, where Omega is considered the lower bound. Theta needs both Big O and Omega, and it's referred to as a tight bound.

Let f(n) and g(n) be functions, if there exist positive constants c, f(n) is your algorithm runtime, and g(n) is an arbitrary time complexity, **n** is input, **T** is time.

Big oh (O): If f(n) & g(n) are two nonnegative functions. Such that, f(n) <= c.g(n)   [For all n>=k & where c is a constant number and we can write:

f(n) =O[g(n)], If f(n)=n^2+n+1 & f(n)=O[g(n)] then g(n)=?
Sol.: n^2+n+1 <= c(n^2)   [where c>=2]
Or, f(n) <=O(n^2) for all n>= 1. ∴ $\underline{g(n) = n^2}$

Big omega (Ω): f (n)>=c.g(n)

Big theta (Θ): c1.g(n)<=f(n)<=c2.g(n)

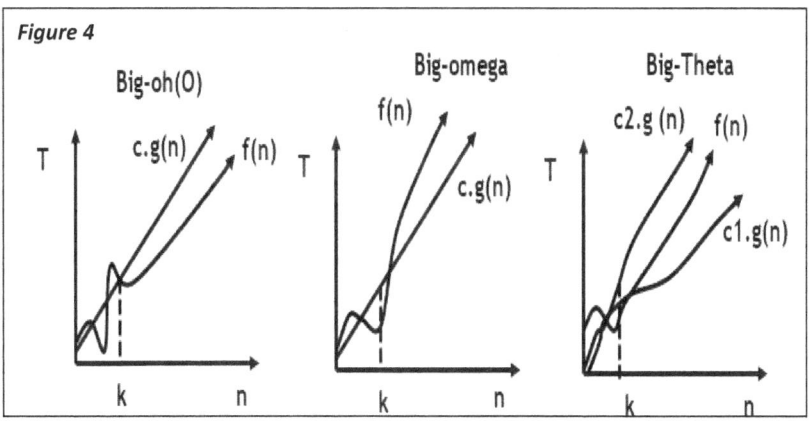

Figure 4

Algorithm

Algorithms and pseudocodes are essential topics to understand before delving into programming. In this context, some source code examples will be accompanied by their corresponding algorithm and pseudocode.

An algorithm is a set of clear and logical instructions designed to solve a specific problem. It should be written in a way that allows it to be implemented in different programming languages. Each step of the algorithm must be precise and unambiguous.

Characteristics of an algorithm:

1. **Finiteness**: An algorithm should have a fixed number of steps, so end after a finite amount of time.
2. **Effectiveness**: Each step of the algorithm must be simple.
3. **Input**: Algorithms may have inputs or no inputs.
4. **Output**: Algorithms must have at least one output.
5. **Definiteness**: Steps if the algorithm must be clear and precise. There should be no vagueness.
6. **Generality**: The algorithm applies to a set of inputs.

Advantages of Algorithms & Disadvantages

1. A step-wise depiction of a given problem and that makes it easy to understand.	1. Writing Algorithms takes lots of time.
2. An algorithm uses a fixed process.	2. Branchings and Loopings are difficult.
3. It is not reliant on any programming language, so it is easy to understand for anyone even without programming knowledge.	3. It is difficult to write algorithms for big problems.
4. The steps of the algorithm have their own logical sequence, so it is easy to correct.	
5. By using algorithms, the problem is fragmented down into tiny pieces or steps that make it easier for programmers to convert it into an actual program.	

Step 1: Accept two values to A and B

Step 2: Store sum of A and B to C

Step 3: Display C

Step 4: End

Pseudocode

Pseudocode literally means 'phony code.' It is an informal, high-level representation of actual code, used to depict the sequence of actions and instructions in an easily understandable format.

Example 20

Begin

    input A,B

    if A>B then

        Print A

    else

        print B

    end if

Array (Program & Examples).

Searching

Searching is a procedure used to find a specific item within a collection, such as an array, linked list, tree, or text file. There are several search algorithms designed to help locate the item you are looking for. Some of the commonly used search algorithms include Linear Search, Binary Search, Interpolation Search, Jump Search, Exponential Search, and Fibonacci Search. However, the first three on this list are the most widely used and will be discussed here.

Linear Search

Linear Search: It is a search method used to find an element within a list of items. A linear search, also known as a sequential search, examines each element of the list one by one. The search continues until a match is found or the entire list has been checked. This method is relatively slow. The time complexity of linear search is divided into two parts: worst case $O(n)$ and best case $O(1)$.

Algorithm.
Step 1: Accept N elements in Arr[N]
Step 2: Accept search value in S
Step 2: set 0 to I
Step 3: if Arr[i] = S then go to step 6
Step 4: Add 1 to I
Step 5: Go to Step 3

Step 6: Display the Element S is Found and go to step 8

Step 7: Display element not found

Step 8: Exit

Pseudocode.

Begin

    for i <- 0 to (n - 1) do

      if (Arr[i] = item) then

         return i-1

      End if

      End for

End

Prog-10. Linear Search

Source Code.

```c
#include <stdio.h>
//Linear Search
 int main()
   {
      int Arr[]={23,45,21,56,98,3,12,5,21},n,num,i=0,flag=0;
      n=sizeof(Arr)/sizeof(Arr[0]);
      printf("\n\tThe List : ");
      for(i=0;i<n;i++)
        {
           printf(" %d ",Arr[i]);
        }
      printf("\n\n\tEnter A Number to Search : ");
      scanf("%d",&num);
      for(i=0;i<n;i++)
        {
           if(num==Arr[i])
             {
                flag=1;
                break;
             }
        }
      if(flag==1)
        {
           printf("\n\t%d is present in %d position ",num,i+1);
        }
      else
        {
```

```
            printf("\n\t%d is not present  ",num);
        }
    return 0;
}
```

The List : 23 45 21 56 98 3 12 5 21
Enter A Number to Search : 32
32 is not present
Enter A Number to Search : 5
5 is present in 8 position

Binary Search

The Binary Search algorithm is an efficient way to search for an element in a sorted list. It is an improvement over linear search, as it divides the array in half rather than sequentially checking each element. Binary search is a 'divide and conquer' algorithm. The process begins by comparing the middle element of the array to the search term, then eliminating half of the array elements that do not meet the criteria. This method is more effective than linear search, especially for large datasets. Binary search requires a sorted list and offers better time complexity, resulting in faster execution. Its time **complexity** is **O(log n)**, making it a much faster search algorithm compared to linear search.

Algorithm.

Step 1: Accept N elements in Arr[N]

Step 2: Accept search value in S

Step 3: Compare the search element S with the middle element in the sorted list.

Step 4: If matched, display "element is found" goto step 9

Step 5: If S is smaller than middle element then repeat steps 3 to 5 with the middle element of the left sublist

Step 6: If S is larger than middle element then repeat steps 3 to 5 with the middle element of the right sublist.

Step 7: Repeat steps 3 to 7 until list or sublist contains only one element.

Step 8: If S is not found display appropriate message.

Step 9: Stop

Original Array (A[8]): (Example 1: When the search element is greater than the middle element)

Index →	0	1	2	3	4	5	6	7
Element→	5	17	3	2	8	29	4	40

After Sort

Index →	0	1	2	3	4	5	6	7
Element→	2	3	4	5	8	17	39	40

Flag Variable	Top	Last = Length-1	M = Middle (Top + Last)/2	A[M]	Search Element (Assume)	N==[M]
F=0	0	= 8-1 = 7	= (0+7)/2 = 3	5	39	False

Index →	0	1	2	3	4	5	6	7
Element→	2	3	4	5	8	17	39	40
Middle Element				↑				

N == A[M] (5 == 39) ? No

N>A[m] (39>5) ? Yes (Move the Top Position, next to M (Middle)) Top= M+1

Top = 3+1 =4 Last =7 New Middle M=(Top + Last)/2 (4+7)/2 = 5

Index →	0	1	2	3	4	5	6	7
Element→	2	3	4	5	8	17	39	40
Middle Element						↑		

N == A[m] (17 == 39) No

N>A[m] (39>17) ? Yes (Move the Top, next to M (Middle)) Top = M+1

Top = 5+1 =6 Last =7 New Middle M=(Top + Last)/2 (6+7)/2 = 6

N==A[m] (39==39) yes Found! F=1 break

Index →	0	1	2	3	4	5	6	7
Element→	2	3	4	5	8	17	39	40
							↑	

Example 1: When the search element is greater than the middle element

Flag Variable	Top	Last = Length-1	M = Middle (Top + Last)/2	A[M]	Search Element N=3 <A[M]
F=0	0	= 8-1 = 7	= (0+7)/2 = 3	5	3

Index →	0	1	2	3	4	5	6	7
Element→	2	3	4	5	8	17	39	40
				↑				

N<A[M]? 3<5 Yes (Move the Last, left of M (Middle)) Last=M-1 (3-1) Last=2

M=(Top + Last)/2 (0+2)/2 = 1

A[M] = N? yes !! Found, F=1, break;

Index →	0	1		2	3	4	5	6	7
Element→	2	3		4	5	8	17	39	40
		↑							

Pseudocode.

Arr[] ← sorted array

N   ← Array Size

S   ← value to be searched

L   ← 0 First Index

U   ← N-1 Last Index

while L<=U

    do

      M ← (U - L) / 2

   if A[M] < S then

     set L ← M + 1

   else if A[M] > x

     set U ← M - 1

   else if Arr[M] == S

    EXIT: S found

  end if

end do

Prog-11. Binary Search

```
#include <stdio.h>
//Binary Search
void sort(int A[],int n)
 {
   int i,j,temp;
   for(i=0;i<n;i++)
    {
       for(j=0;j<n-i-1;j++)
         {
             if(A[j]>A[j+1])
               {
```

```c
                    temp=A[j];
                    A[j]=A[j+1];
                    A[j+1]=temp;
                    }
            }
        }
}
int BSearch(int A[],int L, int U,int S)
    {
    int M=0;
  while(L<=U)
        {
            M=(L+U)/2;
            if(A[M]==S)
                {
                    return M;
                }
            else if(A[M]<S)
                {
                    L=M+1;
                }
            else
                {
                    U=M-1;
                }
        }
        return -1;
    }
int main()
  {
      int N,i,Arr[10],S;
      printf("Enter Size (below 10) : ");
      scanf("%d",&N);
      printf("Enter %d Elements : ",N);
      for(i=0;i<N;i++)
        {
            scanf("%d",&Arr[i]);
        }
      printf("Enter the Element to be Searched : ");
      scanf("%d",&S);
      printf("\n\tOriginal \t");
      for(i=0;i<N;i++)
        {
```

```
        printf("%d ",Arr[i]);
      }
    sort(Arr,N);
    printf("\tAfter Sorting \t");
    for(i=0;i<N;i++)
      {
        printf("%d ",Arr[i]);
      }
    i=BSearch(Arr,0,N-1,S);
    if(i>=0)
      {
        printf("\t %d is found at %d Position",S,i+1);
      }
  else
    {
      printf("\t %d is not found!! ",S);
    }
  return 0;
}
```

Output

```
            Enter the Size (below 20 ) : 5
            Enter 5 Numbers 11 23 45 65 33
            The List :  11  23  45  65  33
            Enter A Number to Search : 45
            45 is present in 3 position
            Enter A Number to Search : 55
             55 is not present
```

Interpolation Search

Interpolation Search is another efficient search technique and an improved version of binary search. One key requirement for interpolation search is that the input array must be sorted, and the values should be uniformly distributed. The algorithm uses the lowest and highest elements in the array, as well as the length of the array, to estimate the position of the searched element. The formula is as follows:

mid = low + ((S - Arr[low]) * (high - low) / (Arr[high] - Arr[low]))

Source Code.

```c
#include <stdio.h>
//Interpolation Search -
//Values already stored in Ascending order
  int InPolSearch(int Arr[],int low, int high, int S)
    {
      int mid;
      while(Arr[high] != Arr[low] && S >= Arr[low] && S <= Arr[high])
        {
          mid = low + ((S - Arr[low]) * (high - low) / (Arr[high] - Arr[low]));
          if(S == Arr[mid])
            return mid;
          if(S < Arr[mid])
            high = mid - 1;
          else
            low = mid + 1;
        }
      return -1;
    }
  int main()
    {
      int Arr[]={12,34,56,78,90,122,123,150}, i, n,S, pos;
      n=sizeof(Arr)/sizeof(Arr[0]);
      printf("\n\t\tArray Elements : ");
      for(i=0;i<n;i++)
        {
          printf("%d ",Arr[i]);
        }
      printf("\n\t\tEnter Search Value : ");
      scanf("%d",&S);
      pos=InPolSearch(Arr, 0, n-1, S);
      if(pos>=0)
        {
          printf("\n\t\t%d is present in %d position",S,pos+1);
        }
      else
        {
          printf("\n\t\t%d is not found", S);
        }
      return 0;
}
```

Array Elements : 12 34 56 78 90 122 123 150
Enter Search Value : 90
90 is present in 5 position
Enter Search Value : 135
135 is not found

**Bubble sort used in above searching, can referred to any sort described Below.

Sorting

Sorting is an algorithm that rearranges the positions of elements in an array so that all of its elements are ordered in either ascending or descending order. In other words, a sorting algorithm performs operations to arrange a list in a specific order, whether alphabetical or numerical. Sorting is used to create a sorted list from a collection of data. The list can be an array, a linked list, a database, etc.

Like searching, there are many sorting algorithms available. In terms of complexity, some of these algorithms perform well on small datasets but become very slow as the data size increases. Some algorithms are faster than others, some use less memory space, and certain sorting algorithms may be more suitable for specific types of data. As the number of inputs grows, the performance of sorting algorithms can vary. It is impossible to find one algorithm that is ideal for every situation. For instance, QuickSort is generally faster than MergeSort, but in certain cases, it can perform as slowly as Bubble Sort.

Some common sorting algorithms include: Bubble Sort, Selection Sort, Insertion Sort, QuickSort, Merge Sort, HeapSort, Radix Sort, ShellSort, Comb Sort, Counting Sort, Bucket Sort, and many more. The first seven algorithms will be discussed here.

Bubble Sort

In the bubble sort algorithm, the list is repeatedly checked starting from the 0th element. Each adjacent pair of elements is compared, and they are swapped if they are not in the desired order. The largest (or smallest) item is pushed to the end of the list, and the process is repeated from the beginning up to the last element that is not yet correctly positioned. This continues until the entire list is sorted..

- Let n = array length = the size of the array

- The outer loop is executed n-1 times
- Each time the outer loop is executed, the inner loop is executed
- The Inner loop executes n-1 times at first, linearly dropping to just once
- On average, the inner loop executes about n/2 times for each execution of the outer loop
- In the inner loop, the comparison is always done (constant time), the swap might be done (also constant time). The number of comparisons is : n −1 + n −2 + ... + 2 + 1 = O(n^2)

Complexity :

Best-Case Analysis

If the elements in the list are in sorted order, then the loop will compare the adjacent pairs but not make any changes.

So the swapping of the elements will still be false and the loop is only done once.

In the best case, there are N - 1 comparisons

Worst-Case Analysis

- If in the best case, the loop is done once, in the worst case, the loop must be done as many as possible times.
- The number of comparisons will be: : n^2

Average-Case Analysis

- We can potentially stop after any of the (at most) N − 1 passes of the loop
- On the first pass, we do N − 1 comparisons and so on the second pass N − 2 comparisons
- Average Case, number of comparisons will be:: n^2

Pass	0	1	2	3	4	Remark
	7	3	5	8	2	Compared the first two numbers 7>3. True, Swap
	3	7	5	8	2	Compared the next two numbers 7>5. True, Swap
Pass-1	3	5	7	8	2	The next two numbers 7<8. False, No changes
	3	5	7	8	2	The next two numbers 8>2. True, Swap
	3	5	7	2	8	After Pass-1 the Largest No. Pushed to the last position, continue same from 0 to rest
	3	5	7	2	8	The next two numbers 3>5 False. No changes
Pass-2	3	5	7	2	8	The next two numbers 5<7. False. No changes
	3	5	7	2	8	The next two numbers 7>2. True, Swap
	3	5	2	7	8	After Pass-2
	3	5	2	7	8	The next two numbers 3<5. False, No changes
Pass-3	3	5	2	7	8	The next two numbers 5>2. True, Swap
	3	2	5	7	8	After Pass-3
Pass-4	3	2	5	7	8	First two numbers 3>2. True, Swap
	2	3	5	7	8	Finally List is Sorted in Ascending order

Algorithm

1. Start first loop from 0 to N-1
2. Starting with the array index of 0, compare the present element with the adjacent element.
3. If the present element is greater than the next element, swap the element.
4. If NOT, then move to the next element. Repeat Step 2 and Step 3 until index <N-1.
5. Repeat step 1

Pseudocode

```
for i ← 0 to n-1
    do
    for j ← 0 to n-i-1
    do
        If A[j] > A[j-1] then
                A[j-1]↔ A[j]
        end for j
    end for i
```

Prog-13. Bubble Sort

```c
#include <stdio.h>
//BUBBLE SORT
  void BubbleSort(int arr[],int size)//Sort Function
    {
        int i,j,tmp;
        for(i=0;i<size;i++)
          {
            for(j=0;j<size-i-1;j++)
              {
                if( arr[j]>arr[j+1] )
                  {
                    tmp = arr[j];
                    arr[j] = arr[j+1];
                    arr[j+1] = tmp;
                  }
              }
          }
    }
//Main Function
 int main()
    {
      int i,n,c=0;
      int Arr[]={45,32,12,88,65,78};
      n=sizeof(Arr)/sizeof(Arr[0]);
      printf("\n\tBefore Sort     : ");
      for(i=0 ;i<n;i++)
        {
          printf("%d ",Arr[i]);
        }
      printf("\n\tAfter Bubble  Sort : ");
      BubbleSort(Arr,n);
      for(i=0 ;i<n;i++)
        {
          printf("%d ",Arr[i]);
        }
    }
```

Output

```
Before Sort     : 45 32 12 88 65 78
After Bubble  Sort : 12 32 45 65 78 88
```

Selection Sort

Selection sort is an improvement over bubble sort, as it makes only one swap per pass. In selection sort, the smallest value in the unsorted portion of the array is found, and after each pass, the minimum value is swapped with the current element (or vice versa). However, selection sort is not recommended for sorting large datasets due to its inefficiency.

- Let n = array length = the size of the array
- The outer loop is executed n-1 times
- Each time the outer loop is executed, the inner loop is executed
- Inner loop executes starting from outer loop +1 to n-1
- In the inner loop, the comparison is always done, swap the current value with the minimum of the list and move down until N-1. The number of comparisons is : n −1 + n −2 + ... + 2 + 1 = $O(n^2)$

Complexity :

Best-Case Analysis

- There are N − 1 comparisons in the best case

Worst-Case Analysis

- The number of comparisons will be: : n^2

Average-Case Analysis

- Average Case: n^2

Index	A[]	@ Pass2	@ Pass3	@ Pass4
0	4	2	2	2
1	9	9	4	4
2	2	4	9	6
3	8	8	8	8
4	6	6	6	9

Pass 1	Pass 2	Pass 3	Pass 4
S=A[0]	S=A[1] S=9 P=1	S=A[2] S=9 P=2	S=A[3] S=8
P=0	A[2]<S →True S=4	A[2]<S →True S=8	P=3
If A[1]<S No – Cont.	P=2	P=3	
A[2]<S →True S=2	A[3]<S →False – Cont.	A[4]<S →True S=6	A[4]<S →False
P=2		P=4	
A[3]<S →False	A[4]<S →False – Cont.	A[2] ↔ A[P]	
A[4]<S →False – Cont.	A[1] ↔ A[P]		
A[0] ↔ A[P]			

Passes	0	1	2	3	4	Remark
	7	3	8	5	2	Start with the 0th element and proceed down to find the smallest finally the 4th element is the smallest in the list. Swap 0th element with 4th element
Pass-1	7 ↑	3	8	5	2 ↑	
	2	3	8	5	7	
Pass-2	2	3 ↑	8	5	7	Move to next and 3 is the smallest in the remaining list, so no change happens
Pass-3	2	3	8 ↑	5 ↑	7	The next 8 and smallest in the list is 5, swap between 2nd element and 3rd
	2	3	5	8	7	
Pass-4	2	3	5	8 ↑	7 ↑	Starts with 3rd and the last element in 4th position is smaller, so swap the value.
	2	3	5	7	8	Final list after completion

Following the first pass, found the smallest no in the third position and swapped it with 0th. Then, starting from the 1st element, finding the smallest at 1st only. Then from 2nd onwards, repeat the same until it is sorted.

Algorithm

1. Step 1 : Execute outer loop from 0 to N-1
2. Step 2 : Store 0 element to MIN
3. Step 3 : Search the minimum in the list
4. Step 4 : Swap the value with the started position
5. Step 5 : Repeat until list is sorted

Pseudocode

```
for i ←1 to n-1
    min ← i;
    x ← A[i]
    for j = i + 1 to n
        do
            If A[j] < min  then
                m← j
                x← A[j]
            end if
        end for j
    A[i] ↔ A [m]
end for i
```

Prog-14. Selection Sort

```
#include <stdio.h>
#include <stdlib.h>   //for malloc()
// SELECTION SORT
void SelectionSort(int arr[],int size) //Function for Sorting the list
    {
        int i,j,min,pos,t;
        for(i = 0;i<size-1;i++)
            {
                min = arr[i];
                pos = i;
                for(j = i+1;j<size;j++)
                    {
                        if(arr[j]<min)
                            {
                                min = arr[j];
                                pos = j;
                            }
```

DS -53

```c
            }
        t=arr[i];
        arr[i]=arr[pos];
        arr[pos]=t;
        }
    }
//Main Function
  int main()
    {
        int i,n,c=0;
        int *Arr;
        printf("\n\tEnter size of Array  : ");
        scanf("%d",&n);
        Arr=(int *)malloc(n*sizeof(int *)); //Dynamic allocation
        printf("\tEnter [%d] Nos. : ",n);
        for(i=0 ;i<n;i++)
          {
            scanf("%d",&Arr[i]);
          }
        printf("\n\tBefore Sort       : ");
        for(i=0 ;i<n;i++)
          {
            printf("%d  ",Arr[i]);
          }
        printf("\n\tAfter Selection  Sort : ");
        SelectionSort(Arr,n);
        for(i=0 ;i<n;i++)
          {
            printf("%d  ",Arr[i]);
          }
    }
```

Output

```
Enter size of Array  : 6
Enter [6] Nos. : 45  32  12  88  65  78
Before Sort       : 45  32  12  88  65  78
After Selection  Sort : 12  32  45  65  78  88
```

*** *For each of the above source codes, a proper main function is included, and arrays are input in various ways. However, for all subsequent programs, the main function will be omitted unless explicitly required. Examples of different methods for inputting arrays are also provided and can be used as needed.*

Insertion Sort

Insertion sort is a simple sorting algorithm that works efficiently for small lists. It assumes the first element of the list is already sorted, then processes the remaining elements one by one, inserting each into its correct position. Unlike other algorithms that rely on swapping, insertion sort shifts elements to achieve the correct order. While effective for small datasets, it is not well-suited for larger ones due to its time complexity.

The outer loop runs N−1N - 1N−1 times, starting from the second element of the list. The inner loop performs most of its work when the current element is smaller than the preceding elements. During each iteration, the current element is compared with all previous elements to find its correct position.

- down until N-1. The number of comparisons is : $n-1 + n-2 + ... + 2 + 1 = O(n^2)$

Complexity :

Best-Case Analysis
- There are $N - 1$ comparisons in the best case

Worst-Case Analysis
- The number of comparisons will be: : n^2

Average-Case Analysis
- Potentially stop after any of the (at most) $N - 1$ passes of the for loop
- Average Case: n^2

AArray [5]: [6, 4, 9, 8, 3]

Pass	Element	Comparing and shifting	Updated Array
Start	-	Initial list	[6, 4, 9, 8, 3]
1	4	Compare 4 with 6, shift 6 to the right	[4, 6, 9, 8, 3]
2	9	9 is larger than 6 (no shifts)	[4, 6, 9, 8, 3]
3	8	Compare 8 with 9, shift 9 to the right	[4, 6, 8, 9, 3]
		Compare 8 with 6 (no further shifts)	[4, 6, 8, 9, 3]
4	3	Compare 3 with 9, shift 9 to the right	[4, 6, 8, 9, -]
		Compare 3 with 8, shift 8 to the right	[4, 6, 8, -, -]
		Compare 3 with 6, shift 6 to the right	[4, -, -, -, -]
		Compare 3 with 4, shift 4 to the right	[-, -, -, -, -]
		Insert 3 in the correct position	[3, 4, 6, 8, 9]

Algorithm

1. Step 1 : Execute outer loop from 1 to N-1
2. Step 2 : Store current element to X
3. Step 3 : Search the lesser in the list
4. Step 4 : Move the value to correct position
5. Step 5: Store value of X in the current position
6. Step 5 : Repeat until list is sorted

Pseudocode

```
for i ← 1 to n-1 do
    do
        value ← A[i];
        j ← i;
        repeat until j>0 && A[j-1] > value
            do
                A[j ] ← A[j-1];
                j ← j - 1;
        end
        A[j] ← value;
    end for i
```

Prog-15. Insertion Sort

```
//Function for Sorting
void InsertionSort(int arr[],int size)
    {
        int i,j;
        int tmp;
        for(i=1;i<size;i++)
          {
              tmp = arr[i];
              j=i;
              while(j>0 && arr[j-1]>tmp)
                 {
                     arr[j] = arr[j-1];
                     j--;
                 }
              arr[j]=tmp;
          }
    }
```

Output

```
Enter size of Array : 5
Before Sort      : 12 43 5 67 3
After Insertion Sort : 3 5 12 43 67
```

Quick Sort

Quicksort is a divide and conquer algorithm. A pivot is selected to partition the array into two parts. Move all smaller elements to the left of the pivot and the greater elements after it. Finally, recursively sort the lesser and greater sub-arrays until the whole array is not properly sorted. The most complex issue in quicksort is choosing a good pivot element. Poor pivot selection can result in extremely slow $O(n^2)$ performance, but if we choose the middle as the pivot at each step, it works in O(n log n).

Complexity :

Quick sort relation

$$T(n)=2T(n2)+O(n)$$

Worst-case

When the unbalanced partitions possible, then the original call takes n time

T(n) = T(n-2) + O(n) time complexity is O(n^2)

Best-case
pivot always middle element

O(n*log n)

- Average-case
- O(n*log n)

Average-Case Analysis

- Potentially stop after any of the (at most) N − 1 passes of the for loop
- Average Case: n^2

Function QSort()

    Left =0   Right =5

    Pivot =A[(Left + Right)/2] A

    i=Left   j=Right

i 0 a[i] =88   j=5 a[j] = 77 Pivot = 55

Step	Current List	Pivot	Left (Smaller)	Right (Larger)	Result
1	[88, 99, 55, 33, 22, 77]	55	[33, 22]	[88, 99, 77]	[33, 22, 55, 88, 99, 77]
2a	[33, 22]	33	[22]	[]	[22, 33]
2b	[88, 99, 77]	99	[88, 77]	[]	[77, 88, 99]
Final	[22, 33] + [55] + [77, 88, 99]	-	-	-	[22, 33, 55, 77, 88, 99]

1. **Initial Split (Pivot = 55):**
   a. Split the list into elements smaller than 55 ([33, 22]) and elements larger than 55 ([88, 99, 77]).
3. **Recursive Steps:**
   b. Sort [33, 22] with pivot 33: [22] (smaller), and nothing larger ([]).
   c. Sort [88, 99, 77] with pivot 99: [88, 77] (smaller), and nothing larger ([]).
4. **Combine Results:**
   d. Combine sorted parts: [22, 33], pivot 55, and [77, 88, 99].

All elements smaller than the pivot will be shifted to the left of the pivot, while the larger one will be shifted to the right. Now repeat the above with both sub-arrays recursively while changing the starting and last position of both sub-arrays.

```
if (left <j)   QSort(a,left,j); // This first half of array
if (i <right)  QSort(a,i,right); // This is second half of aray
```

Algorithm
1. Pick pivot P from the list, left most, right most or middle element.
2. Partition the list into two subgroups. The left subgroup is < P and the right subgroup is > P.
3. Quick sort first subgroup and last subgroup recursively.

Picking the pivot
1. Choose the first element
   - Bad for pre-sorted data
2. Choose randomly

- Random number generation can be very over the odds.
3. Choose median of left, right, and center
    - Good choice!

Pseudocode

```
QSort(A[], left , rightt)
    begin
        i ← left
        j ← right
        Pivot ← A[(left+right)/2]
        Repeat until i<=j
            do
                repeat i<right and A[i] <Pivot i++
                repeat j>left and A[j] >Pivot j--
            swap A[i] ↔ A[j]
        end loop
        if  left >j then Qsort(A,left,j);
        if i<right then Qsort(A,i,right)
    end
```

Prog-16. Quick Sort

Source Code
```
//Function for Sorting Qsort(A,0,n-1)
void QSort(int a[],int left,int right)
    {
        int i,j;
        int x,temp;
        i=left;
        j=right;
        x=a[(left+right)/2];
        do
          {
            while(a[i] <x&& i <right)
                ++i;
            while(a[j] >x && j >left)
                --j;
            if (i <=j)
              {
                temp=a[i];
                a[i]=a[j];
```

```
            a[j]=temp;
            ++i;
            --j;
        }
    } while(i <=j);
    if (left <j)
        QSort(a,left,j);
    if (i <right)
        QSort(a,i,right);
}
```

Output

Enter Size of Array : 6

Enter 6 values in array : 88 99 55 33 22 77

Original : 88 99 55 33 22 77

Sorted Values : 22 33 55 77 88 99

Merge sort

A merge sort follows a divide-and-conquer algorithm. The original array is fragmented into halves and then further subdivided until no further division is possible, as it eventually reaches an array with a single element and no middle number to divide. Each divided sub-array is then sorted and subsequently merged with the other sub-arrays. This process is repeated until all divisions of the array have been merged, resulting in a sorted array.

Complexity :

Best case performance : $O(n \log n)$ *typical,*

 $O(n)$ *natural variant*

Average case performance   : $O(n \log n)$

Worst case space complexity : $O(n \log n)$

$O(n)$ *auxiliary*

Algorithm

1. Start
2. Store N elements in Arr[N]
3. Store 0 to start and N-1 to end
4. Find mid = start+(start + end)/2
5. Procedure msort(Arr,start,,mid) to sort first half recursively

6. Procedure msort(Arr,mid+1,end) to sort second half recursively
7. Procedure merge(Arr, start, mid, end) to merge sorted arrays.
8. End

Array[6] : [9, 8, 22, 11, 10, 2]:

Step	Action	Result
1	Initial List	[9, 8, 22, 11, 10, 2]
2	Split into two halves	[9, 8, 22] and [11, 10, 2]
3	Split [9, 8, 22] further	[9] and [8, 22]
4	Split [8, 22] further	[8] and [22]
5	Merge [8] and [22]	[8, 22]
6	Merge [9] and [8, 22]	[8, 9, 22]
7	Split [11, 10, 2] further	[11] and [10, 2]
8	Split [10, 2] further	[10] and [2]
9	Merge [10] and [2]	[2, 10]
10	Merge [11] and [2, 10]	[2, 10, 11]
11	Merge [8, 9, 22] and [2, 10, 11]	[2, 8, 9, 10, 11, 22]

Explanation:

1. The **list is divided** into halves recursively until each sublist contains only one element.
2. These single-element sublists are considered sorted.
3. The sorted sublists are **merged back together** step by step:
   - First merging pairs of single-element sublists.
   - Then merging the sorted sublists from previous steps.
4. Finally, the entire list is merged into one sorted array: [2, 8, 9, 10, 11, 22].

Pseudocode

```
    Merge_Sort (A, left, right)
if   left ≥ right   return
else
    middle ← b(left+right)/2û
```

Merge-Sort(A, left, middle)

Merge-Sort(A, middle+1, right)

Merge(A, left, middle, right)

Merge(A, left, middle, right)

n1 ← middle − left + 1

n2 ← right − middle

create array L[n1], R[n2]

for i ← 0 to n1-1 do L[i] ← A[left +i]

for j ← 0 to n2-1 do R[j] ← A[middle+j]

k ← i ← j ← 0

while i < n1 & j < n2

if L[i] < R[j]

A[k++] ← L[i++]

else

A[k++] ←R[j++]

while i < n1

A[k++] ← L[i++]

while j < n2

A[k++] ← R[j++]

Prog-17. Merge Sort

```
#include <stdio.h>
 void merge(int Ar[], int l, int m, int r)
   {
     int n1 = m - l + 1;
     int n2 = r - m;
     int i,j;
      //Two Arrays store data into sub-arrays
     int Left[n1], Right[n2];
     for (i = 0; i < n1; i++)
       Left[i] = Ar[l + i];
     for (j = 0; j < n2; j++)
       Right[j] = Ar[m + 1 + j];
     i = 0;
     j = 0;
     int k = l
    //Elements transferred from sub-arrays to the original
    while (i < n1 && j < n2)
       {
         if (Left[i] <= Right[j])
```

```
            {
                Ar[k] = Left[i++];
            }
        else
            {
                Ar[k] = Right[j++];
            }
        k++;
        }
    while (i<n1)
        {
            Ar[k++] = Left[i++];
        }
    while (j < n2)
        {
            Ar[k++] = Right[j++];
        }
}
//Recursively divides the array into halves
 void mergeSort(int Ar[],int left,int right)
    {
        if(left>=right)
            {
                return;
            }
        int mid = (left+right-1)/2;
        mergeSort(Ar,left,mid);
        mergeSort(Ar,mid+1,right);
        merge(Ar,left,mid,right);
    }
 void Display(int A[], int size)
    {
        int i;
        for (i = 0; i < size; i++)
            {
                printf(" %d  ",A[i]);
            }
    }
```

Output

Original Array : 75 22 21 33 54 62 45

After Sorting : 21 22 33 45 54 62 75

Heap sort

Heap Sort is a comparison-based sorting algorithm that uses a binary heap data structure to sort elements. It is efficient and has a time complexity of O(n log n) for all cases. The Heap Sort algorithm is highly efficient. It determines the largest or smallest element of a list, places it at the end (or beginning), and repeats this process for the remaining elements. This is achieved using a data structure called a heap, a specialized binary tree. Once the list is transformed into a heap, the root node is guaranteed to be the largest (or smallest) element. After removing and placing this element at the list's end, the heap is reorganized so the next largest element becomes the root. Using a heap allows finding the next largest element in O(log n) time, compared to O(n).

Heapify: is an operation that is used to sustain the heap property of the binary heap. The heap property is that in max heap, every parent node is greater than or equal to its child nodes, and, in min heap, every parent node is smaller than or equal to its child nodes.

Heapification: Building a heap from an unordered array.

Removing the root element and replacing it with the last element of the heap.

How Heapify Works

The procedure repairs the heap property by checking if a node is smaller or larger than its children, and swaps them accordingly

Max Heapify Procedure for a Max Heap:

Start with a node (the root of the subtree). Compare the node with its left and right children. if one of the children is larger than the node, swap the node with the largest child.

Recursively apply the process to the affected child node until the heap property is restored. For a min heap, the steps are similar but you compare the node with its children and swap it with the smallest child.

###Max Heap Construction**

Input array: [13, 19, 12, 11, 14, 15]

1. Represent the array as a binary tree.

```
        13
       /  \
      19   12
     / \  /
    11 14 15
```

2. Start heapifying from the last non-leaf node (`index = ⌊n/2⌋ - 1` where `n = 6`).
   - Last non-leaf node: Index 2 (value 12).
3. Perform **heapify** on index 2 (value 12):
   - Compare value 12 with its children (15). Swap 12 with 15.

```
        13
       /  \
      19   15
     / \  /
    11 14 12
```

4. Move to index 1 (value 19):
   - Compare value 19 with its children (11, 14). No swap needed.
5. Move to index 0 (value 13):
   - Compare value 13 with its children (19, 15). Swap 13 with 19.
   - - Updated tree:

```
        19
       /  \
      13   15
     / \  /
    11 14 12
```

   - Compare 13 with its new children (11, 14). Swap 13 with 14.
   - Final tree:

```
        19
       /  \
      14   15
     / \  /
    11 13 12
```

Max heap result: **[19, 14, 15, 11, 13, 12]**

Min Heap Construction**

Input array: [13, 19, 12, 11, 14, 15]

1. Represent the array as a binary tree.

```
        13
       /  \
      19   12
     / \  /
    11 14 15
```

2. Start heapifying from the last non-leaf node (`index = ⌊n/2⌋ - 1` where `n = 6`).
   - Last non-leaf node: Index 2 (value 12).
3. Perform **heapify** on index 2 (value 12):
   - Compare value 12 with its children (15). No swap needed.
4. Move to index 1 (value 19):
   - Compare value 19 with its children (11, 14). Swap 19 with 11.

```
        13
       /  \
      11   12
     / \  /
    19 14 15
```

5. Move to index 0 (value 13):
- Compare value 13 with its children (11, 12). Swap 13 with 11.
   - Updated tree:

```
        11
       /  \
      13   12
     / \  /
    19 14 15
```

Min heap result: **[11, 13, 12, 19, 14, 15]**

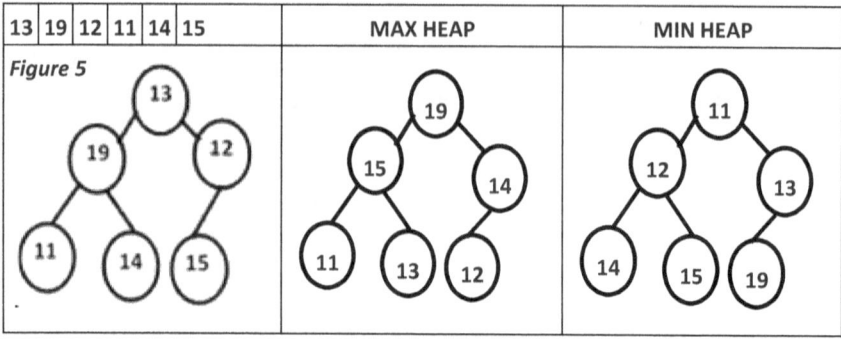

| 13 | 19 | 12 | 11 | 14 | 15 | MAX HEAP | MIN HEAP |

Figure 5

Figure 6

| 16 | 20 | 11 | 8 | 18 | 17 |

1. 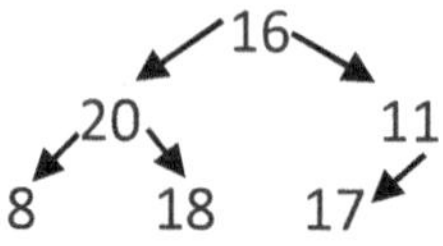
```
      16
   20      11
  8  18  17
```

2. 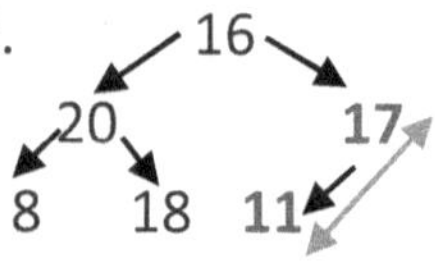
```
      16
   20      17
  8  18  11
```

3. 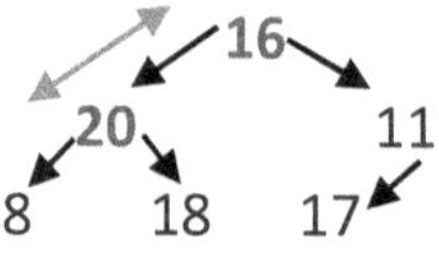
```
      16
   20      11
  8  18  17
```

4. 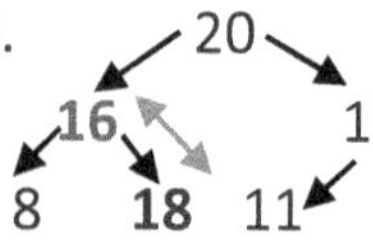
```
      20
   16      17
  8  18  11
```

5. 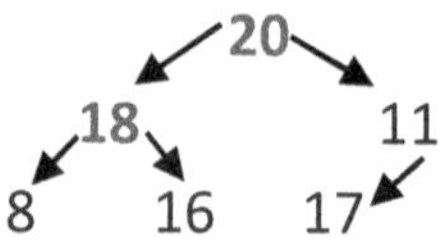
```
      20
   18      11
  8  16  17
```

6. 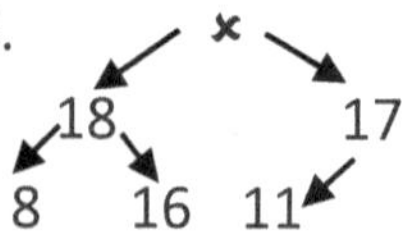
```
      ✗
   18      17
  8  16  11
```

Remove the top element and store it in a temporary variable and then swap with last element and rebuild the heap

20

	18	17	8	16	11
11	18	17	8	16	20

7. 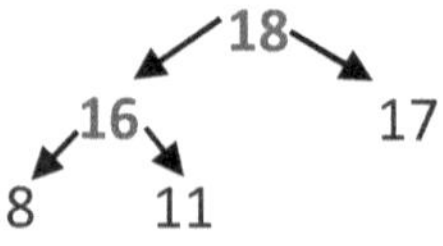
```
      18
   16      17
  8  11
```

18	16	17	8	11	20

18

| 11 | 16 | 17 | 8 | 18 | 20 |

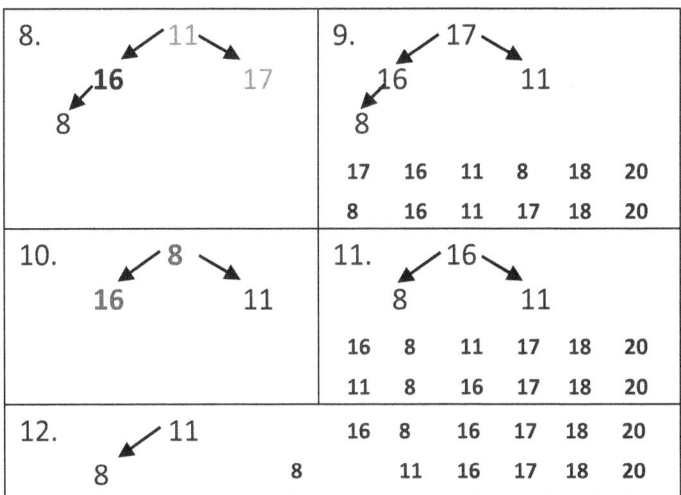

8.	9.
	17 16 11 8 18 20
	8 16 11 17 18 20
10.	11.
	16 8 11 17 18 20
	11 8 16 17 18 20
12.	16 8 16 17 18 20
	11 16 17 18 20

Complexity :

Best case performance :   O(n log n) typical,

Average case performance   :   O(n log n)

Worst case space complexity :   O(n log n)

Space Complexity: O(1), as heapify works in-place.

Algorithm

1. Start
2. Step 1 : Creating a Heap of the unsorted list/array.
3. Step 2 : Turn the Binary Tree into Min Heap or Max Heap as needed.
4. Step 3 : Remove the root element.
5. Step 4 : Place the deleted element at the end of the list.
6. Step 5 : Repeat until Min Heap or Max Heap is left with zero element
7. Stop

Pseudocode

BUILD_HEAP

```
    Size (A) ←length [A]
    for i ←length[A]/2 down to 1 do
        Heapify (A, i)
```

SORT

```
    BUILD_HEAP (A)
    for i ← length (A) down to 2 do
        exchange A[1] ⮀ A[i]
    Size [A] ← heap-size [A] - 1
```

Heapify (A, 1)

HEAPIFY

    l ← left [i]

    r← right [i]

    if l ≤ Size [A] and A[l] > A[i] then

        largest ← l

    else

        largest ← i

    if r ≤ Size [A] and A[i] > A[largest] then

        largest ← r

    if largest ≠ i

        then exchange A[i] ←A[largest]

    Heapify (A, largest)

Prog-18. Heap Sort

```c
#include <stdio.h>
//Heapsort
 void HeapSort(int ar[], int n)
    {
      int i,j;
      int lf, rt, mid, val, num;
      val = (n-1)/2;
      for(j=val;j>=0;j--)
        {
          for(i=val;i>=0;i--)
            {
              lf = (2*i)+1;
              rt = (2*i)+2;
              if ((lf <= n) && (rt <= n))
                {
                  if(ar[rt] >= ar[lf])
                    {
                              mid = rt;
                    }
                  else
                    {
                              mid = lf;
                    }
                }
              else
                {
```

```
                  if(rt > n)
                    {
                              mid = lf;
                    }
                  else
                    {
                              mid = rt;
                    }
                }
            if (ar[i] < ar[mid])
              {
                 num = ar[i];
                 ar[i] = ar[mid];
                 ar[mid] = num;
              }
          }
      }
    num = ar[0];
    ar[0] = ar[n];
    ar[n] = num;
  }
//Main Function
  void main(void)
  {
      int i,n;
      int a[]={45,34,12,326,76,98,76};
      n=sizeof(a)/sizeof(a[0]);
      printf("\n\tOriginal   : ");
      for(i=0 ;i<n;i++)
        {
          printf("%d ",a[i]);
        }
      for(i=n; i>1; i--)
        {
          HeapSort(a,i-1);
        }
      printf("\n\tAfter Sort : ");
      for(i=0 ;i<n;i++)
        {
          printf("%d ",a[i]);
        }
  }
```

Output

> Original : 45 34 12 326 76 98 76
>
> After Sort : 12 34 45 76 76 98 326

Radix Sort

Instead of sorting the entire list using whole numbers, radix sort focuses on sorting the digits of the numbers individually, from right to left. The radix sort algorithm works exclusively for a list of integers. The numbers are sorted based on their individual digits. Radix sort is applied to each digit of the numbers, starting with the least significant digit least significant digit (right most -LSD) to the most significant digit (left most - MSD).

465	21	1	654	83	7

Sort by LSB			Sort by Last Digit		Move left ←	Sort middle Digit	Move Left ←		First Digit Sorted
4	5	6	0	2	1	0	0	1	001
0	2	1	0	0	1	0	0	7	007
0	0	1	0	8	3	0	2	1	021
6	5	4	6	5	4	6	5	4	083
0	8	3	4	5	6	4	5	6	456
0	0	7	0	0	7	0	8	3	654

Prog-19. Radix Sort

```c
#include <stdio.h>
#include <stdlib.h>
//find the Maximum element
  int maximum(int arr[], int n)
    {
      int max = arr[0], i;
    for (i = 1; i < n; i++)
        {
        if (arr[i] > max)
        max = arr[i];
        }
    return max;
}
```

```c
//sorting using Radix sort technique
void rsort(int arr[], int n)
{
    int *buck[n], Count[n];
    int i, j, k, rem, nd = 0, div = 1, max, i1;
    max = maximum(arr, n);
    while (max > 0)
      {
       nd++;
        max/= 10;
      }
    for(i=0;i<n;i++)
      {
         buck[i]=(int *)malloc(nd*sizeof(int *));
      }
    for (i1 = 0; i1 < nd; i1++)
      {
        for (i = 0; i < n; i++)
          {
          Count[i] = 0;
          }
      for (i = 0; i < n; i++)
        {
      // sort the digit merrit on its place LSB to MSB
       rem = (arr[i] / div) % n;
       buck[rem][Count[rem]] = arr[i];
       Count[rem] += 1;
        }
    // collecting the numbers from the bucket to the array
      i = 0;
      for (k = 0; k < n; k++)
         {
        for (j = 0; j < Count[k]; j++)
             {
            arr[i] = buck[k][j];
            i++;
          }
         }
        div *= n;
        }
}
void main()
```

```
{
  int *arr, i, n;
  //enter the numbers of elements in array
  printf("\n Enter the number of elements in the array: ");
  scanf("%d", &n);
  arr=(int *)malloc(n*sizeof(int *)); //enter array elements
  printf("\nEnter %d elements (Positive Integer only): ");
  for (i = 0; i < n; i++)
    {
      scanf("%d", &arr[i]);
    }
    printf("\nOriginal Input : ");
  for (i = 0; i < n; i++)
  {
      printf(" %d ", arr[i]);
      }
//calling the radix sort function
  rsort(arr, n);
  printf("\nAfter Sorting : ");
  for (i = 0; i < n; i++)
  {
      printf(" %d ", arr[i]);
  }
}
```

Output

Enter the number of elements in the array: 8
Enter 1 elements (Positive Integer only): 12 43 21 89 11 3 9 8 32
Original Input : 12 43 21 89 11 3 9 8
After Sorting : 3 8 9 11 12 21 89 43

Queue and Stack

Queue

A queue is an abstract data type. The queue follows the FIFO (First In First Out) norm. Data is inserted from one end and deleted from the other end. The insertion took place from the end and the deletion took place from the front. There are four types of queues :

1. Simple Queue or Linear Queue : Added from the rear and deleted from the front. Adding an element into a queue is called enqueue, and removing process known as dequeue.

1	2	3	4	
front↑				Rear↑

2. Circular Queue: A circular queue is an extended form of a linear queue. In a circular queue, the last element points to the first element, making a circular relation. It solves the major drawback of the normal queue. In a linear queue, there will be non-usable empty space after the insertion and deletion. That can be utilised in a circular queue.

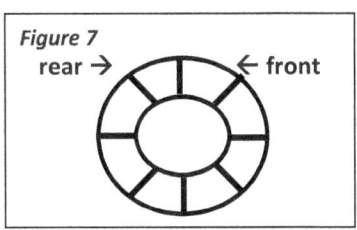

Figure 7
rear → ← front

3. Priority Queue : In a priority queue, a priority clause is connected with each element, and the queue is worked according to the priority.

Element with Highest → Priority	Front↓				Rear↓
	(1,X)	(2,S)	(3,T)	(4,U)	(5,A)

4. Deque (Double Ended Queue) : The Double Ended Queue (Deque) does not follow the FIFO (First In First Out) rule. In Deque, insertion and removal of elements can be performed from both the sides, from the front, as well as from the rear.

Insertion/ Deletion		1	2	3	4		Insertion/ Deletion

Queue using Array

Prog-20. Simple Queue

```
#include<stdio.h>
#include <ctype.h>
#define SIZE 5

//Declaration
int queue[SIZE];
int front,rear;
```

```c
//Adding elements in queue
int Enqueue()
 {
   if(rear == SIZE-1)
    {
      printf("\n\t\tQueue is Full!!");
      return 0;
    }
    printf("\n\t\tEnter an Element : ");
    scanf("%d",&queue[++rear]);
 }
//Removing data from Queue
int Dequeue()
{
   if(front == rear)
     {
      printf("\n\t\tQueue is Empty!!");
      return 0;
     }
     return queue[++front];
 }
//Display Items
void Print()
{
   int i;
   if(rear == front)
     printf("\n\t\tQueue is Empty!!");
   else
     {
     printf("\n\t\tElements in Queue :");

     for(i = front+1; i <= rear; i++)
        printf("%d ",queue[i]);
 }
}
//Menu driven main function
int main()
 {
    char ch;
    int num,e;
   front=rear=-1;
   do
```

```
{
    printf("\n\n\t\t(E) Enueue\n\t\t(D) Dequeue\n\t\t(P) Print\n\t\t(X) Exit");
        printf("\n\t\tEnter a choice (E/D/P/X)");
        ch=getche();
        ch=toupper(ch);
        fflush(stdin);    //clearing buffer
        switch(ch)
         {
          case 'E': Enqueue(num);
                    break;
          case 'D': num=Dequeue();
                        if(num>0)
                                printf("\n\t\tThe Element %d : ",num);
                    break;
          case 'P': Print();
                    break;
         }
    }while(ch!='X');
  return 0;
}
```

Output

```
                (E) Enueue
                (D) Dequeue
                (P) Print
                (X) Exit
                Enter a choice (E/D/P/X)E
                Elements in Queue :9
                Elements in Queue :7
                Elements in Queue :6
                Elements in Queue :5
                Elements in Queue :4
                Queue is Full!!

                (E) Enueue
                (D) Dequeue
                (P) Print
                (X) Exit
                Enter a choice (E/D/P/X)P
        Elements in Queue :9 7 6 5 4
```

Prog-21. Priority Queue-1

```
#include<stdio.h>
#include <ctype.h>
```

```c
#include <limits.h>
#define SIZE 5

//Declaration
int queue[SIZE];
int rear;
//Adding elements in queue
int Enqueue()
 {
   if(rear == SIZE-1)
   {
     printf("\n\t\tQueue is Full!!");
     return 0;
   }
    printf("\n\t\tEnter an Element : ");
     scanf("%d",&queue[++rear]);
 }
//Removing data from Queue
int Dequeue()
{
   int num;
   if(rear==-1)
     {
     printf("\n\t\tQueue is Empty!!");
     return 0;
   }
   int i, max = INT_MIN,p;
     // find the position of maximum value
     for (i = 0; i <=rear; i++)
         {
       if (max < queue[i])
           {
           max = queue[i];
           p=i;
         }
       }
     num = queue[p];
     // Maximum replaced with the Last element
     queue[p] = queue[rear];
     rear = rear - 1;
     return num;
 }
//Display Items
```

```c
void Print()
{
    int i;
    if(rear == -1)
        printf("\n\t\tQueue is Empty!!");
    else
        {
        printf("\n\t\tElements in Queue :");

        for(i = 0; i <= rear; i++)
        {
            printf("%d ",queue[i]);
        }
    }
}
//Menu driven main function
int main()
{
    char ch;
    int num,e;
    rear=-1;
    do
        {
        printf("\n\n\t\t\t(E) Enqueue\n\t\t\t(D) Dequeue\n\t\t\t(P) Print\n\t\t\t(X) Exit");
        printf("\n\t\tEnter a choice (E/D/P/X)");
        ch=getche();
        ch=toupper(ch);
        fflush(stdin);     //clearing buffer
        switch(ch)
         {
          case 'E': Enqueue();
                    break;
          case 'D': num=Dequeue();
                    if(num>0)
                            printf("\n\t\tThe Element %d : ",num);
                    break;
          case 'P': Print();
                    break;
         }
        }while(ch!='X');
    return 0;
}
```

(E) Enqueue
(D) Dequeue
(P) Print
(X) Exit
Enter a choice (E/D/P/X)e
Enter an Element : 23
Enter an Element : 45
Enter an Element : 56
Enter an Element : 67
Enter an Element : 32

(E) Enqueue
(D) Dequeue
(P) Print
(X) Exit
Enter a choice (E/D/P/X)e
Queue is Full!!

(E) Enqueue
(D) Dequeue
(P) Print
(X) Exit
Enter a choice (E/D/P/X)p
Elements in Queue :23 45 56 67 32

(E) Enqueue
(D) Dequeue
(P) Print
(X) Exit
Enter a choice (E/D/P/X)d
The Element 67 :
The Element 56 :
The Element 45 :
The Element 32 :
The Element 23 :
Queue is Empty!!

Prog-22. Priority Queue-2

```
//Using a structure with priority
#include<stdio.h>
#include <ctype.h>
#include <limits.h>
#define SIZE 5

//Declaration
```

```c
struct Qu{int queue,prty;}pq[SIZE];
int rear;
//Inserting elements
int Enqueue()
 {
   if(rear == SIZE-1)
    {
      printf("\n\t\tQueue is Full!!");
      return 0;
    }
    printf("\n\t\tEnter Queue Element : ");
     scanf("%d",&pq[++rear].queue);
         printf("\t\tEnter Priority : ");
     scanf("%d",&pq[rear].prty);
 }
//Removing data from Queue
void Dequeue()
{
   if(rear==-1)
     {
     printf("\n\t\tQueue is Empty!!");
     return;
     }
   int i, max = INT_MIN,p;
     // find the position of maximum value
     for (i = 0; i <=rear; i++)
        {
       if (max < pq[i].prty)
          {
          max = pq[i].prty;
          p=i;
        }
       }
       printf("\n\t\tRemoved Highest Priority %d, %d",pq[p].queue,pq[p].prty);
     // Maximum replaced with the Last element
     pq[p].queue = pq[rear].queue;
     pq[p].prty = pq[rear].prty;
     rear = rear - 1;
 }
//Display Items
void Print()
{
   int i;
```

```c
    if(rear == -1)
        printf("\n\t\tQueue is Empty!!");
    else
        {
        printf("\n\t\tElements in Queue :");
        printf("\n\t\tQueue Elem   Priority");
        for(i = 0; i <= rear; i++)
        {
            printf("\n\t\t%d\t\t %d",pq[i].queue,pq[i].prty);
        }
    }
}
//Menu driven main function
int main()
 {
    char ch;
   rear=-1;
   do
     {
       printf("\n\n\t\t(E) Enueue\n\t\t(D) Dequeue\n\t\t(P) Print\n\t\t(X) Exit");
        printf("\n\t\tEnter a choice (E/D/P/X)");
        ch=getche();
        ch=toupper(ch);
        fflush(stdin);    //clearing buffer
        switch(ch)
         {
          case 'E': Enqueue();
                  break;
          case 'D': Dequeue();
                  break;
          case 'P': Print();
                  break;
          }
      }while(ch!='X');
    return 0;
 }
```

Prog-23. Circular Queue

```c
#include<stdio.h>
#include<ctype.h>
# define SIZE 5
int cq[SIZE],front,rear;
```

```c
void Enqueue(int item)
  {
      if((front == 0 && rear == SIZE-1) || (front == rear+1))
         {
            printf("\n\t\tQueue is Overflow!!");
             return;
         }
      if(front==-1)
         {
             front= rear=0;
         }
      else
         {
           if(rear==SIZE-1)
              rear = 0;
           else
              rear = rear+1;
         }
      cq[rear] = item ;
  }
void Dequeue()
  {
      if(front==-1)
        {
           printf("\n\t\tQueue is Empty!!");
           return;
        }
      printf("\n\t\tElement Removed : %d ",cq[front]);
      if(front == rear)
        {
            front=rear=-1;
        }
      else
        {
            if(front==SIZE-1)
               front=0;
            else
              front=front+1;
        }
  }
void Print()
  {
     int i=front,j= rear;
```

```c
        if(front==-1)
          {
            printf("\n\nt\tQueue is Empty!!");
            return;
          }
        printf("\n\t\tElements In Queue : ");
        if( i<=j )
          {
            while(i<=j)
              {
                  printf("%d ",cq[i++]);
              }
          }
        else
          {
            while(i<=SIZE-1)
              {
                printf(" %d ",cq[i++]);
              }
            i=0;
            while(i<=j)
              {
                  printf("%d ",cq[i++]);
              }
          }
      }
    }
//Menu driven main function
int main()
  {
      char ch;
      int num;
    front=rear=-1;
    do
      {
        printf("\n\n\t\t(E) Enueue\n\t\t(D) Dequeue\n\t\t(P) Print\n\t\t(X) Exit");
        printf("\n\t\tEnter a choice (E/D/P/X)");
        ch=getche();
        ch=toupper(ch);
        fflush(stdin);    //clearing buffer
        switch(ch)
          {
            case 'E': printf("\n\t\tEnter an Element : ");
                    scanf("%d",&num);
```

```
                    Enqueue(num);
            break;
    case 'D': Dequeue();
            break;
    case 'P': Print();
            break;
    }
}while(ch!='X');
return 0;
}
```

Output

```
                (E) Enqueue
                (D) Dequeue
                (P) Print
                (X) Exit
                Enter a choice (E/D/P/X)e

                Enter an Element : 1
                Enter an Element : 3
                Enter an Element : 4
                Enter an Element : 5
                Enter an Element : 6
                Queue is Overflow!!
                Enter a choice (E/D/P/X)p

                Elements in Queue : 1 3 4 5 6

                Enter a choice (E/D/P/X)d
                Element Removed : 1

                Enter a choice (E/D/P/X)e
                Enter an Element : 5
                Enter a choice (E/D/P/X)p
                Elements In Queue :  3  4  5  6 5
```

Prog-24. Double Ended Queue

```
#include <stdio.h>
#include <conio.h>
#include <stdlib.h>
#define SIZE 5
int dq[SIZE];
int front,rear;
```

DS -83

```c
void Enq_Right()
  {
     if((front==0 && rear==SIZE-1) || (front== rear+1))
       {
           printf("\n\tQueue is Full\n");
           return;
       }
     if (front==-1)
       {
           front=rear = 0;
       }
     else  if(rear==SIZE-1)
       {
           rear=0;
       }
     else
       {
           rear=rear+1;
       }
     printf("\n\tEnter An Element : ");
     scanf("%d", &dq[rear]);
  }
void Enq_Left()
  {
     if((front==0 && rear==SIZE-1) || (front==rear+1))
       {
           printf("\n\tQueue is Full \n");
           return;
       }
     if (front==-1)
       {
           front=rear = 0;
       }
     else if(front== 0)
       {
           front=SIZE-1;
       }
     else
       {
           front=front-1;
       }
     printf("\n\tEnter an Eelement : ");
     scanf("%d", &dq[front]);
```

```c
        }
void Deq_Left()
  {
      if (front==-1)
        {
            printf("\n\tQueue is Empty!\n");
            return ;
        }
      printf("\n\tElement Removed from Queue = : %d",dq[front]);
      if(front==rear)
        {
            front=rear=-1;
        }
      else if(front==SIZE-1)
        {
            front=0;
        }
      else
        {
            front=front+1;
        }
  }
void Deq_Right()
  {
      if (front==-1)
        {
            printf("\n\tQueue is Empty!\n");
            return ;
        }
      printf("\n\tElement Removed  : %d",dq[rear]);
      if(front==rear)
        {
            front=rear=-1;
        }
      else if(rear==0)
        {
            rear=SIZE-1;
        }
      else
        {
            rear=rear-1;
        }
  }
```

```c
void Disp()
  {
    int i=front;
    if(front==-1)
      {
        printf("\n\tQueue is Empty!\n");
        return;
      }
    printf("\n\tQueue elements : \t ");
    if( i<=rear )
      {
        while(i<=rear)
          {
            printf("%d ",dq[i]);
            i++;
          }
      }
    else
      {
        while(i<=SIZE-1)
          {
            printf("%d ",dq[i]);
            i++;
          }
        i=0;
        while(i<=rear )
          {
            printf("%d ",dq[i]);
            i++;
          }
      }
    printf("\n");
  }
void Input_Menu()
  {
    char ch=0;
    do
      {
        printf("\n\t * Input Restricted Menu *\n");
        printf("\n\t1. Insert at Rear");
        printf("\n\t2. Delete from front");
        printf("\n\t3. Delete from rear");
        printf("\n\t4. Display");
```

```c
            printf("\n\t5. Quit");
            printf("\n\tEnter your choice : ");
            fflush(stdin);
                    ch=getche();
            switch(ch)
                {
                    case '1':Enq_Right();break;
                    case '2':Deq_Left();break;
                    case '3':Deq_Right();break;
                    case '4':Disp();break;
                }
        }while(ch!='5');
    }
void Output_Menu()
  {
        char ch;
        do
          {
            printf("\n\t * Output Restricted Menu *\n");
            printf("\n\t1. Push at Rear");
            printf("\n\t2. Push at Front");
            printf("\n\t3. Pop from Front");
            printf("\n\t4. Display");
            printf("\n\t5. Quit");
            printf("\n\tEnter A choice : ");
            fflush(stdin);
            ch=getche();
            switch(ch)
                {
                    case '1': Enq_Right();break;
                    case '2': Enq_Left();break;
                    case '3': Deq_Left();break;
                    case '4': Disp();break;
                }
        }while(ch!='5');
    }
int main()
  {
        rear=front=-1;
        char ch;
        do
          {
            printf("\n\t * Main Menu *\n");
```

```c
        printf("\n\t1. Input Restricted");
        printf("\n\t2. Output Restricted");
        printf("\n\t3. Exit");
        printf("\n\tEnter A choice : ");
        fflush(stdin);
            ch=getche();
        switch(ch)
           {
              case '1':Input_Menu();break;
              case '2':Output_Menu();break;
              case '3':printf("\n\t..Quit...");exit(0);
              default: printf("Wrong choice\n");
           }
     }while(ch!='3');
   }
```

Output (Showing Menus Only)

```
        * Main Menu *
        1. Input Restricted
        2. Output Restricted
        3. Exit
        Enter A choice : 1

        * Input Restricted Menu *
        1. Insert at Rear
        2. Delete from front
        3. Delete from rear
        4. Display
        5. Quit
        Enter your choice : 5

        * Main Menu *
        1. Input Restricted
        2. Output Restricted
        3. Exit
        Enter A choice : 2

        * Output Restricted Menu *
        1. Push at Rear
        2. Push at Front
        3. Pop from Front
        4. Display
        5. Quit
        Enter A choice :
```

Stack

Stack is also a linear data structure but follows the LIFO (Last-in-First-out) norm. Data is inserted from one end and deleted from the same end too. That means the last element that is inserted will be removed first.

Push	Push	Push		Pop
1	2	3		

1	2	3	After Push
	1	2	After 1st POP
		1	After 2nd POP

Stack Applications

These are the few areas where the stack is implemented.

1. Expression Evaluation and Conversion.

    a. Infix to Prefix
    b. Infix to Postfix
    c. Prefix to Infix
    d. Postfix to Infix

2. Memory Management : Stack also have a key role in Memory Management

3. Backtracking : A recursive algorithm for building a set of all the solutions gradually

4. Function Call : When a function is called from another function, the address of the calling function is stored in the stack

5. Parenthesis Checking : Help to check balanced Parenthesis.

6. Syntax Parsing : Stack is also used for Syntax analyzing in most of the Compilers.

7. String Reversal : Used for reversing the string.

Similarity and Difference between Queue and Stack

STACK	QUEUE
1. Stacks are an abstract and Linear Data Structure	1. Queues too are abstract and Linear Data Structure
2. In Stacks, elements are inserted from the same end, and it follows the Last In First Out (LIFO) principle.	2. In Queues, elements are inserted from one end, known as the rear, and deleted from the other end, known as the front. Queues are based on the First In First out (FIFO) principle.
3. Operations in Stack are called push and pop.	3. Operations in aQueue are called enqueue and dequeue.
4. A stack is a recursive data structure..	4. A queue is a sequential data structure..

Prog-25. Stack using Array

```
#include<stdio.h>
#include<conio.h>
#define MAX 5
int stk[MAX],rear;

  void Push(int num)
    {
      if(rear==-1)
        {
         rear=0;
        }
      if(rear>=MAX)
        {
           printf("\n\t Stack is full");
        }
      else
        {
           stk[rear++]=num;
        }
    }
```

```c
int PoP()
  {
    int P;
    if(rear<=0)
      {
        printf("\n\t Stack is empty");
        return 0;
      }
    else
      {
        P=stk[rear-1];
        rear--;
        return P;
      }
  }
void Display()
  {
    int i;
    if(rear<=0)
      {
        printf("\n\t Stack is empty");
        return;
      }
    printf("\n\tValues in Stack : ");
    for(i=0;i<rear;i++)
      {
        printf("%d ",stk[i]);
      }
  }
void main()
  {
    char ch,n,i=0;
    rear=-1;
    do
      {
        printf("\n\t1. Push \n\t2. Pop \n\t3. Display \n\t4. Exit");
        printf("\n\n\tEnter your choice : ");
        fflush(stdin);
        ch=getche();
        switch(ch)
          {
            case '1':
```

```
                printf("\n\tEnter a No. ");
                scanf("%d",&n);
                Push(n);
                break;
        case '2':
                n=PoP();
                if(n>0)
                  {
                            printf("\n\tNo. is Popped - %d",n);
                  }
                break;
        case '3': Display();
                break;
      }
    }while(ch!='4');
  }
```

Output

1. Push	Enter your choice : 1
2. Pop	Enter a No. 33
3. Display	Enter your choice : 3
4. Exit	Values in Stack : 11 22 33
Enter your choice : 1	
Enter a No. 11	Enter your choice : 2
Enter your choice : 1	No. is Popped - 33
Enter a No. 22	

Infix – Postfix – Prefix Expression

When in an expression operators are written in between their operands is called **Infix Notations**. E.g. A + B, 4 + 5,

Where operators are written before the operand is known as **Prefix Notations**. E.g. +AB, +45

Finally in **Postfix Notations**, operators used after the operand. E.g. AB+, 45+.

Stack is also used to convert the readable infix notation, which is used by humans, to postfix, because the computer failed to distinguish between the different operators and parenthesis.

More examples of the above three expressions are given below:

Infix	Postfix	Prefix
x + y + z	x y + z +	+ + x y z
x + y * z	x y z * +	+ x *y z
(x + y) * (z - x)	x y + z x - *	* + x y - z x

Infix	Result		Postfix	Result		Prefix	Result
2 + 3 * 4	14		2 3 4 * +	14		+2 * 3 4	14
(2+3)*4	20		2 3+ 4*	20		* +2 3 4	20

Infix to Postfix using Stack

A + (B * C + D) / E

Input	Stack	Output
A		A
+	+	A
(	+(	A
B	+(	AB
*	+(*	AB
C	+(*	ABC
+	+(+	ABC*
D	+(+	ABC*D
)	+	ABC*D+
/	+/	ABC*D+
E	+/	ABC*D+E
		ABC*D+E/+

Prog-26. Infix to Postfix

```
#include<ctype.h>
#include <stdio.h>

char Stk[50]; //Global Variables
int top=-1;

 push(char expr)
  {
     Stk[++top]=expr;
```

```c
        }
    char pop()
     {
     return(Stk[top--]);
     }
//Checking precedence in order ^, *, /, +, -
 int Op_Pre(char Opertr)
    {
       if(Opertr == '^')
        {
           return 3;
        }
       else if(Opertr == '*' || Opertr == '/')
       {
           return 2;
       }
       else if(Opertr == '+' || Opertr == '-')
        {
           return 1;
        }
       else
        {
           return 0;
        }
    }
    //Main Function
 int main()
{
    int i=0,j=0;
    char infix[50],post[50],ch,expr;
    printf("\n\tEnter a valid Infix Notation : ");
    scanf("%s",infix);
    push('~');
    for(i=0;infix[i]!='\0';i++)
     {
       ch=infix[i];
        if( ch == '(')
                push(ch);
        else
          if(isalnum(ch))
                   post[j++]=ch;
```

```
        else
          if( ch == ')')
            {
              while( Stk[top] != '(')
                 post[j++]=pop();
              expr=pop();
            }
          else
            {
              while( Op_Pre(Stk[top]) >= Op_Pre(ch) )
                 post[j++]=pop();
              push(ch);
            }
    }
  while( Stk[top] != '~' )
    post[j++]=pop();
  post[j+1]='\0';        // Remove Garbage
  printf("\n\tInfix : %s to Postfix :  %s\n",infix,post);
}
```

Output

Enter a valid Infix Notation : (a+b)*c/d+(a-b)
Infix : (a+b)*c/d+(a-b) to Postfix : ab+c*d/ab-+

Prog-27. Infix to Prefix

```
#include<string.h>
#include <ctype.h>
#include<stdio.h>
#define SIZE 50

char Stk[SIZE];
int top=-1;

  push(char expr)
    {
       Stk[++top]=expr;
    }
  char pop()
    {
       return Stk[top--];
    }
```

```c
int pred(char expr)
  {
    switch(expr)
      {
        case '#': return 0;
        case ')': return 1;
        case '+':
        case '-': return 2;
        case '*':
        case '/': return 3;
      }
  }
void toPrefix(char infix[],char prefix[])
  {
  char ch,expr;
  int i=0,k=0;
  while( (ch=infix[i++]) != '\0')
  {
  if( ch == ')')
        {
            push(ch);
        }
    else if(isalnum(ch))
        {
            prefix[k++]=ch;
        }
    else if( ch == '(')
      {
        while( Stk[top] != ')')
         {
            prefix[k++]=pop();
              }
            expr=pop();
      }
    else
      {
        while( pred(Stk[top]) >= pred(ch) )
         {
            prefix[k++]=pop();
              }
            push(ch);
      }
  }
}
```

```
    while( Stk[top] != '#')
      {
        prefix[k++]=pop();
      }
      prefix[k]='\0';
    strrev(prefix);
      strrev(infix);
      printf("\n\n\tInfix : %s  To Prefix : %s\n",infix,prefix);
  }

int main()
  {
    char infix[SIZE],prefix[SIZE];
    printf("\n\tEnter a Valid Infix Expression : ");
    gets(infix);
    push('#');
    strrev(infix);
    toPrefix(infix,prefix);
  }
```

Output

Enter a Valid Infix Expression : (a+b)*(c+d)/e
Infix : (a+b)*(c+d)/e To Prefix : *+ab/+cde

Linked List

A linked list is a linear data structure consisting of a collection of objects called nodes. Linked lists are made up of a series of connected nodes. Each node in a linked list contains data fields and a field that links to the next node, typically referred to as next. Unlike arrays, linked lists can dynamically grow or shrink by adding or removing nodes as needed. In a linked list, data is stored in a non-contiguous manner.

Types of Linked List

There are four common types of Linked List.

1. Singly Linked List
2. Doubly Linked List
3. Circular Linked List
4. Doubly Circular Linked List

Singly Linked List

A singly linked list is the most common, and navigation is possible in a forward direction. In other words, a singly linked list is unidirectional and traverse is possible in a forward direction too.

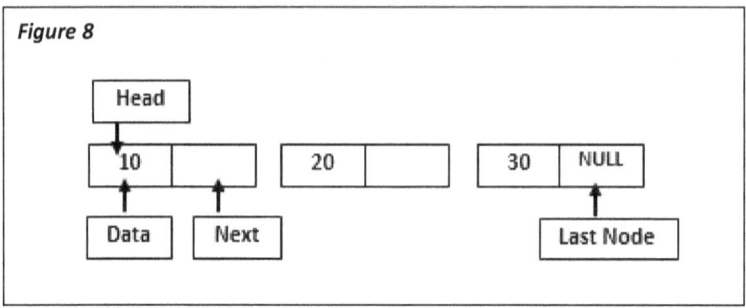

Doubly Linked List

A doubly linked list is bidirectional, enabling traversal in both forward and backward directions. Each node in a doubly linked list contains an additional field to store the address of the previous node.

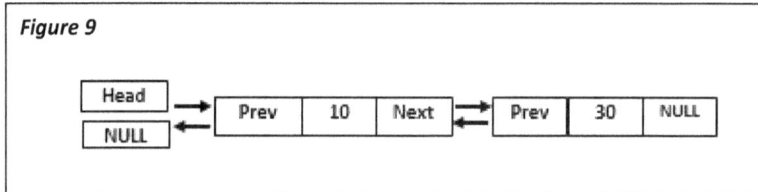

Circular linked list

Like a singly linked list, a circular linked list is also unidirectional, but with the key difference that the last node is linked to the first node, forming a circle. Similar to a singly linked list, traversal in a circular linked list occurs in the forward direction.

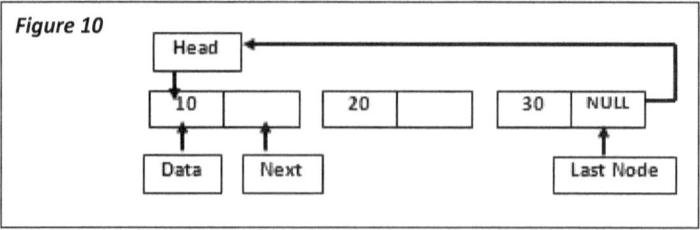

Doubly Circular linked list

A doubly circular linked list combines the features of a ***circular linked*** list and a ***doubly linked list.***

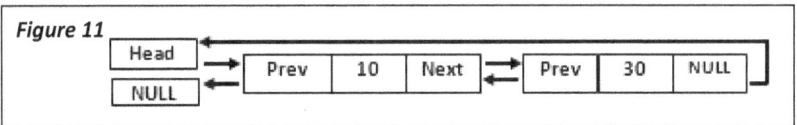

Figure 11

Head
NULL
Prev
10
Next
Prev
30
NULL

A complete Menu-Driven Singly Linked List Program, using typedef. Apart from typedef, the dynamic memory allocation using malloc() has already been described briefly.

Linked List

Create New Node and add a Node

When Head is NULL, new Node assigned as Head

Figure 12

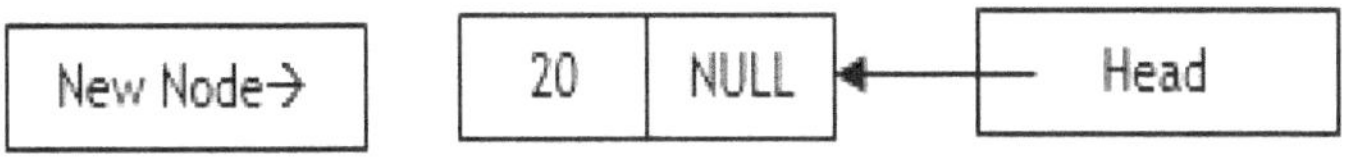

New Node→
20
NULL
Head

Otherwise Search for Next Pointer with NULL value and add the address of New Node into it.

Figure 13

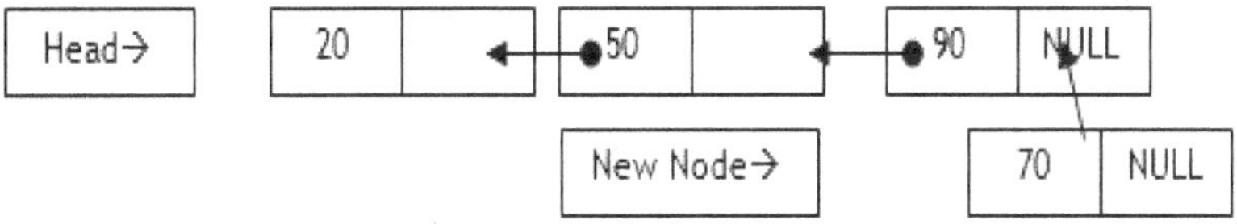

Head→
20
50
90
NULL
New Node→
70
NULL

Insert Before Head

Figure 14

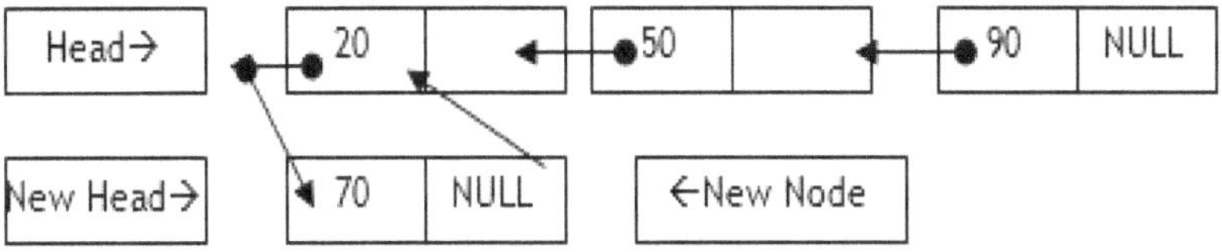

Head→
20
50
90
NULL
New Head→
70
NULL
←New Node

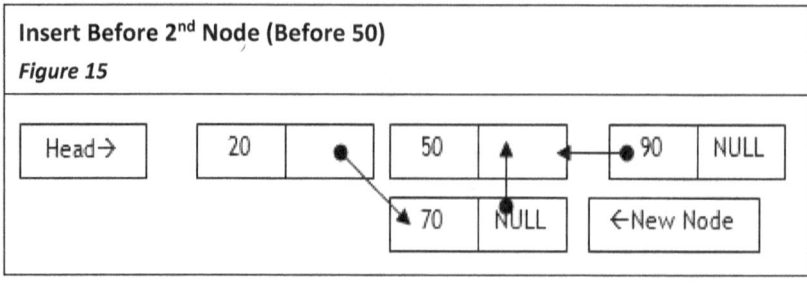

Insert Before 2ⁿᵈ Node (Before 50)

Figure 15

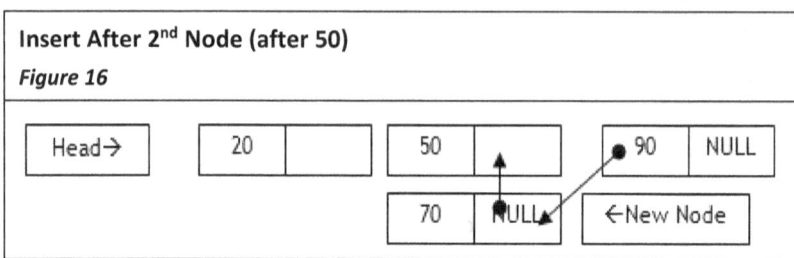

Insert After 2ⁿᵈ Node (after 50)

Figure 16

Delete : Delete Head : Deleting Head means the adjacent node of the head will be the new Head.

Figure 17

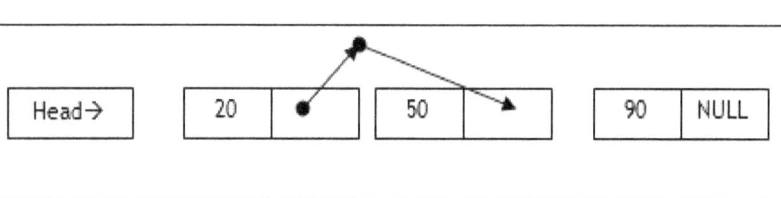

Delete Other Node

Figure 18

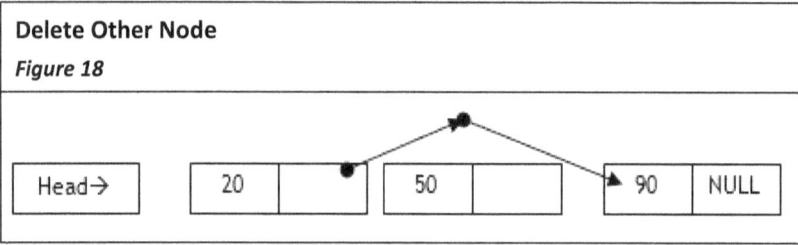

Prog-28. Singly Linked List

```
#include <stdio.h>
#include<stdlib.h>

typedef struct LList{int n;struct LList *Next;}List;
List *Last;
   void chkMsg()
     {
       printf("\n\t** List is Empty ** \n");
```

```
      }
List * addNew(List *hd, int num)
  {
    List *Ptr;
    Ptr=(List *)malloc(sizeof(List *));
    Ptr->Next=NULL;
    Ptr->n=num;
    if(hd==NULL)
      {
        hd=Last=Ptr;
      }
    else
      {
        Last->Next=Ptr;
        Last=Ptr;
      }
    return hd;
  }
void dispList(List *hd)
  {
    List *Ptr;
    if(hd==NULL)
      {
        chkMsg();return;
      }
    else
      {
        printf("\n\tData in the List : ");
        for(Ptr=hd;Ptr!=NULL;Ptr=Ptr->Next)
          {
            printf(" %d ",Ptr->n);
          }
      }
  }

List * delNode(List *hd)
  {
    int num;
    List *Ptr,*Pptr;
    if(hd==NULL)
      {
        chkMsg();return;
      }
```

```c
        printf("\n\tEnter a No. to Delete : ");
        scanf("%d",&num);
        for(Ptr=hd;Ptr!=NULL;Ptr=Ptr->Next)
          {
            if(num==Ptr->n)
              {
                 break;
              }
                 Pptr=Ptr;
          }
        if(Ptr==hd)              //Delete First
          {
             hd=hd->Next;
          }
        else if(Ptr==NULL)
          {
             printf("\n\tNumber is not in the List");
          }
        else if(Ptr->Next!=NULL)                      //Delete Last
          {
             Pptr->Next=Ptr->Next;

          }
        else          //Delete from Middle
          {
             Last=Pptr;
             Pptr->Next=Ptr->Next;
             Last->Next=NULL;
          }
        return hd;
    }

List * insBefo(List *hd)
   {
      int pos;
      List *Ptr,*Pptr,*Ptmp;
      if(hd==NULL)
        {
           chkMsg();return hd;
        }
      printf("\tEnter the Position : ");
      scanf("%d",&pos);
      for(Pptr=hd;Pptr!=NULL;Pptr=Pptr->Next)
```

```c
        {
          pos--;
          if(pos<1)
            {
              break;
            }
            Ptmp=Pptr;
        }
      if(Pptr==NULL)
        {
          printf("\n\tPosition is Out! ");
          return hd;
        }
      else
        {
          Ptr=(List *)malloc(sizeof(List *));
          printf("\n\tEnter a No. to Insert :");
          scanf("%d",&Ptr->n);
          Ptr->Next=NULL;
          if(Pptr==hd)
            {
              Ptr->Next=hd;
              hd=Ptr;
            }
          else
            {
              Ptr->Next=Pptr;
              Ptmp->Next=Ptr;
            }
        }
      return hd;
  }

List * insAfter(List *hd)
  {
    int pos;
    List *Ptr,*Pptr;
    if(hd==NULL)
      {
        chkMsg();return hd;
      }
    printf("\tEnter the Position : ");
    scanf("%d",&pos);
```

```
        for(Pptr=hd;Pptr->Next!=NULL;Pptr=Pptr->Next)
          {
             pos--;
             if(pos<1)
               {
                  break;
               }
          }
        Ptr=(List *)malloc(sizeof(List *));
        printf("\tEnter a No. to Insert :");
        scanf("%d",&Ptr->n);
        Ptr->Next=NULL;
        if(Pptr->Next==NULL)
          {
             printf("\n\tPosition is Out of range, Adding at the Last! ");
             Last->Next=Ptr;
             Last=Ptr;
             return hd;
          }
        else
          {
             Ptr->Next=Pptr->Next;
             Pptr->Next=Ptr;
          }
        return hd;
     }
  List * revList(List *hd)
     {
        List *Ptr,*Pptr,*Ptmp;
        if(hd==NULL)
          {
             chkMsg();return hd;
          }
        Ptr=hd;
        Pptr=NULL;
        while(Ptr!=NULL)
          {
             Ptmp=Pptr;
             Pptr=Ptr;
             Ptr=Ptr->Next;
             Pptr->Next=Ptmp;
          }
```

```
        hd=Pptr;
        for(Last=Pptr;Last->Next!=NULL;Last=Last->Next);
        return hd;
  }
void sortList(List *hd)
  {
     List *Ptr,*Pptr;
     int num;
     if(hd==NULL)
       {
          chkMsg();return;
       }
     for(Ptr=hd;Ptr->Next!=NULL;Ptr=Ptr->Next)
       {
          for(Pptr=Ptr->Next;Pptr!=NULL;Pptr=Pptr->Next)
            {
              if(Ptr->n>Pptr->n)
                {
                   num=Ptr->n;
                   Ptr->n=Pptr->n;
                   Pptr->n=num;
                }
            }
       }
  }

void searchList(List *hd)
  {
     List *Ptr;
     int num,Pos=0;
     if(hd==NULL)
       {
          chkMsg();return;
       }
     printf("\tEnter a Number to Search ; ");
     scanf("%d",&num);
     for(Ptr=hd;Ptr!=NULL;Ptr=Ptr->Next)
       {
          Pos++;
          if(Ptr->n==num)
            {
               break;
```

```c
            }
         }
      if(Ptr!=NULL)
        {
           printf("\n\t%d is Found in %d Position!\n ",num,Pos);
        }
      else
        {
           printf("\n\t%d is Not Found !\n ",num);
        }
   }
int main()
  {
     List *Head;
     Head=Last=NULL;
     int c,num;
     do
       {
          printf("\n\t\t** Menu **");
          printf("\n\t1. Add New\n\t2. Display\n\t3. Delete");
          printf("\n\t4. Insert Before\n\t5. Insert After");
          printf("\n\t6. Reverse\n\t7. Sort\n\t8. Search\n\t9. Exit");
          printf("\n\tEnter a choice : ");
          scanf("%d",&c);
          switch(c)
            {
               case 1: printf("\n\tEnter a No. to Add : ");
                          scanf("%d",&num);
                          Head=addNew(Head,num);
                          break;
               case 2:dispList(Head);break;
               case 3:Head=delNode(Head);break;
               case 4:printf("\n\tInsert Before");Head=insBefo(Head);break;
               case 5:;printf("\n\tInsert After");Head=insAfter(Head);break;
               case 6:Head=revList(Head);printf("\n\tReversed:
");dispList(Head);break;
               case 7:sortList(Head);printf("\n\tSorted ");dispList(Head);break;
               case 8:printf("\n\tSearch");searchList(Head);break;
            }
       }while(c!=9);
       free(Head);
       free(Last); }
```

Output

```
        ** Menu **
    1. Add New
    2. Display
    3. Delete
    4. Insert Before
    5. Insert After
    6. Reverse
    7. Sort
    8. Search
    9. Exit
    Enter a choice : 1
    Enter a No. to Add : 1
    Enter a No. to Add : 2
    Enter a No. to Add : 3
    Enter a No. to Add : 4
    Enter a No. to Add : 6
    Enter a choice : 2
    Data in the List :  1  2  3  4  6
    Enter a choice : 3
    Enter a No. to Delete : 1
    Enter a choice : 2
    Data in the List :   2  3  4  6
```

```
Enter a choice : 4

Insert Before   Enter the Position : 1
Enter a No. to Insert :11

Enter a choice : 2
Data in the List :  11  2  3  4  6

Enter a choice : 5
Insert After    Enter the Position : 2
Enter a No. to Insert :45
Enter a choice : 2
Data in the List :  11  2  45  3  4  6
Enter a choice : 6
Reversed:
Data in the List :  6  4  3  45  2  11
Enter a choice : 7
Sorted
Data in the List :  2  3  4  6  11  45
Enter a choice : 8
Search  Enter a Number to Search : 3
3 is Found in 2 Position!
```

Prog-29. Circular Linked List

```c
#include <stdio.h>
#include<stdlib.h>

typedef struct LList{int n;struct LList *Next;}List;
List *Last;
  void chkMsg()
    {
      printf("\n\t** List is Empty ** \n");
    }
  List * newNod(List *hd)
    {
      List *Ptr;
      Ptr=(List *)malloc(sizeof(List *));
      printf("\n\tEnter a No. to Insert :");
      scanf("%d",&Ptr->n);
      return Ptr;
    }
  List * addNew(List *hd, int num)
    {
```

DS -107

```
          List *Ptr;
          Ptr=(List *)malloc(sizeof(List *));
          Ptr->Next=NULL;
          Ptr->n=num;
          if(hd==NULL)
            {
               hd=Last=Ptr;
               Ptr->Next=hd;
            }
          else
            {
               Last->Next=Ptr;
               Last=Ptr;
               Last->Next=Ptr->Next=hd;
            }
          return hd;
       }
    void dispList(List *hd)
      {
         List *Ptr;
         if(hd==NULL)
           {
              chkMsg();return;
           }
         else
           {
              Ptr=hd;
              printf("\n\tData in the List : %d ",Ptr->n);
              Ptr=Ptr->Next;
              while(Ptr!=hd)
                {
                   printf(" %d ",Ptr->n);
                   Ptr=Ptr->Next;
                }
           }
      }

    List * delNode(List *hd)
      {
         int num;
         List *Ptr,*Pptr;
         if(hd==NULL)
           {
```

```
          chkMsg();return;
        }
      printf("\n\tEnter a No. to Delete : ");
      scanf("%d",&num);
      if(hd->n==num)                    //Delete First
        {
          hd=hd->Next;
          Last->Next=hd;
          return hd;
        }
        Pptr=hd;
      for(Ptr=hd->Next;Ptr!=hd;Ptr=Ptr->Next)
        {
          if(num==Ptr->n)
            {
              break;
            }
                Pptr=Ptr;
        }
      if(Ptr==hd)
        {
            printf("\n\tNumber is not in the List ");
        }
      else if(Ptr->Next==hd)
        {
          Pptr->Next=hd;
          Last->Next=Pptr->Next;
          Last=Pptr;
        }
      else
        {
          Pptr->Next=Ptr->Next;            //Delete from Middle
        }
      return hd;
    }
List * insBefo(List *hd)
  {
    int pos;
    List *Ptr,*Pptr,*Ptmp;
    if(hd==NULL)
      {
        chkMsg();return hd;
      }
```

```
        printf("\n\tEnter the Position : ");
        scanf("%d",&pos);
        if(pos==1)
          {
            Ptr=newNod(hd);
            Last->Next=Ptr;
            Ptr->Next=hd;
            hd=Ptr;
            return hd;
          }
        Ptmp=hd;
        for(Pptr=hd->Next;Pptr!=hd;Pptr=Pptr->Next)
          {
            pos--;
            if(pos<2)
              {
                break;
              }
            Ptmp=Pptr;
          }
        if(Pptr==hd)
          {
            printf("\n\tPosition is Out! ");
            return hd;
          }
        else
          {
            Ptr=newNod(hd);
            Ptr->Next=Ptmp->Next;
            Ptmp->Next=Ptr;
          }
        return hd;
      }
    List * insAfter(List *hd)
      {
        int pos;
        List *Ptr,*Pptr,*Ptmp;
        if(hd==NULL)
          {
            chkMsg();return hd;
          }
        printf("\n\tEnter the Position : ");
        scanf("%d",&pos);
```

```c
        Ptmp=hd;
        for(Pptr=hd->Next;Pptr!=hd;Pptr=Pptr->Next)
          {
             pos--;
             if(pos<1)
               {
                 break;
               }
             Ptmp=Pptr;
          }
        Ptr=newNod(hd);
        Ptr->Next=NULL;
        if(Pptr==hd)
          {
             printf("\n\tPosition is Out of range, Adding at the Last! ");
             Ptmp->Next=Ptr;
             Ptr->Next=hd;
             Last=Ptr;
             return hd;
          }
        else
          {
             Ptr->Next=Ptmp->Next;
             Ptmp->Next=Ptr;
          }
        return hd;
     }
int main()
  {
     List *Head;
     Head=Last=NULL;
     int c,num;
     do
       {
          printf("\n\t1. Add New\n\t2. Display\n\t3. Delete");
          printf("\n\t4. Insert Before\n\t5. Insert After\n\t6. Exit");
          printf("\n\tEnter a choice : ");
          scanf("%d",&c);
          switch(c)
            {
               case 1: printf("\n\tEnter a No. to Add : ");
                       scanf("%d",&num);
                       Head=addNew(Head,num);
```

```
                    break;
            case 2:dispList(Head);break;
            case 3:Head=delNode(Head);break;
            case 4:Head=insBefo(Head);break;
            case 5:Head=insAfter(Head);break;
        }
    }while(c!=6);
    free(Last);
    free(Head);
    return 0;
}
```

Output

```
1. Add New                    Enter a choice : 2
2. Display
3. Delete                     Data in the List : 2  3  4
4. Insert Before
5. Insert After               Enter a choice : 4
6. Exit
Enter a choice : 1            Enter the Position : 1
                             Enter a No. to Insert :1
Enter a No. to Add : 1
Enter a No. to Add : 2        Enter a choice : 2
Enter a No. to Add : 3        Data in the List : 1  2  3  4
Enter a No. to Add : 4
                             Enter a choice : 5
Enter a choice : 2
Data in the List : 1  2  3  4   Enter the Position : 3
                             Enter a No. to Insert :4
Enter a choice : 3
                             Enter a choice : 2
Enter a No. to Delete : 1     Data in the List : 1  2  3  4  4  6
```

Prog-30. Queue using Linked List

```
#include <stdio.h>
#include<stdlib.h>

typedef struct Queue{int n;struct Queue *Next;}Qu;
Qu *Rear;
    void chkOver()
    {
        printf("\n\t** Queue is Overflow ** \n");
    }
    void chkUnder()
```

```c
    {
      printf("\n\t** Queue is Underflow ** \n");
    }
Qu * Enqueue(Qu *First, int num)
  {
    Qu *Ptr;
    Ptr=(Qu *)malloc(sizeof(Qu *));
    if(Ptr==NULL)
      {
        chkOver();
        return First;
      }
    Ptr->Next=NULL;
    Ptr->n=num;
    if(First==NULL)
      {
        First=Rear=Ptr;
      }
    else
      {
        Rear->Next=Ptr;
        Rear=Ptr;
      }
    return First;
  }
void dispQueue(Qu *First)
  {
    Qu *Ptr;
    if(First==NULL)
      {
        chkUnder();return;
      }
    else
      {
        printf("\n\tValues in the Queue : ");
        for(Ptr=First;Ptr!=NULL;Ptr=Ptr->Next)
          {
            printf(" %d ",Ptr->n);
          }
      }
  }
Qu * Dequeue(Qu *First)
```

```c
{
    int num;
    Qu *Ptr;
    if(First==NULL)
      {
        chkUnder();
        return First;
      }
    printf("\n\tValue removed from List : %d",First->n);
    First=First->Next;
    return First;
  }
int main()
  {
    Qu *Front;
    Front=Rear=NULL;
    int c,num;
    do
      {
        printf("\n\t1. Enqueue\n\t2. Dequeue\n\t3. Display\n\t4. Exit");
        printf("\n\tEnter a choice : ");
        scanf("%d",&c);
        switch(c)
          {
            case 1: printf("\n\tEnter a No. : ");
                        scanf("%d",&num);
                        Front=Enqueue(Front,num);
                        break;
            case 2:Front=Dequeue(Front);break;
            case 3:dispQueue(Front);break;
          }
      }while(c!=4);
    free(Front);
    free(Rear);
  }
```

Output

1. Enqueue	Enter a choice : 2
2. Dequeue	Value removed from List : 1
3. Display	
4. Exit	Enter a choice : 2
Enter a choice : 1	Value removed from List : 2

```
Enter a No. : 1                    Enter a choice : 2
Enter a No. : 2                    Value removed from List : 3
Enter a No. : 3
                                   Enter a choice : 2
Enter a choice : 3                 ** Queue is Underflow **
Values in the Queue :  1  2  3
```

Prog-31. *Double Ended Queue using Linked List*

```c
#include <stdio.h>
#include<stdlib.h>

typedef struct deList{int n;struct deList *Next;}List;

  void chkMsg()
    {
      printf("\n\t** List is Empty ** \n");
    }

  List * addBeg(List *hd, int num)
    {
      List *Ptr;
      Ptr=(List *)malloc(sizeof(List *));
      Ptr->Next=NULL;
      Ptr->n=num;
      Ptr->Next=hd;
      hd=Ptr;
      return hd;
    }
  List * addEnd(List *hd,int num)
    {
      List *Ptr,*Pptr;
      Ptr=(List *)malloc(sizeof(List *));
      Ptr->n=num;
      Ptr->Next=NULL;
      if(hd==NULL)
        {
          hd=Ptr;
          return hd;
        }
    for(Pptr=hd;Pptr->Next!=NULL;Pptr=Pptr->Next);
    Pptr->Next=Ptr;
    return hd;
```

DS -115

```
        }
    void dispList(List *hd)
      {
        List *Ptr;
        if(hd==NULL)
          {
            chkMsg();return;
          }
        else
          {
            printf("\n\tData in the List : ");
            for(Ptr=hd;Ptr!=NULL;Ptr=Ptr->Next)
              {
                printf(" %d ",Ptr->n);
              }
          }
      }

    List * delBeg(List *hd)
      {
        if(hd==NULL)
          {
            chkMsg();return;
          }
        hd=hd->Next;
        return hd;
      }
    List * delEnd(List *hd)
      {
        List *Ptr,*Pptr;
        if(hd==NULL)
          {
            chkMsg();
            return hd;
          }
        for(Ptr=hd;Ptr->Next!=NULL;Ptr=Ptr->Next)
          {
                Pptr=Ptr;
          }

        Pptr->Next=Ptr->Next;
        if(Ptr==hd)
          {
```

```c
            hd=NULL;
        }
      return hd;
  }
int main()
  {
     List *Head;
     Head=NULL;
     int c,num;
     do
       {
          printf("\n\t\t** Menu **");
          printf("\n\t1. Insert at Begin\n\t2. Insert at End");
          printf("\n\t3. Delete from Begining\n\t4. Delete at End");
          printf("\n\t5. Display\n\t6. Exit");
          printf("\n\tEnter a choice : ");
          scanf("%d",&c);
          switch(c)
            {
              case 1: printf("\n\tEnter a No. to Add : ");
                           scanf("%d",&num);
                           Head=addBeg(Head,num);break;
              case 2:     printf("\n\tEnter a No. to Add : ");
                           scanf("%d",&num);
                           Head=addEnd(Head,num);break;
              case 3:     Head=delBeg(Head);break;
              case 4:     Head=delEnd(Head);break;
              case 5:     dispList(Head);break;
            }
       }while(c!=6);
     free(Head);
  }
```

Output

```
                ** Menu **
          1. Insert at Begin
          2. Insert at End
          3. Delete from Begining
          4. Delete at End
          5. Display
          6. Exit
          Enter a choice :
```

```c
#include <stdio.h>
#include<stdlib.h>

typedef struct Stack{int n;struct Stack *Next;}Stk;
//Stk *Rear;
  void chkOver()
    {
      printf("\n\t** Stack is Overflow ** \n");
    }
    void chkUnder()
    {
      printf("\n\t** Stack is Underflow ** \n");
    }
  Stk * Push(Stk *Last, int num)
    {
      Stk *Ptr;
      Ptr=(Stk *)malloc(sizeof(Stk *));
      if(Ptr==NULL)
        {
          chkOver();
          return Last;
        }
      Ptr->Next=NULL;
      Ptr->n=num;
      Ptr->Next=Last;
      Last=Ptr;
      return Last;
    }
  void dispStack(Stk *Last)
    {
      Stk *Ptr;
      if(Last==NULL)
        {
          chkUnder();return;
        }
      else
        {
          printf("\n\tValues in the Stack : ");
          for(Ptr=Last;Ptr!=NULL;Ptr=Ptr->Next)
            {
              printf(" %d ",Ptr->n);
            }
```

```
            }
      }
   Stk * Pop(Stk *Last)
     {
        int num;
        Stk *Ptr;
        if(Last==NULL)
          {
             chkUnder();
             return Last;
          }
        printf("\n\tNumber Popped : %d ",Last->n);
        Last=Last->Next;
        return Last;
     }
   int main()
     {
        Stk *Rear;
        Rear=NULL;
        int c,num;
        do
          {
             printf("\n\t1. Push\n\t2. Pop\n\t3. Display\n\t4. Exit");
             printf("\n\tEnter a choice : ");
             scanf("%d",&c);
             switch(c)
               {
                  case 1: printf("\n\tEnter a No. : ");
                          scanf("%d",&num);
                          Rear=Push(Rear,num);
                          break;
                  case 2:Rear=Pop(Rear);break;
                  case 3:dispStack(Rear);break;
               }
          }while(c!=4);
     }
```

Output

1. Push	Enter a choice : 2
2. Pop	Number Popped : 3
3. Display	
4. Exit	Enter a choice : 2

Enter a choice : 1   Number Popped : 2

Enter a No. : 1   Enter a choice : 2
Enter a No. : 2   Number Popped : 1
Enter a No. : 3
                                      Enter a choice : 2
Enter a choice : 3   ** Stack is Underflow **
Values in the Stack : 3 2 1

Prog-33. *Polynomial Addition using Linked List*

```c
#include <stdio.h>
#include<stdlib.h>

typedef struct Poly{float coff;int exp; struct Poly *Next;}Pol;
Pol *Last;

   Pol * addNew(Pol *First, float c, int e)
     {
        Pol *Ptr;
        Ptr=(Pol *)malloc(sizeof(Pol *));
        if(Ptr==NULL)
          {
             return First;
          }
        Ptr->Next=NULL;
        Ptr->exp=e;
        Ptr->coff=c;
        if(First==NULL)
          {
             First=Last=Ptr;
          }
        else
          {
             Last->Next=Ptr;
             Last=Ptr;
          }
        return First;
     }
   void dispPoly(Pol *First,int c)
     {
        Pol *Ptr;
        if(First==NULL)
          {
             printf("\n\tEmpty Poly %d :",c);return;
```

DS -120

```
            }
        else
            {
                printf("\n\tValues in %d Poly : ",c);
                for(Ptr=First;Ptr!=NULL;Ptr=Ptr->Next)
                    {
                        printf(" %.00fx^%d ",Ptr->coff,Ptr->exp);
                    }
            }
    }
Pol * addPoly(Pol *First1, Pol *First2)
    {
        Pol *First3,*Ptr,*Pptr;
        First3=NULL;
        for(Ptr=First1;Ptr!=NULL;Ptr=Ptr->Next)
            {
                float cf=0;
                int flag=0;
                for(Pptr=First2;Pptr!=NULL;Pptr=Pptr->Next)
                    {
                        if(Ptr->exp==Pptr->exp)
                            {
                                cf=Ptr->coff+Pptr->coff;
                                flag=1;
                            }
                    }
                if(flag==1)
                    {
                        First3=addNew(First3,cf,Ptr->exp);
                    }
                else
                    {
                        First3=addNew(First3,Ptr->coff,Ptr->exp);
                    }
            }
        for(Pptr=First2;Pptr!=NULL;Pptr=Pptr->Next)
            {
                int flag=0;
                for(Ptr=First1;Ptr!=NULL;Ptr=Ptr->Next)
                    {
                        if(Ptr->exp==Pptr->exp)
                            {
                                flag=1;
```

```c
                break;
            }
        }
        if(flag==0)
        {
            First3=addNew(First3,Pptr->coff,Pptr->exp);
        }
    }
    return First3;
}
int main()
{
    Pol *Head1,*Head2,*Head3;
    Head1=Head2=Head3=NULL;
    int c,c1,ex;
    float cf;
    do
    {
        printf("\n\t1. Append\n\t2. Display\n\t3. Add\n\t4. Exit");
        printf("\n\tEnter a choice : ");
        scanf("%d",&c);
        switch(c)
        {
            case 1:
                do
                {
                    printf("\n\t1. Poly-1\n\t2. Poly-2\n\t3. Exit");
                    printf("\n\tEnter a choice : ");
                    scanf("%d",&c1);
                    if(c1<3)
                        {
                                        printf("\n\tEnter Coeficient : ");
                                        scanf("%f",&cf);
                                        printf("\n\tEnter a Exponent : ");
                                        scanf("%d",&ex);
                        }
                    switch(c1)
                        {
                                        case 1:Head1=addNew(Head1,cf,ex);break;
                                        case 2:Head2=addNew(Head2,cf,ex);break;
                        }
                }while(c1!=3);break;
            case 2:
```

```
            printf("\n\t1. Poly-1\n\t2. Poly-2\n\t3. Poly-3");
            printf("\n\tEnter a Choice : ");
            scanf("%d",&c1);
            switch(c1)
              {
                case 1:dispPoly(Head1,1);break;
                case 2:dispPoly(Head2,2);break;
                case 3:dispPoly(Head3,3);break;
              }
            break;
          case 3:Head3=addPoly(Head1,Head2);break;
        }
    }while(c!=4);
}
```

Output

1. Append
2. Display
3. Add
4. Exit
Enter a choice : 1

1. Poly-1
2. Poly-2
3. Exit
Enter a choice : 1
Enter Coeficient : 2
Enter a Exponent : 2

1. Poly-1
2. Poly-2
3. Exit
Enter a choice : 1
Enter Coeficient : 3
Enter a Exponent : 3

1. Poly-1
2. Poly-2
3. Exit
Enter a choice : 1
Enter Coeficient : 4
Enter a Exponent : 4

1. Poly-1
2. Poly-2
3. Exit
Enter a choice : 2
Enter Coeficient : 3
Enter a Exponent : 2

1. Poly-1
2. Poly-2
3. Exit
Enter a choice : 2
Enter Coeficient : 4
Enter a Exponent : 3

1. Poly-1
2. Poly-2
3. Exit
Enter a choice : 2
Enter Coeficient : 5
Enter a Exponent : 5

1. Append
2. Display
3. Add
4. Exit
Enter a choice : 3

Values in 1 Poly : 2x^2 3x^3 4x^4
Values in 2 Poly : 3x^2 4x^3 5x^5
Values in 3 Poly : 5x^2 7x^3 4x^4 5x^5

```c
#include <stdio.h>
#include<stdlib.h>

typedef struct DList{int n;struct DList *Next,*Prev;}DLst;
DLst *Last;
  void chkMsg()
    {
      printf("\n\t** List is Empty ** \n");
    }
  DLst * addNew(DLst *hd, int num)
    {
      DLst *Ptr;
      Ptr=(DLst *)malloc(sizeof(DLst *));
      Ptr->Next=NULL;
      Ptr->n=num;
      Ptr->Prev=NULL;
      if(hd==NULL)
        {
          hd=Last=Ptr;
        }
      else
        {
          Ptr->Prev=Last;
          Last->Next=Ptr;
          Last=Ptr;
        }
      return hd;
    }
  void dispList(DLst *hd)
    {
      DLst *Ptr;
      if(hd==NULL)
        {
          chkMsg();return;
        }
      else
        {
          printf("\n\tData in the List : ");
          for(Ptr=hd;Ptr!=NULL;Ptr=Ptr->Next)
            {
              printf(" %d ",Ptr->n);
```

```
            }
        }
    }
void dispRevList(DLst *hd)
  {
    DLst *Ptr;
    if(hd==NULL)
      {
        chkMsg();return;
      }
    else
      {
        printf("\n\tData in Reverse Order : ");
        for(Ptr=Last;Ptr!=NULL;Ptr=Ptr->Prev)
          {
            printf(" %d ",Ptr->n);
          }
      }
  }
DLst * delNode(DLst *hd)
  {
    int num;
    DLst *Ptr,*Pptr;
    if(hd==NULL)
      {
        chkMsg();return hd;
      }
    printf("\n\tEnter a No. to Delete : ");
    scanf("%d",&num);
    for(Ptr=hd;Ptr!=NULL;Ptr=Ptr->Next)
      {
        if(num==Ptr->n)
          {
            break;
          }
            Pptr=Ptr;
      }
    if(Ptr==NULL)
      {
        chkMsg();
        return hd;
      }
```

```
        if(Ptr==hd)              //Delete First
          {
            hd=hd->Next;
            hd->Prev=NULL;
          }
        else if(Ptr->Next==NULL)
          {
            Pptr->Next=Ptr->Next;
            Last->Next=NULL;
            Last=Pptr;
            return hd;
          }
        else if(Ptr->Next!=NULL)                    //Delete Last
          {

            Pptr->Next=Ptr->Next;
            Ptr=Ptr->Next;
            Ptr->Prev=Pptr;
          }
        return hd;
      }
    DLst * insBefo(DLst *hd)
      {
        int pos;
        DLst *Ptr,*Pptr,*Ptmp;
        if(hd==NULL)
          {
            chkMsg();return hd;
          }
        printf("\n\tEnter the Position : ");
        scanf("%d",&pos);
        for(Pptr=hd;Pptr!=NULL;Pptr=Pptr->Next)
          {
            pos--;
            if(pos<1)
              {
                break;
              }
              Ptmp=Pptr;
          }
        if(Pptr==NULL)
          {
```

```c
            printf("\n\tPosition is Out! ");
            return hd;
        }
      else
        {
          Ptr=(DLst *)malloc(sizeof(DLst *));
          printf("\n\tEnter a No. to Insert :");
          scanf("%d",&Ptr->n);
          Ptr->Next=NULL;
          Ptr->Prev=NULL;
          if(Pptr==hd)
            {
              Ptr->Next=hd;
              hd->Prev=Ptr;
              hd=Ptr;


            }
          else
            {
              Ptmp->Next=Ptr;
              Ptr->Prev=Ptmp;
              Ptr->Next=Pptr;
              Pptr->Prev=Ptr;
            }
        }
      return hd;
    }
DLst * insAfter(DLst *hd)
  {
    int pos;
    DLst *Ptr,*Pptr;
    if(hd==NULL)
      {
        chkMsg();return hd;
      }
    printf("\n\tEnter the Position : ");
    scanf("%d",&pos);
    for(Pptr=hd;Pptr->Next!=NULL;Pptr=Pptr->Next)
      {
        pos--;
        if(pos<1)
          {
```

```c
                break;
            }
        }
    Ptr=(DLst *)malloc(sizeof(DLst *));
    printf("\n\tEnter a No. to Insert :");
    scanf("%d",&Ptr->n);
    Ptr->Next=NULL;
    Ptr->Prev=NULL;
    if(Pptr->Next==NULL)
        {
            printf("\n\tPosition is Out of range, Adding at the Last! ");
            Last->Next=Ptr;
            Ptr->Prev=Last;
            Last=Ptr;
            return hd;
        }
    else
        {
            Ptr->Prev=Pptr;
            Pptr->Next->Prev=Ptr;
            Ptr->Next=Pptr->Next;
            Pptr->Next=Ptr;
        }
    return hd;
    }
int main()
    {
        DLst *Head;
        Head=Last=NULL;
        int c,num;
        do
            {
                printf("\n\t1. Add New\n\t2. Display\n\t3. Display-Reverse\n\t4. Delete");
                printf("\n\t5. Insert Before\n\t6. Insert After\n\t7. Exit");
                printf("\n\tEnter a choice : ");
                scanf("%d",&c);
                switch(c)
                    {
                        case 1: printf("\n\tEnter a No. to Add : ");
                                scanf("%d",&num);
                                Head=addNew(Head,num);
                                break;
```

```
                case 2:dispList(Head);break;
                case 3:dispRevList(Head);break;
                case 4:Head=delNode(Head);break;
                case 5:Head=insBefo(Head);break;
                case 6:Head=insAfter(Head);break;
            }
        }while(c!=7);        }
```

Output

1. Add New	Enter a choice : 4
2. Display	Enter a No. to Delete : 1
3. Display-Reverse	Enter a choice : 4
4. Delete	Enter a No. to Delete : 3
5. Insert Before	Enter a choice : 2
6. Insert After	Data in the List : 2
7. Exit	Enter a choice : 5
Enter a choice : 1	Enter the Position : 1
Enter a No. to Add : 1	Enter a No. to Insert :12
Enter a choice : 1	Enter a choice : 6
Enter a No. to Add : 2	Enter the Position : 2
Enter a choice : 1	Enter a No. to Insert :44
Enter a No. to Add : 3	Position is Out of range, Adding at
Enter a choice : 2	the Last!
Data in the List : 1 2 3	Enter a choice : 2
Enter a choice : 3	Data in the List : 12 2 44
Data in Reverse Order : 3 2 1	

Prog-35. Doubly Circular Linked List

```
#include<stdio.h>
#include<stdlib.h>
 typedef struct dList{
   struct dList *Prev;
   struct dList *Next;
   int val;}Node;

   Node * insBeg(Node *head)
     {
        Node *Ptr,*Pptr;
        int num;
        Ptr=(Node *)malloc(sizeof(Node *));
        if(Ptr==NULL)
          {
             printf("\n\tAllocation is Failed!!");
```

DS -129

```c
                }
            else
                {
                    printf("\n\tEnter the Value : ");
                    scanf("%d",&num);
                    Ptr->val=num;
                    if(head==NULL)
                        {
                            head=Ptr;
                            Ptr->Next=head;
                            Ptr->Prev=head;
                        }
                    else
                        {
                            Pptr=head;
                            while(Pptr->Next!=head)
                                {
                                    Pptr=Pptr->Next;
                                }
                            Pptr->Next=Ptr;
                            Ptr->Prev=Pptr;
                            head->Prev=Ptr;
                            Ptr->Next=head;
                            head=Ptr;
                        }
                }
            return head;
        }
Node * insEnd(Node *head)
    {
        Node *Ptr,*Pptr;
        int num;
        Ptr=(Node *) malloc(sizeof(Node *));
        if(Ptr==NULL)
            {
                printf("\n\tFailed to Allocate!!");
            }
        else
            {
                printf("\n\tEnter the Value : ");
                scanf("%d",&num);
                Ptr->val=num;
                if(head == NULL)
```

```
          {
            head=Ptr;
            Ptr->Next=head;
            Ptr->Prev=head;
          }
        else
          {
            Pptr=head;
            while(Pptr->Next!=head)
              {
                Pptr= Pptr->Next;
              }
            Pptr->Next=Ptr;
            Ptr->Prev=Pptr;
            head->Prev=Ptr;
            Ptr->Next=head;
          }
      }
    return head;
  }
Node * delBeg(Node *head)
  {
    Node *Pptr;
    if(head==NULL)
      {
        printf("\n\tList is Empty");
      }
    else if(head->Next==head)
      {
        head=NULL;
        printf("\n\tDelete from Top");
      }
    else
      {
        Pptr=head;
        while(Pptr->Next!=head)
          {
            Pptr=Pptr->Next;
          }
        Pptr->Next=head->Next;
        head->Next->Prev=Pptr;
        head=Pptr->Next;
      }
```

```c
        return head;
    }
Node * delEnd(Node *head)
  {
    Node *Pptr;
    if(head==NULL)
      {
        printf("\n\tList is Empty");
      }
    else if(head->Next==head)
      {
        head=NULL;
      }
    else
      {
        //Pptr=head;
        for(Pptr=head->Next;Pptr->Next!=head;Pptr=Pptr->Next);
        Pptr->Prev->Next= head;
        free(Pptr);
      }
    return head;
  }
void Display(Node *head)
  {
    Node *Ptr;
    Ptr=head;
    if(head==NULL)
      {
        printf("\n\tList is Empty!! ");
      }
    else
      {
        printf("\n\tData in the List : ");
        while(Ptr->Next!=head)
          {
            printf("%d ",Ptr->val);
            Ptr=Ptr->Next;
          }
        printf("%d ", Ptr->val);
      }
  }
int main ()
  {
```

```
    int ch;
    Node *head;
    head=NULL;
    do
      {
        printf("\n\t1. Insert At Begining\n\t2. Insert At End\n\t3. Delete From
Beginning");
        printf("\n\t4. Delete from End\n\t5. Display\n\t6. Exit\n");
        printf("\n\tEnter the Choice : ");
        scanf("%d",&ch);
        switch(ch)
          {
            case 1:
              head=insBeg(head);
              break;
            case 2:
              head=insEnd(head);
              break;
            case 3:
              head=delBeg(head);
              break;
            case 4:
              head=delEnd(head);
              break;
            case 5:
              Display(head);
              break;
            case 6:
              printf("\n\tQuit....");
              exit(0);
            default:
              printf("\n\tEnter a Valid Choice");
          }
      }while(ch!=6);
    free(head);
    return 0;
  }
```
**Not Providing any output, it is almost like Double Ended Queue.

Tree

A tree, also known as a general tree, is a recursive data structure where
each node can have an unlimited number of children. In contrast, a

binary tree is a specific type of data structure in which each node can have at most two children, referred to as the left and right nodes. Subtrees in a binary tree are always ordered, whereas subtrees in a general tree are not necessarily ordered.

Advantages of Trees

- Trees reproduce structural associations in the facts.
- Trees are used to denote hierarchies.
- Used for an efficient way of inserting and searching.
- It is very flexible.

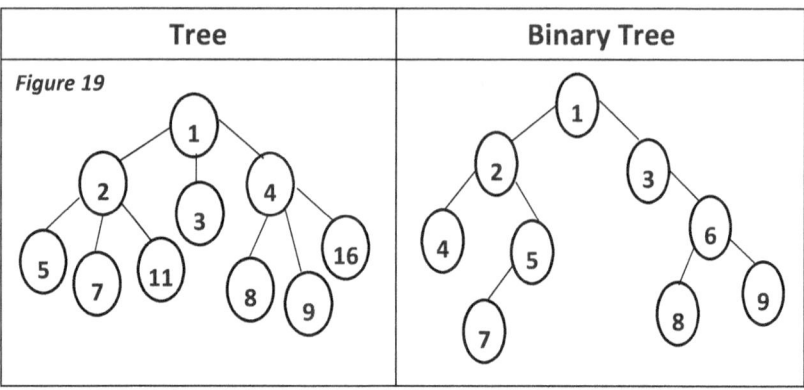

Tree	Binary Tree

Figure 19

Binary Tree

A binary tree is a non-linear data structure composed of nodes, similar to linked lists. However, each node in a binary tree can have at most two children, referred to as the left and right children. The first node of the tree is called the root. Searching in a binary tree is generally faster than in a sorted array or a linked list.

Some of Terminologies of Binary Trees

- **Root:** The topmost node in a tree is called **Root**.
- **Parent:** Apart from the root, every node in a binary tree has an upward edge to a node called a **Parent**.
- **Child:** The node below a node linked by its edge downward is called its **Child Node**.
- **Siblings**: Children of the same parent are said to be **Siblings**.
- **Leaf/External node:** Nodes which do not have a child are called as **Leaf Nodes**.

- **Internal node:** An Internal Node is a node that has at least one child.
- **Edge:** Connecting links between the nodes is called an **Edge**
- **Path:** The sequence of nodes and edges that connects one node to another is referred to as a Path between those two nodes.
- **Height:** The height of a node is the number of edges that make up the lengthiest downward path between that node and a leaf.
- **Level:** Level is defined by considering the **root** at level 0. If a node is at level *n*, then its children are at level *n* + 1.
- **Depth:** the total number of edges from a root node to a particular node is called as the **Depth** of that Node.
- **Degree:** The number of subtrees of a node is called the **degree of the node.**

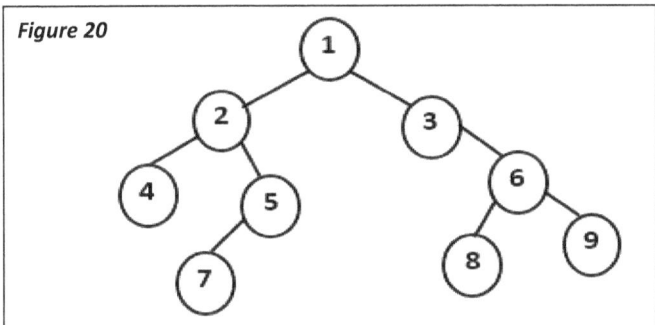

Figure 20

1. The Tree have N nodes (9) and N-1 edges (8).
2. ① is Root
3. 2 and 3 is left and right child of 1
4. 1 is 2 and 3's Parent
5. 2 and 3 are siblings
6. 3 is 8's ancestor (grandparent)
7. 8 and 9 is 3's descendent (grandchild)
8. 4, 7, 8, and 9 Leaf Node
9. Level of the tree 3 (root at 0)

Types of Binary Trees

1. **Complete Binary Tree** : A complete binary tree is a binary tree in which every level, except possibly the last, is completely filled, and all nodes are as far left as possible. A complete binary tree should not be confused with a perfect binary tree, where all levels are completely filled, including the last.

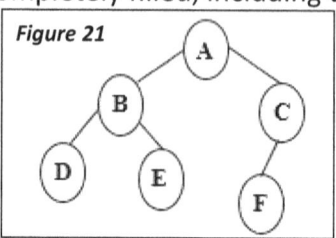

Figure 21

2. **Full Binary Tree** : A full binary tree is a binary tree in which every node has either no children or exactly two children. This means all non-leaf nodes have exactly two children.

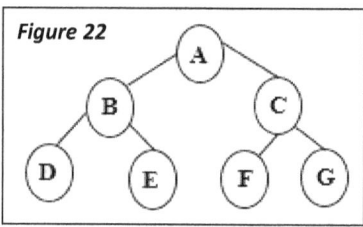

Figure 22

3. **Balanced Binary Tree**: A balanced binary tree is a tree with a height of of **O(log₂N)**, where **N** is the number of nodes. In a balanced binary tree, the height difference between the left and right subtrees of any node is at most one. Common examples of balanced binary search trees include AVL trees and Red-Black trees.

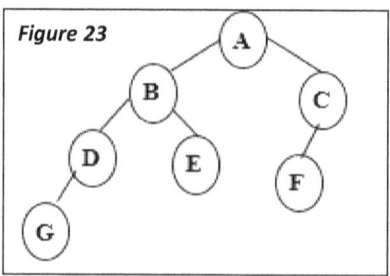

Figure 23

4. **Degenerate Binary Tree:** A degenerate tree, also known as a pathological tree, is a type of binary tree in which each node has only one child, either left or right.

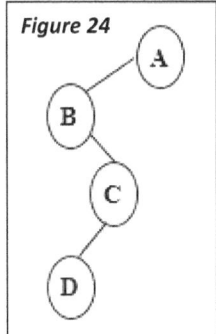

Figure 24

Threaded Binary Tree: A threaded binary tree is a type of binary tree in which the null pointers of leaf nodes are used to point to their inorder predecessor or inorder successor, facilitating faster traversal.

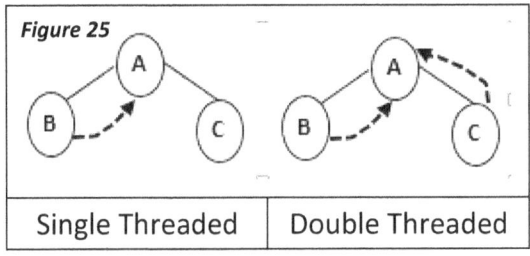

Figure 25

Single Threaded	Double Threaded

Binary Tree Traversal

Tree traversal refers to the process of visiting each node in a tree. In linear data structures like arrays, queues, stacks, and linked lists, traversal occurs in a single direction. However, in a hierarchical data structure like a tree, traversal can be performed in three different ways.

The three different ways of traversal:

1. **Inorder traversal:**
2. **Preorder traversal**
3. **Postorder traversal**

Inorder Traversal: Inorder traversal processes the root node between the left and right subtrees. In this traversal, the nodes are visited in the following order: first the left subtree, then the root, and finally the right subtree. **(Left → Root → Right).**

Preorder Traversal: Preorder traversal processes nodes in the following order: first the root, then the left subtree, and finally the right subtree. **(Root → Left → Right).**

Postorder traversal: Postorder traversal takes place from the left subtree to the right subtree and then to the root. **(Left → Right →Root).**

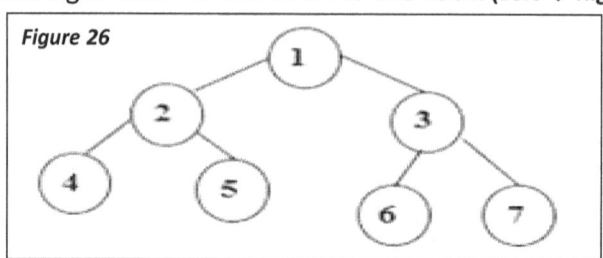

Figure 26

Preorder – Root-Left-Right: 1 2 4 5 3 6 7 : Start from the Root and then to the left child of the Left subtree and then to the Right. After completing Left subtree traversing move to the right subtree with same rule.

Inorder – Left-Root-Right: 4 2 5 1 6 3 7: Begin with the leftmost child of the left subtree, then move to the root, and finally to the right.

Postorder –Left-Right-Root: 4 5 2 6 7 3 1: Start from the leftmost child of the left subtree and then to the right and finally to the root.

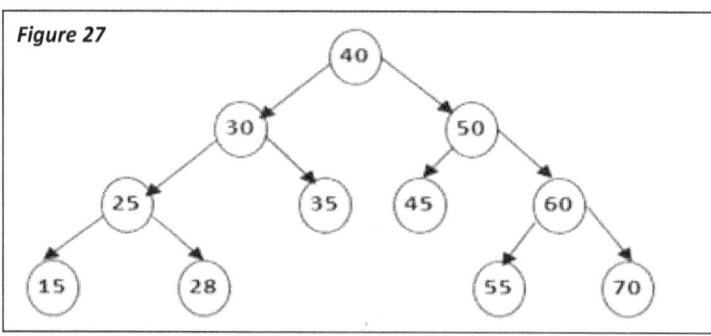

Figure 27

Preorder: 40, 30, 25, 15, 28, 35, 50, 45, 60, 55, 70

Inorder: 15, 25, 28, 30, 35, 40, 45, 50, 55, 60, 70

Postorder: 15, 28, 25, 35, 30, 45, 55, 70, 60, 50, 40

Prog-36. Tree (User's Choice Insert at Left / Right)

The tree is a recursive data structure, so recursive functions are commonly used for operations such as creation, addition, and traversal. This program allows nodes to be added to either the left or right, based on the user's choice.

```c
#include<stdio.h>
#include<stdlib.h>
 struct tree {
   int val;
   struct tree *Left;
   struct tree *Right;};
 typedef struct tree node;
 int c=0;
 node *createTree()        //Creating the tree
    {
      node *Ptr;
      int num;
      Ptr=(node*)malloc(sizeof(node *));
      printf("\n\tEnter the Value : ");
      scanf("%d",&num);
      Ptr->val=num;
      Ptr->Left=NULL;
      Ptr->Right=NULL;
      return (Ptr);
    }
 void buildTree(node *root)  //Adding a Node at Left or Right
    {
      char ch;
      printf("\n\t(L)eft / (R)ight child / Any Key to Exit : ");
      fflush(stdin);
      ch=getchar();
      if(toupper(ch)=='L')
        {
          root->Left=createTree();
          buildTree(root->Left);
        }
      else if(toupper(ch)=='R')
        {
          root->Right=createTree();
```

```c
          buildTree(root->Right);
        }
      else
        {
          return;
        }
  }
int nodeCount(node *root)
  {
    if(root!=NULL)
      {
        nodeCount(root->Left);
        c+=1;
        nodeCount(root->Right);
      }
    return c;
  }
void inorder(node *root)          //Inorder-Traversal
  {
    if(root!=NULL)
      {
        inorder(root->Left);
        printf(" --> %d",root->val);
        inorder(root->Right);
      }
  }
void preorder(node *root)          //Preorder-Traversal
  {
    if(root!=NULL)
      {
        printf(" --> %d",root->val);
        preorder(root->Left);
        preorder(root->Right);
      }
  }
void postorder(node *root)          //Postorder-Traversal
  {
    if(root!=NULL)
      {
        postorder(root->Left);
        postorder(root->Right);
        printf(" --> %d",root->val);
      }
```

```c
        }
int main()
    {
        node *root;
        int ch;
        int tot=0;
        do
          {
            printf("\n\t1. Insert a Node.");
            printf("\n\t2. Pre-Order Traversal.");
            printf("\n\t3. In-Order Traversal.");
            printf("\n\t4. Post-Order Traversal");
            printf("\n\t5. Counting Nodes");
            printf("\n\t6. EXIT.");
            printf("\n\tENTER CHOICE::");
            scanf("%d",&ch);
            switch(ch)
              {
                case 1:
                  root=createTree();
                  buildTree(root);
                  break;
                case 2:
                  printf("\n\tPre-order Traversal : ");
                  preorder(root);
                  break;
                case 3:
                  printf("\n\tIn-order Traversal : ");
                  inorder(root);
                  break;
                case 4:
                  printf("\n\tPost-order Traversal : ");
                  postorder(root);
                  break;
                case 5:
                  tot=nodeCount(root);
                  printf("\n\tNumber of Total Nodes : %d ",tot);
                  break;
                case 6:
                  printf("\n\tQuiting...");
                  exit(0);
                default:
```

```
        printf("\n\tWrong Choice ");
    }
   }while(ch!=6);
   return 0;
}
```

Output

1. INSERT A NODE. 2. PRE-Order Traversal. 3. IN-Order Traversal. 4. Post-Order Traversal 5. Counting Nodes 6. EXIT. ENTER CHOICE::1 Enter the Value : 5 (L)eft / (R)ight child / Any Key to Exit : L Enter the Value : 7 (L)eft / (R)ight child / Any Key to Exit : R Enter the Value : 8	(L)eft / (R)ight child / Any Key to Exit : X ENTER CHOICE::2 Pre-order Traversal : --> 5 --> 7 --> 8 ENTER CHOICE::3 In-order Traversal : --> 7 --> 8 --> 5 ENTER CHOICE::4 Post-order Traversal : --> 8 --> 7 --> 5 ENTER CHOICE::5 Number of Total Nodes : 3

Binary Search Tree

The Binary Search Tree, also known as the Ordered Binary Tree. In a BST, all the nodes in the left subtree have values that are less than the value of the root node. All nodes in the right subtree have values that are greater than the root node. The Binary Search Tree is ideal for searching for data in $O(\log(n))$ time. Both the subtrees of each node are also BST. They also have the above properties.

Building a Binary Search Tree

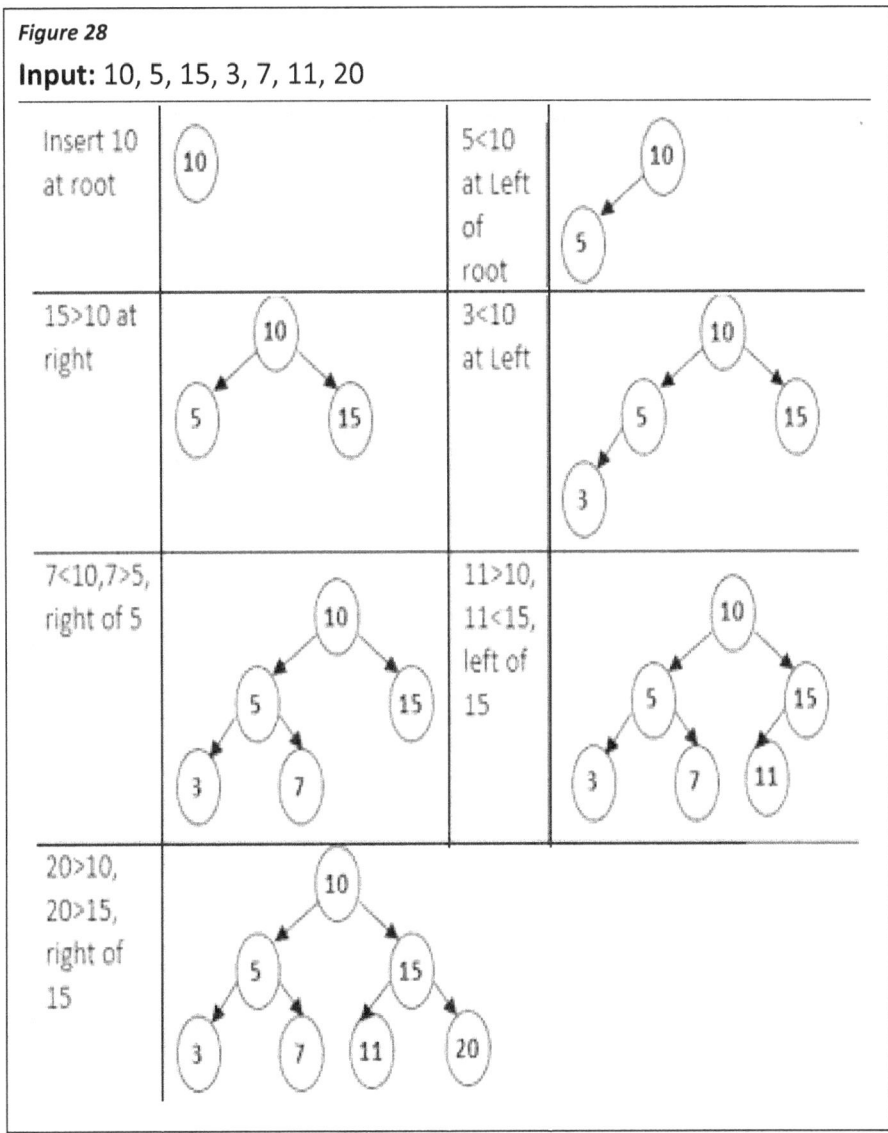

Figure 28

Input: 10, 5, 15, 3, 7, 11, 20

Input : 15, 5, 6, 14, 16, 12, 7, 3, 10, 4, 9, 11, 13, 8, 20

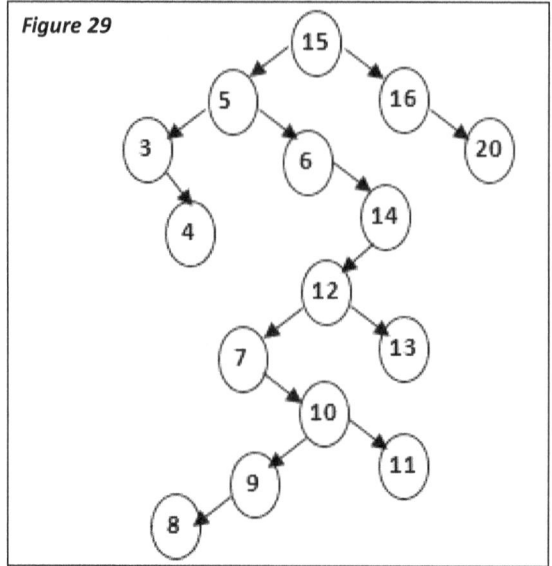

Figure 29

Delete a Node

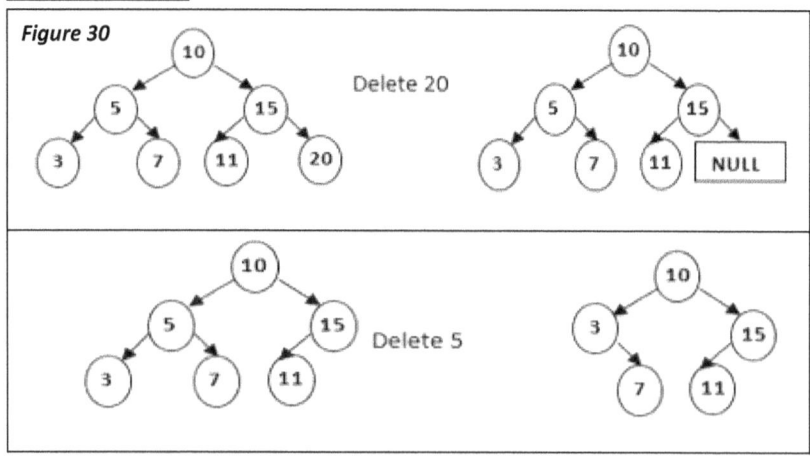

Figure 30

Complexity of Binary Tree

Process	Average Case	Worst Case
Insert Node	O(log n)	O(n)
Delete Node	O(log n)	O(n)
Searching	O(log n)	O(n)
Find Minimum	O(log n)	O(n)
Find Maximum	O(log n)	O(n)

Predecessor	O(log n)	O(n)
Successor	O(log n)	O(n)

Prog-37. Binary Search Tree

```c
#include <stdio.h>
#include <stdlib.h>

    typedef struct BST
      {
      int val;
      struct BST *right, *left;
      }Node;
    int c=0;
    Node* searchNode(Node *root, int N)
      {
      if(root==NULL || root->val==N) //Element found, if the condition
        {
          return root;
          }
      else if(N>root->val) // Search right subtree
      {
          return searchNode(root->right, N);
          }
      else //search left subtree
        {
          return searchNode(root->left,N);
          }
  }
//Minimum Element
  Node *minimum( Node *root)
    {
    if(root == NULL)
      {
        return NULL;
        }
    else if(root->left != NULL)
      {
        return minimum(root->left); // Minimum is either Root or left most value
        }
  return root;
  }
//Maximum Element
```

```
Node *maximum( Node *root)
  {
  if(root == NULL)
    {
       return NULL;
       }
  else if(root->right != NULL)
    {
       return maximum(root->right); // Maximum is either root or Right most
value
       }
  return root;
  }
  int countNodes(Node *root)
    {
       if(root!=NULL)
         {
            countNodes(root->left);
            c+=1;
            countNodes(root->right);  //Counting right and left subtree
         }
       return c;
    }

  Node* createNode(int N) //creating Node
    {
    Node *Ptr;
    Ptr = malloc(sizeof(Node *));
    Ptr->val = N;
    Ptr->left = NULL;
    Ptr->right = NULL;
    return Ptr;
    }

  Node* insertNode(Node *root, int N)
    {
    if(root==NULL)
      {
         return createNode(N);
         }
    else if(N>root->val) // Larger than root inserted in right
      {
         root->right = insertNode(root->right, N);
```

```
        }
   else if(N<root->val) // Smaller than root inserted in Left//
      {
          root->left = insertNode(root->left,N);
        }
  return root;
  }


Node* delNode(Node *root, int N)
  {
  if(root==NULL)
     {
        return NULL;
        }
  if (N>root->val) //Searching node to be Deleted
    {
      root->right = delNode(root->right, N);
        }
   else if(N<root->val)
    {
      root->left = delNode(root->left, N);
        }
   else
     {
     if(root->left==NULL && root->right==NULL) //No Child
       {
       free(root);
       return NULL;
       }
     else if(root->left==NULL || root->right==NULL) //One Child
       {
       Node *tmp;
       if(root->left==NULL)
         {
            tmp = root->right;
              }
       else
         {
            tmp = root->left;
              }
         free(root);
       return tmp;
       }
```

```c
        else
         {
         Node *tmp = minimum(root->right); //Two Children
         root->val = tmp->val;
         root->right = delNode(root->right, tmp->val);
         }
        }
      return root;
      }
      void preorder(Node *root)
       {
       if(root!=NULL)
         {
            printf(" %d ", root->val); // Printing root
            preorder(root->left); // left child
            preorder(root->right);// right child
         }
       }
      void inorder(Node *root)
       {
       if(root!=NULL)
         {
            inorder(root->left); //left child
            printf(" %d ", root->val); // printing root
            inorder(root->right);// right child
         }
       }
      void postorder(Node *root)
       {
       if(root!=NULL)
         {
            inorder(root->left); // visiting left
            inorder(root->right);// visiting right
            printf(" %d ", root->val); // printing root
         }
       }
// Height of a tree
   int Height(Node* root)
     {
     if (!root)
       {
          return 0;
       }
```

```c
        else
          {
             int lh = Height(root->left);
             int rh = Height(root->right);
             if (lh >= rh)
               {
                  return lh + 1;
               }
        else
          {
             return rh + 1;
          }
      }
    }
int main()
{
    int c,num;
    Node *root=NULL,*Ptr=NULL;
    do
      {
        printf("\n\t1. Insert\n\t2. Traverse\n\t3. Delete\n\t4. Search");
        printf("\n\t5. Minimum\n\t6. Maximum\n\t7. Count Nodes");
        printf("\n\t8. Height\n\t9. Exit");
        printf("\n\tEnter a Choice : ");
        scanf("%d",&c);
        switch(c)
          {
            case 1:
                  printf("\n\tEnter a Number to Insert :");
                  scanf("%d",&num);
                  if(root==NULL)
                    {
                                  root = createNode(num);
                    }
                  else
                        {
                                  insertNode(root,num);
                        }
                break;
              case 2:
                  printf("\nPreorder  : ");
                  preorder(root);
```

```c
        printf("\nInorder  : ");
          inorder(root);
        printf("\nPostorder : ");
        postorder(root);
        printf("\n");
          break;
    case 3:
        printf("\n\tEnter a Number to Delete :");
        scanf("%d",&num);
        Ptr=searchNode(root,num);
        if(Ptr==NULL)
          {
                    printf("\n\t%d is not found!!!",num);
          }
        else
          {
                    root = delNode(root, num);
          }
        break;
    case 4:
        printf("\n\tEnter a Number to Search :");
        scanf("%d",&num);
        Ptr=searchNode(root,num);
        if(Ptr==NULL)
          {
                    printf("\n\t%d is not found!!!",num);
          }
        else
          {
                    printf("\n\t%d  is Present ",Ptr->val);
          }
        break;
    case 5:
        Ptr=minimum(root);
        printf("\n\tMinimum : %d  ",Ptr->val);
        break;
    case 6:
        Ptr=maximum(root);
        printf("\n\tMaximum : %d  ",Ptr->val);
        break;
    case 7:
        num=countNodes(root);
        printf("\n\tNumber of Total Nodes of Tree : %d  ",num);
```

```
                break;
            case 8:
                num=Height(root);
                printf("\n\tHeight of Tree : %d  ",num);
                break;
        }
    }while(c!=9);
    return 0;
}
```

Output

1. Insert	Enter a Choice : 2
2. Traverse	Preorder : 5 4 3 7 8
3. Delete	Inorder : 3 4 5 7 8
4. Search	Postorder : 3 4 7 8 5
5. Minimum	
6. Maximum	Enter a Choice : 4
7. Count Nodes	Enter a Number to Search :8
8. Height	
9. Exit	8 is Present
Enter a Choice : 1	
Enter a Number to Insert :5	Enter a Choice : 5
	Minimum : 3
Enter a Choice : 1	
Enter a Number to Insert :7	Enter a Choice : 6
	Maximum : 8
Enter a Choice : 1	
Enter a Number to Insert :4	Enter a Choice : 8
	Height of Tree : 3
Enter a Choice : 1	
Enter a Number to Insert :3	Enter a Choice : 3
	Enter a Number to Delete :5
Enter a Choice : 1	
Enter a Number to Insert :8	Enter a Choice : 2
	Preorder : 7 4 3 8
	Inorder : 3 4 7 8
	Postorder : 3 4 8 7

Balanced Tree

A balanced binary tree is also known as a height-balanced tree. It is called a balanced binary tree when the difference between the height of the left and right subtrees is no more than 1. An AVL Tree and a Red-Black Tree are common examples of data structures that can produce a balanced binary search tree.

AVL Tree

The AVL tree is a height-balanced tree, named after its inventors, Adelson-Velsky and Landis. In an AVL tree, the height of the left and right subtrees is checked to ensure that the height difference between them is limited to 1. The difference in heights between the subtrees is known as the balance factor. If a node becomes imbalanced, a rotation technique can be applied to restore balance.

BalanceFactor = height(left sub-tree) − height(right sub-tree)

AVL Rotations

In an AVL tree, rotations are used to restore balance when the tree becomes unbalanced due to insertions or deletions. There are four types of rotations in an AVL tree, based on the balance factors of the nodes. The balance factor is the difference in height between the left and right subtrees of a node. If the balance factor exceeds 1 or is less than -1, a rotation is required.

1. Left rotation.
2. Right rotation.
3. Left-Right rotation.
4. Right-Left rotation

Here are the four types of rotations:

1. **Right Rotation (Single Rotation)**
   - This is used when the left subtree of a node is higher than the right subtree, specifically in a **Left-Left (LL)** case.

   Steps:
   - Make the left child of the unbalanced node the new root of the subtree.
   - The old root becomes the right child of the new root.

- The right subtree of the new root becomes the left subtree of the old root.

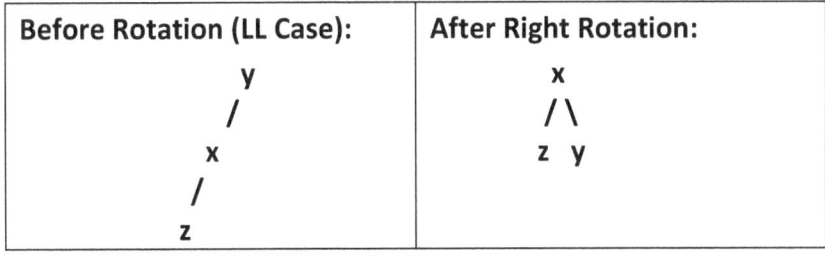

Before Rotation (LL Case):	After Right Rotation:
y / x / z	x / \\ z y

2. **Left Rotation (Single Rotation)**
   - This is used when the right subtree of a node is higher than the left subtree, specifically in a Right-Right (RR) case.

   Steps:
   - Make the right child of the unbalanced node the new root of the subtree.
   - The old root becomes the left child of the new root.
   - The left subtree of the new root becomes the right subtree of the old root.

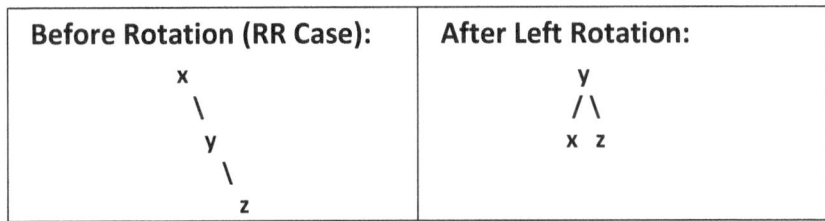

Before Rotation (RR Case):	After Left Rotation:
x \\ y \\ z	y / \\ x z

3. **Left-Right Rotation (Double Rotation)**
   Let's break down the **Left-Right (LR) Case** further, with detailed steps and explanations.

Initial Structure Before Rotation

The unbalanced node is **z**, its left child is **x**, and the right child of **x** is **y**.

z
/
x
\\
Y

1. This structure is imbalanced because:
2. The height difference between the left and right subtrees of z exceeds 1 (AVL property violated).
3. The imbalance occurs due to the growth in the right subtree of x, creating the Left-Right (LR) imbalance.

Steps to Fix LR Imbalance, to fix this imbalance, **two rotations** are required:

1. A **Left Rotation** on **x** to straighten the zigzag structure.
2. A **Right Rotation** on **z** to balance the subtree.

Step 1: Perform a Left Rotation on x

The goal here is to bring **y** up as the new root of the subtree rooted at **x**. The left child of **y** (if any) becomes the right child of **x**.

Before Left Rotation on x:	After Left Rotation on x:

<pre>   z
     /
    x
     \
      Y</pre>
	<pre> z
	     /
	    y
	    /
	   x</pre>

Explanation:

- **y** becomes the new root of the subtree rooted at **x**.
- **x** becomes the left child of **y**.
- Any left child of **y** (if it exists) becomes the right child of **x**.

Step 2: Perform a Right Rotation on z

Now that the subtree rooted at **x** is straightened, we perform a **Right Rotation** on **z** to make **y** the new root of the entire subtree.

Before Right Rotation on z:	After Right Rotation on z:

<pre>   z
     /
    y
   /
  x</pre>
	<pre> y
	    /\
	   x z</pre>

Explanation:
- **y** becomes the new root of the subtree.
- **z** becomes the right child of **y**.
- **x** remains the left child of **y**.

The **Right-Left (RL) Rotation** occurs when a node in an AVL tree becomes unbalanced because its **right child** has a **left-heavy subtree**. This creates a **zigzag pattern**, which cannot be resolved with a single rotation. A double rotation (right rotation followed by left rotation) is required.

Analyze and resolve the imbalance for the given tree structure:

Initial Structure Before Rotation:

```
x
 \
  z
 /
y
```

- Node x: Unbalanced node, balance factor = -2 (right-heavy).
- Node z: Balance factor = +1 (left-heavy).
- The imbalance occurs because the left subtree of z (node y) has grown.

Steps to Resolve RL Imbalance

To fix this imbalance, we perform **two rotations**:

1. A **Right Rotation** on z to straighten the structure.
2. A **Left Rotation** on x to balance the tree.

Step 1: Perform a Right Rotation on z

The goal of this step is to make **y** the new root of the subtree rooted at **z**.

Before Right Rotation on z:

```
x
 \
  z
 /
y
```

Right Rotation Steps:

1. Promote **y** to the position of **z**.
2. Make **z** the right child of **y**.

3. Transfer the right child of **y** (if any) to the left child of **z**.

After Right Rotation on z:

```
x
 \
  y
   \
    z
```

Explanation:

- **y** becomes the root of the subtree previously rooted at **z**.
- **z** becomes the right child of **y**.
- Any right child of **y** (if it exists) is transferred to the left child of **z**.

Step 2: Perform a Left Rotation on x

Now that the subtree rooted at **z** is straightened, we perform a **Left Rotation** on **x** to make **y** the new root of the entire subtree.

Before Left Rotation on x:

```
x
 \
  y
   \
    z
```

Left Rotation Steps:

1. Promote **y** to the position of **x**.
2. Make **x** the left child of **y**.
3. Transfer the left child of **y** (if any) to the right child of **x**.

After Left Rotation on x:

```
  y
 / \
x   z
```

Explanation:

- **y** becomes the new root of the entire subtree.
- **x** becomes the left child of **y**.
- **z** remains the right child of **y**.

Performing just one rotation (either left or right) would not fix the imbalance and might violate the BST property.

Key Concepts

1. **Imbalance Source**:
   - The RL case occurs when the right subtree of a node is left-heavy.
   - The zigzag pattern demands two rotations to fix.
2. **Time Complexity**:
   - Rotations are local operations and take O(1) time.
   - Maintaining balance during insertions or deletions in an AVL tree, including rotations, ensures an overall time complexity of O(log n)
   - At every step, the left subtree contains nodes smaller than the root, and the right subtree contains nodes larger than the root.

Left Rotation

The tree is unbalanced as balance factor>1	Left Rotation	Balanced Tree
Figure 31		

Right Rotation

The tree is unbalanced as balance factor>1	Right Rotation	Balanced Tree
Figure 32		

Left-Right Rotation

2 is inserted at right of left node and the tree is unbalance as balanced factor is 2. Then Right Rotation to Balance	First perform Left Rotation.	First perform Right Rotation.	**Balanced Tree**
Figure 33			

Right-Left Rotation

Following tree also an unbalanced tree because 2 is inserted at left of right sub-tree.	First perform Right Rotation.	First perform Left Rotation.	Balanced Tree
Figure 34			

Insert Node

Insert 15, 18, 12, 8, 5, 54, 14, 13 into an empty AVL tree

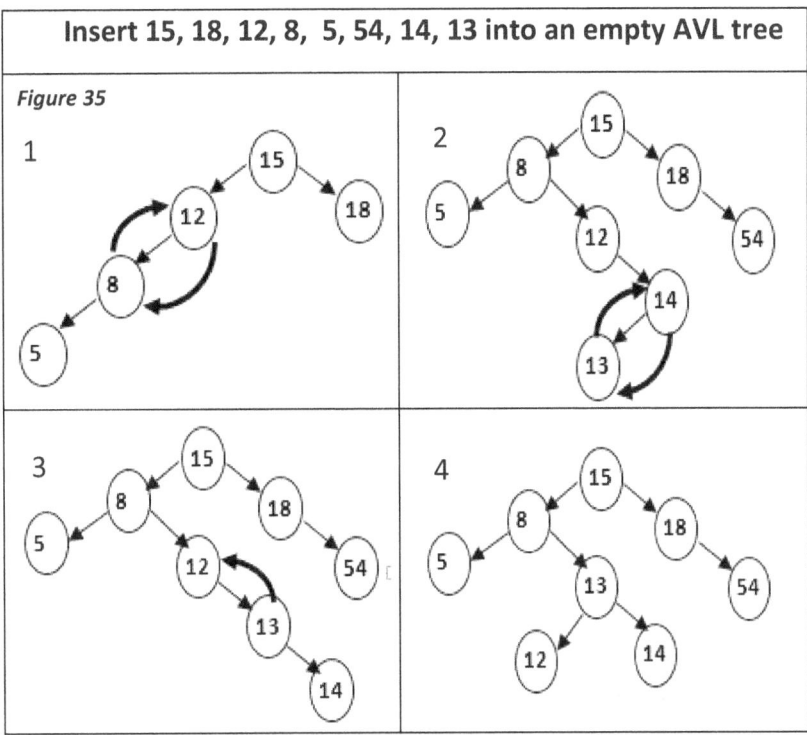

Figure 35

Delete Node

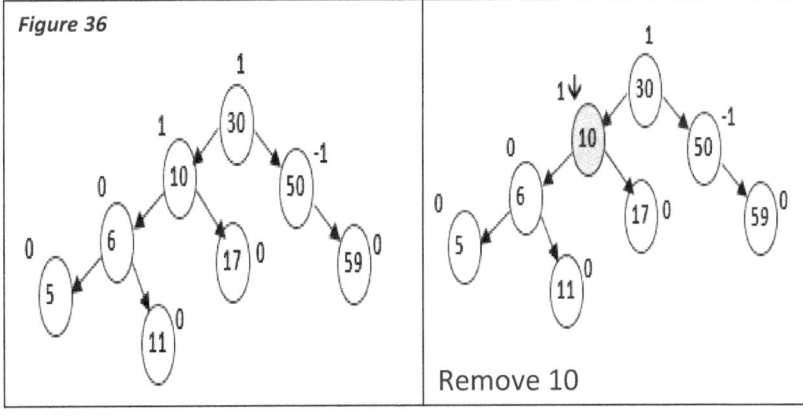

Figure 36

Remove 10

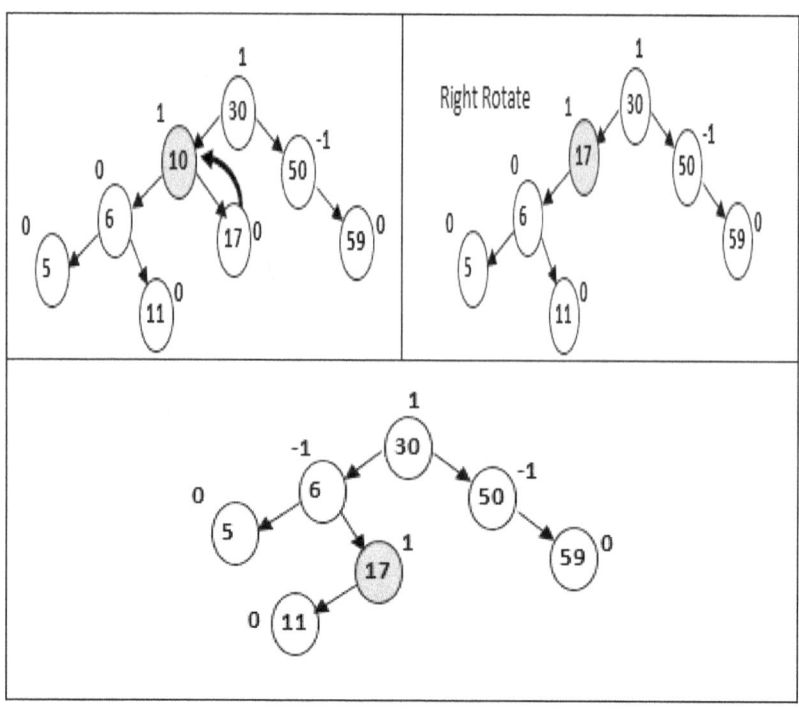

Prog-38. AVL Tree

```
//  AVL Tree
//  AVL Tree
#include <stdio.h>
#include <stdlib.h>
#define FALSE 0
#define TRUE 1
 typedef  struct node
    {
    struct  node *Left;
    int Data;
    struct  node *Right;
    int height;
    }aNode;

  aNode *LeftRoataion(aNode *Ptr)
    {
    aNode *Pptr;
    Pptr = Ptr->Right; // right child
    Ptr->Right = Pptr->Left; //Rotate
    Pptr->Left = Ptr;
```

```
  return Pptr;
 }

aNode *RightRoataion(aNode *Ptr)
 {
 aNode *Pptr;
 Pptr = Ptr->Left;  //Left Child
 Ptr->Left = Pptr->Right;  //Rotate
 Pptr->Right = Ptr;
 return Pptr;
 }
aNode *insert_Left(aNode *Ptr) //Insert Left Child
 {
 aNode *Pptr, *Tptr;
 Pptr = Ptr->Left;
 if(Pptr->height == 1)
  {
    Ptr->height = 0;
    Pptr->height = 0;
    Ptr = RightRoataion(Ptr);
  }
  else
  {
    Tptr = Pptr->Right;
    switch(Tptr->height)
     {
      case -1:
       Ptr->height = 0;
       Pptr->height = 1;
       break;
      case 1:
       Ptr->height = -1;
       Pptr->height = 0;
       break;
      case 0:
       Ptr->height = 0;
       Pptr->height = 0;
     }
    Tptr->height = 0;
    Ptr->Left = LeftRoataion(Pptr);
    Ptr = RightRoataion(Ptr);
  }
```

```
    return Ptr;
   }
aNode *insert_Right(aNode *Ptr)          //Insert Right Child
  {
 aNode *Pptr, *Tptr;
 Pptr = Ptr->Right;
 if(Pptr->height == -1)
  {
    Ptr->height = 0;
    Pptr->height = 0;
    Ptr = LeftRoataion(Ptr);
  }
 else
  {
    Tptr = Pptr->Left;
    switch(Tptr->height)
     {
      case -1:
       Ptr->height = 1;
       Pptr->height = 0;
       break;
           case 1:
       Ptr->height = 0;
       Pptr->height = -1;
       break;
      case 0:
       Ptr->height = 0;
       Pptr->height = 0;
     }
    Tptr->height = 0;
    Ptr->Right = RightRoataion(Pptr);
    Ptr = LeftRoataion(Ptr);
  }
  return Ptr;
  }
aNode *Del_Left(aNode *Ptr,int *MinPtr)          //Delete Left Child
  {
 aNode *Pptr, *Tptr;
 Pptr = Ptr->Left;
 if( Pptr->height == 0)
  {
    Ptr->height = 1;
```

```
      Pptr->height = -1;
      *MinPtr = FALSE;
      Ptr = RightRoataion(Ptr);
   }
  else if(Pptr->height == 1 )
   {
     Ptr->height = 0;
     Pptr->height = 0;
     Ptr = RightRoataion(Ptr);
   }
  else
   {
     Tptr = Pptr->Right;
     switch(Tptr->height)
      {
        case 0:
          Ptr->height = 0;
          Pptr->height = 0;
          break;
        case 1:
          Ptr->height = -1;
          Pptr->height = 0;
          break;
        case -1:
          Ptr->height = 0;
          Pptr->height = 1;
       }
     Tptr->height = 0;
     Ptr->Left = LeftRoataion(Pptr);
     Ptr = RightRoataion(Ptr);
   }
  return Ptr;
  }


aNode *Del_Right(aNode *Ptr,int *MinPtr)          //Delete Right Child
  {
  aNode *Pptr, *Tptr;
     Pptr = Ptr->Right;
  if (Pptr->height == 0)
   {
     Ptr->height = -1;
     Pptr->height = 1;
     *MinPtr = FALSE;
```

```
        Ptr = LeftRoataion(Ptr);
      }
    else if(Pptr->height == -1 )
      {
        Ptr->height = 0;
        Pptr->height = 0;
        Ptr = LeftRoataion(Ptr);
      }
    else
      {
        Tptr = Pptr->Left;
        switch(Tptr->height)
          {
            case 0:
              Ptr->height = 0;
              Pptr->height = 0;
              break;
            case 1:
              Ptr->height = 0;
              Pptr->height = -1;
              break;
             case -1:
              Ptr->height = 1;
              Pptr->height = 0;
            }
        Tptr->height = 0;
        Ptr->Right = RightRoataion(Pptr);
        Ptr = LeftRoataion(Ptr);
      }
    return Ptr;
    }
aNode *Right_Del(aNode *Ptr, int *MinPtr)
  {
   switch(Ptr->height)
    {
      case 0:
        Ptr->height = 1;
        *MinPtr = FALSE;
        break;
      case -1:
        Ptr->height = 0;
        break;
      case 1:
```

```
      Ptr = Del_Left(Ptr, MinPtr );
    }
  return Ptr;
}
aNode *Left_Chk(aNode *Ptr, int *MaxPtr )
  {
  switch(Ptr->height)
   {
     case 0:
      Ptr->height = 1;
      break;
     case -1:
      Ptr->height = 0;
      *MaxPtr = FALSE;
      break;
     case 1:
      Ptr = insert_Left(Ptr);
      *MaxPtr = FALSE;
   }
  return Ptr;
  }
aNode *Check_Right(aNode *Ptr, int *MaxPtr )
  {
  switch(Ptr->height)
   {
     case 0:
      Ptr->height = -1;
      break;
     case 1:
      Ptr->height = 0;
      *MaxPtr = FALSE;
      break;
     case -1:
      Ptr = insert_Right(Ptr);
      *MaxPtr = FALSE;
   }
  return Ptr;     }
void Disp(aNode *ptr,int level)
  {
  int i;
  if(ptr == NULL )
    return;
```

```
      else
        {
        Disp(ptr->Right, level+1);
        printf("%d ", ptr->Data);
        Disp(ptr->Left, level+1);
      }
    }
aNode *Chk_Left(aNode *Ptr, int *MinPtr)
    {
    switch(Ptr->height)
      {
        case 0: // Balanced
          Ptr->height = -1;  //Check right
          *MinPtr = FALSE;
          break;
        case 1:     //Check left
          Ptr->height = 0;
          break;
        case -1: // Check right
          Ptr = Del_Right(Ptr, MinPtr); /*Right Balancing*/
      }
    return Ptr;
    }

aNode *del(aNode *Ptr, int PKey)
    {
    aNode *tmp, *succ;
    static int Min;
    if( Ptr == NULL)
      {
        printf("\n\tNumber not Present");
        Min = FALSE;
        return(Ptr);
      }
    if( PKey < Ptr->Data )
      {
        Ptr->Left = del(Ptr->Left, PKey);
        if(Min == TRUE)
          Ptr = Chk_Left(Ptr, &Min);
      }
    else if( PKey > Ptr->Data )
      {
        Ptr->Right = del(Ptr->Right, PKey);
```

```
    if(Min==TRUE)
      Ptr = Right_Del(Ptr, &Min);
   }
  else
   {
    if( Ptr->Left!=NULL && Ptr->Right!=NULL ) //With 2 children
     {
      succ = Ptr->Right;
      while(succ->Left)
       succ = succ->Left;
      Ptr->Data = succ->Data;
      Ptr->Right = del(Ptr->Right, succ->Data);
      if( Min == TRUE )
        Ptr = Right_Del(Ptr, &Min);
     }
    else  //With left child
     {
      tmp = Ptr;
      if( Ptr->Left != NULL )
      Ptr = Ptr->Left;
      else if( Ptr->Right != NULL) // With right child
       Ptr = Ptr->Right;
      else
       Ptr = NULL; // nil children
            free(tmp);
            Min = TRUE;
        }
   }
  return Ptr;
  }
void inorder(aNode *ptr)
  {
  if(ptr!=NULL)
   {
    inorder(ptr->Left);
    printf("%d ",ptr->Data);
    inorder(ptr->Right);
   }
  }
void preorder(aNode *ptr)
  {
  if(ptr!=NULL)
```

```c
      {
        printf("%d  ",ptr->Data);
           inorder(ptr->Left);
        inorder(ptr->Right);
      }
    }
void postorder(aNode *ptr)
   {
   if(ptr!=NULL)
    {
       inorder(ptr->Left);
       inorder(ptr->Right);
       printf("%d  ",ptr->Data);
    }
    }
aNode *insert(aNode *Ptr, int Num)
    {
     static int Max;
    if(Ptr==NULL)
     {
       Ptr = (aNode *) malloc(sizeof(aNode));
       Ptr->Data = Num;
       Ptr->Left = NULL;
       Ptr->Right = NULL;
       Ptr->height = 0;
       Max = TRUE;
     }
    else if(Num < Ptr->Data)      //Inserting left subtree
     {
       Ptr->Left = insert(Ptr->Left, Num);
       if(Max==TRUE)
         Ptr = Left_Chk( Ptr, &Max );
     }
    else if(Num > Ptr->Data)      //Inserting right subtree
     {
       Ptr->Right = insert(Ptr->Right, Num);
       if(Max==TRUE)
         Ptr = Check_Right(Ptr, &Max);
     }
    else
     {
       printf("\n\tDuplicate key\n");
       Max = FALSE;
```

```c
    }
  return Ptr;
  }

int main()
 {
 int choice,num;
 aNode *root = NULL;
 while(1)
  {
    printf("\n\n\t1. Insert\n\t2. Display\n\t3. Delete\n\t4. Inorder");
        printf("\n\t5. Preorder\n\t6. PostOrder \n\t7. Quit");
    printf("\n\tEnter Your Choice : ");
        scanf("%d",&choice);
    switch(choice)
     {
       case 1:
        printf("\n\tEnter the key to be inserted : ");
        scanf("%d",&num);
        root = insert(root,num);
        break;
            case 2:
                printf("\n\tDisplay : \t ");
        Disp(root,0);
        break;
          case 3:
        printf("\n\tEnter the Number to Delete : ");
        scanf("%d",&num);
        root = del(root,num);
        break;
        case 4:
          printf("\n\tInorder : \t ");
        inorder(root);
        break;
        case 5:
          printf("\n\tPreorder : \t ");
        preorder(root);
        break;
        case 6:
          printf("\n\tPostorder : \t ");
        postorder(root);
        break;
            case 7:
```

```c
        printf("\n\t***Quiting...");
    exit(0);
      default:
      printf("\n\t***Wrong choice***");
    }
  }
return 0;
}
```

Output

1. Insert	Enter Your Choice : 2
2. Display	Display : 98 77 44 33 22
3. Delete	
4. Inorder	Enter Your Choice : 4
5. Preorder	Inorder : 22 33 44 77 98
6. PostOrder	Enter Your Choice : 5
7. Quit	Preorder : 44 22 33 77 98
Enter Your Choice : 1	
Enter the key to be inserted : 77	Enter Your Choice : 6
	Postorder : 22 33 77 98 44
Enter Your Choice : 1	Enter Your Choice : 3
Enter the key to be inserted : 44	Enter the Number to Delete : 77
Enter Your Choice : 1	1. Insert
Enter the key to be inserted : 22	2. Display
	3. Delete
Enter Your Choice : 1	4. Inorder
Enter the key to be inserted : 33	5. Preorder
	6. PostOrder
Enter Your Choice : 1	7. Quit
Enter the key to be inserted : 98	Enter Your Choice : 2
	Display : 98 44 33 22

Red and Black Tree

Properties of the Red Black Tree

1. Red - Black Tree is a Binary Search Tree.
2. The ROOT node must be BLACK.
3. The children of Red node must be BLACK. (There should not be two consecutive RED nodes).
4. There should be the same number of BLACK nodes in all the paths of a tree.

5. Every new node must be inserted with RED colour.
6. Every leaf (ex. NULL node) must be coloured BLACK.

All Red Black Tree is a binary search tree, although all Binary Search Trees are not Red Black tree.

Insertion into RED BLACK Tree

The root node of a Red-Black Tree must be black. Every new node is inserted with the color **red**. The insertion operation in a Red-Black Tree is similar to that of a Binary Search Tree but includes an additional color property. After each insertion, verify that all the Red-Black Tree properties are satisfied. If all properties are maintained, proceed as usual. Otherwise, take the necessary steps outlined below to restore the Red-Black Tree properties.

1. **Change Colour (Red or Black)**
2. **Rotate if necessary**
3. **Recolor after Rotation**

The insertion operation in the Red Black Tree is performed using the following steps:

Key Properties of a Red-Black Tree

1. **Node Color**:
   - Each node is either **red** or **black**.
2. **Root Property**:
   - The root node must always be **black**.
3. **Red Property** (No two consecutive red nodes):
   - A **red** node cannot have a **red** parent or child.
4. **Black Height**:
   - Every path from the root to a leaf or null node must have the **same number of black nodes**.
5. **Leaf Property**:
   - All leaf (null) nodes are considered **black**.

Why Red-Black Trees?

Red-Black Trees ensure that the tree remains balanced, preventing degenerative cases (e.g., a skewed BST) and ensuring efficient *O(log n)* operations for:

- Insertion
- Deletion
- Search

Insertion in a Red-Black Tree

1. BST Insertion:

   - Insert the new node as in a standard BST based on key comparison.
   - Assign the new node a **red** color.

2. **Check** for **Violations**:

   - After insertion, check whether the Red-Black Tree properties are violated.
   - If violated, fix the tree using **recoloring** and/or **rotations**.

3. **Fix Violations**:

   - Case 1: Parent is black:

     - No violation; tree remains valid.

   - Case 2: Parent is red:

     - Violation occurs due to the Red Property (no consecutive red nodes). Fix this based on the uncle node's color:

   - Uncle is red:

     - Recolor the parent and uncle as black and the grandparent as red. Then, check the grandparent for further violations.

   - Uncle is black:

     - Perform rotations (Left/Right or combinations) to balance the tree and recolor nodes as needed.

2. **Ensure Root is Black**:

   - If the root becomes red during the process, recolor it to black.

Rotations in a Red-Black Tree

Rotations are used to restore balance after insertion or deletion:

1. **Left Rotation**:
   - Promotes the right child of a node to its parent's position.
   - Used in Right-Right (RR) imbalances.
2. **Right Rotation**:
   - Promotes the left child of a node to its parent's position.
   - Used in Left-Left (LL) imbalances.
3. **Double Rotations**:
   - Left-Right (LR): Perform a left rotation on the parent, then a right rotation on the grandparent.
   - Right-Left (RL): Perform a right rotation on the parent, then a left rotation on the grandparent.

Deletion in a Red-Black Tree

1. **BST Deletion**:
   - Remove the node as in a standard BST.
   - If the deleted node is black, balance the tree to ensure all Red-Black properties are maintained.
2. **Fix Violations**:
   - If a double-black node (extra black height) is created, perform recoloring and/or rotations to fix the violation.
   - Propagate fixes upward as necessary.

Red-Black Tree in Action : Initial Tree:

```
        10(B)
        / \
     5(R)   15(B)
```

Inserting 1:

1. **Insert 1 as a red node:**

```
        10(B)
        / \
     5(R)   15(B)
     /
    1(R)
```

2. Fix Violations:

- Both 5 and 1 are red (violates the Red Property).
- Perform a right rotation on 10:

```
         5(B)
         / \
      1(R)  10(R)
               \
              15(B)
```

Insert

All white circles taken as black and light grey to be considered as red

12, 5, 4, 16, 20, 25, 3, 2, 50

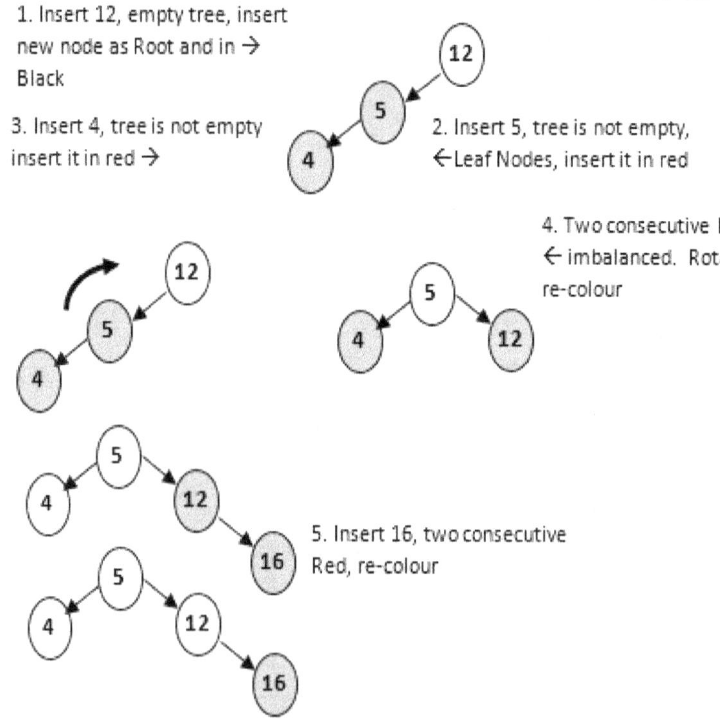

1. Insert 12, empty tree, insert new node as Root and in → Black

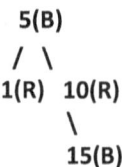

Figure 37

3. Insert 4, tree is not empty insert it in red →

2. Insert 5, tree is not empty, ←Leaf Nodes, insert it in red

4. Two consecutive Red and ← imbalanced. Rotate and re-colour

5. Insert 16, two consecutive Red, re-colour

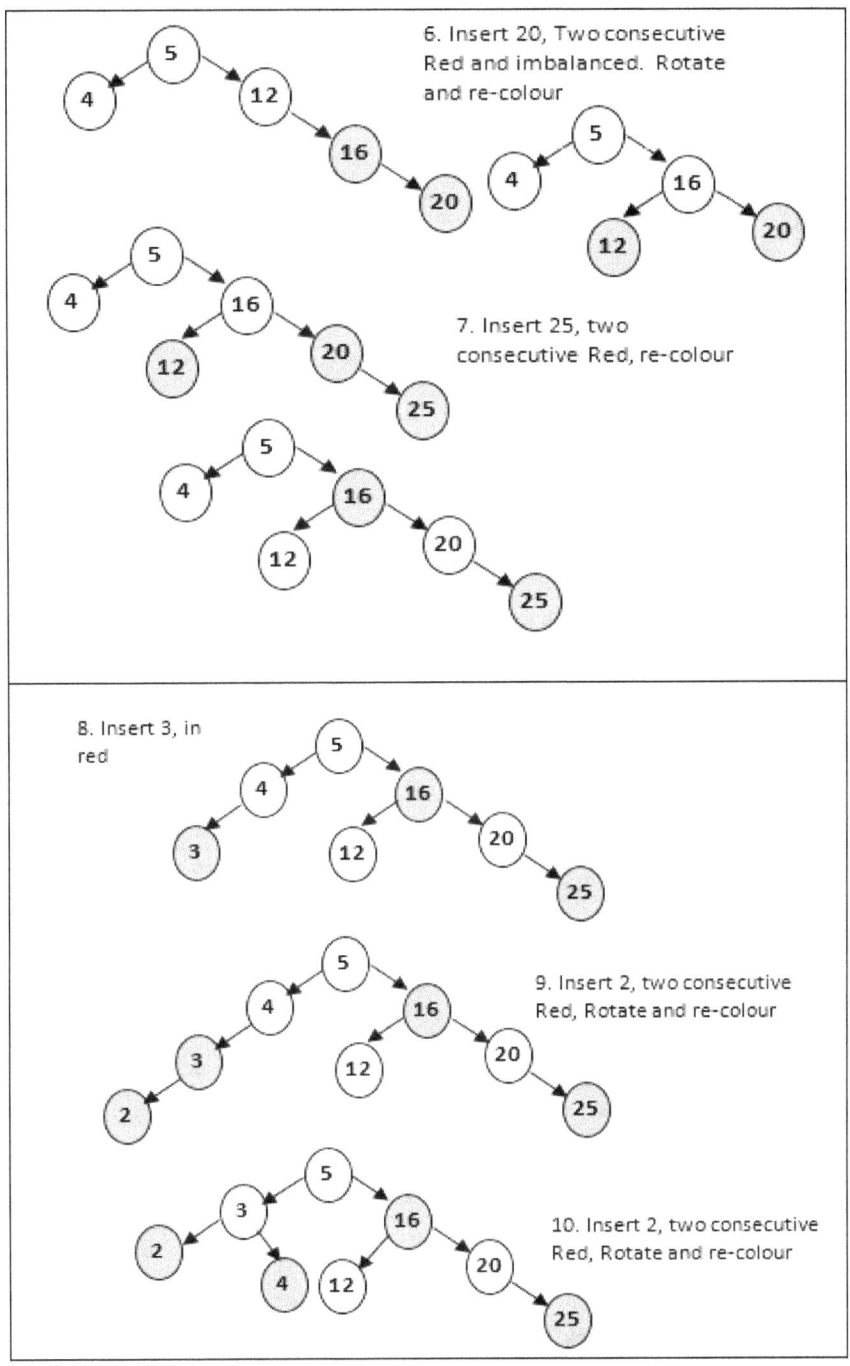

6. Insert 20, Two consecutive Red and imbalanced. Rotate and re-colour

7. Insert 25, two consecutive Red, re-colour

8. Insert 3, in red

9. Insert 2, two consecutive Red, Rotate and re-colour

10. Insert 2, two consecutive Red, Rotate and re-colour

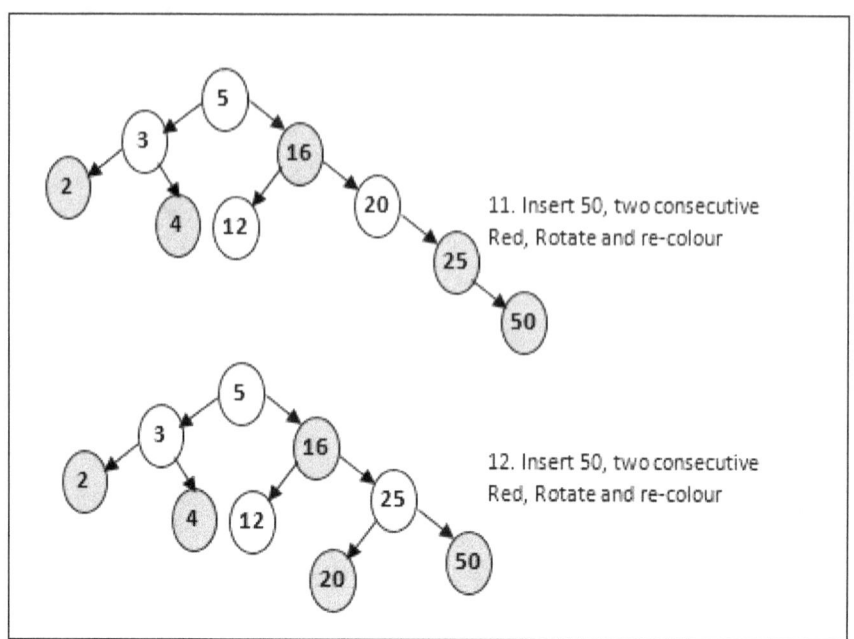

11. Insert 50, two consecutive Red, Rotate and re-colour

12. Insert 50, two consecutive Red, Rotate and re-colour

Delete

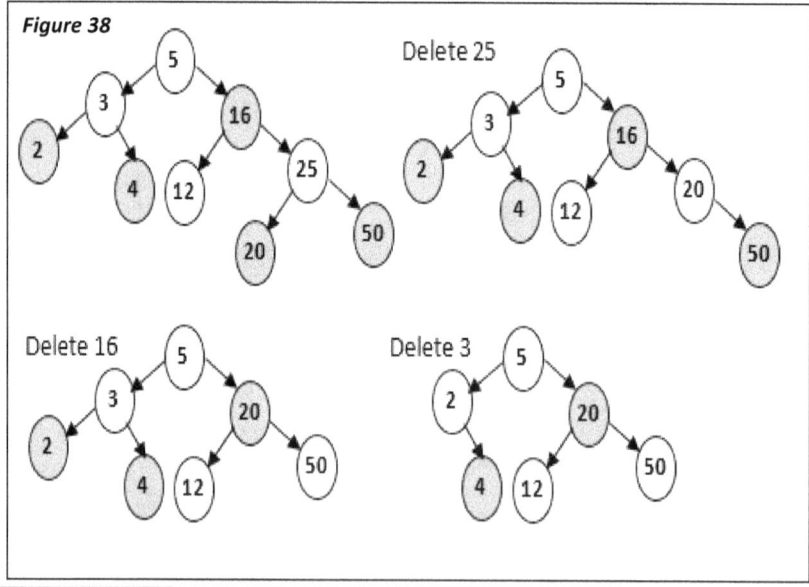

Figure 38

Delete 25

Delete 16

Delete 3

Prog-39. Red and Black Tree

```c
#include <stdio.h>
#include <stdlib.h>
```

```c
#define RED 0
#define BLACK 1

typedef struct RbTree
    {
      int Data;
      int Color;
      struct RbTree *parent;
      struct RbTree *left;
      struct RbTree *right;
    }Node;

  Node *root;
  Node *Ptr;
//Tree Traversal
  void preOrder(Node *Pptr)
    {
     if(Pptr != Ptr)
      {
         printf("\t%3d - %c, ", Pptr->Data,Pptr->Color==0?'R':'B');
         preOrder(Pptr->left);
         preOrder(Pptr->right);
      }
    }
  void inOrder(Node *Pptr)
    {
     if(Pptr != Ptr)
      {
         inOrder(Pptr->left);
         printf("\t%3d - %c, ", Pptr->Data,Pptr->Color==0?'R':'B');
         inOrder(Pptr->right);
      }
    }

  void postOrder(Node *Pptr)
    {
     if(Pptr != Ptr)
      {
         postOrder(Pptr->left);
         postOrder(Pptr->right);
         printf("\t%3d - %c, ", Pptr->Data,Pptr->Color==0?'R':'B');
      }
    }
```

```
//Search a Node
Node *Search(int Data)
  {
    Node *Pptr=NULL;
    Pptr = root;
    while(Pptr != Ptr && Pptr->Data != Data)
      {
        if(Data < Pptr->Data)
          {
            Pptr = Pptr->left;
          }
        else
          {
            Pptr = Pptr->right;
          }
      }
    return Pptr;
  }
//Returning Minimun Value
  Node *findMin(Node *Pptr)
    {
      while(Pptr->left != Ptr)
      {
          Pptr = Pptr->left;
      }
      return Pptr;
    }
  //Returning Maximum Value
  Node *findMax(Node *Pptr)
    {
      while(Pptr->right != Ptr)
        {
          Pptr = Pptr->right;
        }
      return Pptr;
    }

  void rightRotation(Node *Pptr)
    {
      Node *Ptmp;
      Ptmp = Pptr->left;
      Pptr->left = Ptmp->right; //Pptr left to Ptmp right
      if(Ptmp->right != Ptr)
```

```
      {
        Ptmp->right->parent = Pptr;
      }
    Ptmp->parent = Pptr->parent;
    if(Ptmp->parent == Ptr)
      {
        root = Ptmp;
      }
    else if(Pptr == Pptr->parent->left)
      {
        Pptr->parent->left = Ptmp;
      }
    else
      {
        Pptr->parent->right = Ptmp;
      }
    Ptmp->right = Pptr; ///* Ptmp is PPyt parent
    Pptr->parent = Ptmp;
  }

void leftRotation(Node *Pptr)
  {
    Node *Ptmp;
    Ptmp = Pptr->right;
    Pptr->right = Ptmp->left;
    if(Ptmp->left != Ptr)
      {
        Ptmp->left->parent = Pptr;
      }
    Ptmp->parent = Pptr->parent;
    if(Ptmp->parent == Ptr)
      {
        root = Ptmp;
      }
    else if(Pptr == Pptr->parent->left)
      {
        Pptr->parent->left = Ptmp;
      }
    else
      {
        Pptr->parent->right = Ptmp;
      }
    Ptmp->left = Pptr;
```

```
           Pptr->parent = Ptmp;  // Pptr is Ptmp left child and Ptmp is Pptr parent
       }
   //After insertion the reposition of the node should follow the the rule mention
for Red/Black Tree
   void rbInsRearrange(Node *Ptmp)
     {
       while(Ptmp->parent->Color == RED)
         {
           if(Ptmp->parent == Ptmp->parent->parent->left)
             {
               if(Ptmp->parent->parent->right->Color == RED)
                 {
                   Ptmp->parent->Color = BLACK;
                   Ptmp->parent->parent->right->Color = BLACK;
                   Ptmp->parent->parent->Color = RED;
                   Ptmp = Ptmp->parent->parent;
                 }
               else
                 {
                   if(Ptmp == Ptmp->parent->right)
                     {
                               Ptmp = Ptmp->parent;
                               leftRotation(Ptmp);
                     }
                   Ptmp->parent->Color = BLACK;
                   Ptmp->parent->parent->Color = RED;
                   rightRotation(Ptmp->parent->parent);
                 }
             }
           else
             {
               if(Ptmp->parent->parent->left->Color == RED)
                 {
                   Ptmp->parent->Color = BLACK;
                   Ptmp->parent->parent->left->Color = BLACK;
                   Ptmp->parent->parent->Color = RED;
                   Ptmp = Ptmp->parent->parent;
                 }
               else
                 {
                   if(Ptmp == Ptmp->parent->left)
                     {
                               Ptmp = Ptmp->parent;
```

```
                        rightRotation(Ptmp);
                }
            Ptmp->parent->Color = BLACK;
            Ptmp->parent->parent->Color = RED;
            leftRotation(Ptmp->parent->parent);
          }
      }
  }
    root->Color = BLACK;
  }

void rbInsert(int Data)
  {
    Node *Ptmp, *Pptr, *Ptp;
    Ptmp = (Node *)malloc(sizeof(Node));
    Ptmp->Data = Data;
    Ptmp->Color = RED;
    Ptmp->left = Ptr;
    Ptmp->right = Ptr;
    Pptr = root;
    Ptp = Ptr;
    while(Pptr != Ptr)
      {
        Ptp = Pptr;
        if(Ptmp->Data <= Pptr->Data)
          {
            Pptr = Pptr->left;
          }
        else
          {
            Pptr = Pptr->right;
          }
      }
    if(Ptp == Ptr)
      {
        root = Ptmp;
      }
    else if(Ptmp->Data <= Ptp->Data)
      {
        Ptp->left = Ptmp;
      }
    else
      {
```

```
                Ptp->right = Ptmp;
            }
        Ptmp->parent = Ptp;
        rbInsRearrange(Ptmp);
    }
    void rbReposition(Node *Pptr, Node *Ptmp)
    {
        if(Pptr->parent == Ptr)
        {
            root = Ptmp;
        }
        else if(Pptr == Pptr->parent->left)
        {
            Pptr->parent->left = Ptmp;
        }
        else
        {
            Pptr->parent->right = Ptmp;
        }
        Ptmp->parent = Pptr->parent;
    }
//After Deletion the reposition of the node should follow the the rule mention for
Red/Black Tree
    void rbDelRearrange(Node *Pptr)
    {
        Node *Ptmp;
        while(Pptr != root && Pptr->Color == BLACK)
        {
            if(Pptr == Pptr->parent->left)
            {
                Ptmp = Pptr->parent->right;
                if(Ptmp->Color == RED)
                {
                    Ptmp->Color = BLACK;
                    Pptr->parent->Color = RED;
                    leftRotation(Pptr->parent);
                    Ptmp = Pptr->parent->right;
                }
                if(Ptmp->left->Color == BLACK && Ptmp->right->Color == BLACK)
                {
                    Ptmp->Color = RED;
                    Pptr->parent->Color = BLACK;
                    Pptr = Pptr->parent;
```

```
          }
       else
         {
           if(Ptmp->right->Color == BLACK)
            {
                     Ptmp->Color = RED;
                     Ptmp->left->Color = BLACK;
                     rightRotation(Ptmp);
                     Ptmp = Pptr->parent->right;
             }
           Ptmp->Color = Pptr->parent->Color;
           Pptr->parent->Color = BLACK;
           Pptr->right->Color = BLACK;
           leftRotation(Pptr->parent);
           Pptr = root;
         }
    }
  else
    {
      Ptmp = Pptr->parent->left;
      if(Ptmp->Color == RED)
        {
          Ptmp->Color = BLACK;
          Pptr->parent->Color = BLACK;
          rightRotation(Pptr->parent);
          Ptmp = Pptr->parent->left;
        }
      if(Ptmp->left->Color == BLACK && Ptmp->right->Color == BLACK)
        {
          Ptmp->Color = RED;
          Pptr->parent->Color = BLACK;
          Pptr = Pptr->parent;
        }
      else
        {
          if(Ptmp->left->Color == BLACK)
           {
                    Ptmp->Color = RED;
                    Ptmp->right->Color = BLACK;
                    leftRotation(Ptmp);
                    Ptmp = Pptr->parent->left;
            }
          Ptmp->Color = Pptr->parent->Color;
```

```c
                    Pptr->parent->Color = BLACK;
                    Ptmp->left->Color = BLACK;
                    rightRotation(Pptr->parent);
                    Pptr = root;
                }
        }


    }
    Pptr->Color = BLACK;
}
void rbDel(Node *Ptmp)
{
    Node *Ptp, *Pptr;
    int Col;
    Ptp = Ptmp;
    Col = Ptp->Color;
    if(Ptmp->left == Ptr)
        {
            Pptr = Ptmp->right;
            rbReposition(Ptmp, Ptmp->right);
        }
    else if(Ptmp->right == Ptr)
        {
            Pptr = Ptmp->left;
            rbReposition(Ptmp, Ptmp->left);
        }
    else
        {
            Ptp = findMin(Ptmp->right);
            Col = Ptp->Color;
            Pptr = Ptp->right;
            if(Ptp->parent == Ptmp)
                {
                    Pptr->parent = Ptp;
                }
            else
                {
                    rbReposition(Ptp, Ptp->right);
                    Ptp->right = Ptmp->right;
                    Ptp->right->parent = Ptp;
                }
            rbReposition(Ptmp, Ptp);
            Ptp->left = Ptmp->left;
```

```c
          Ptp->left->parent = Ptp;
          Ptp->Color = Ptmp->Color;
        }
    if(Col == BLACK)
      {
        rbDelRearrange(Pptr);
      }
  }
}

int main()
  {
    int c=0,n;
    char col;
    Ptr = (Node* )malloc(sizeof(Node));
    Ptr->Color = BLACK;
    root = Ptr;
    do
      {
        printf("\n\t1. Insert \n\t2. Traversal \n\t3. Search\n");
        printf("\t4. Delete\n\t5. Minimum \n\t6. Maximum\n\t7.Exit");
        printf("\n\tEnter a Choice : ");
        scanf("%d",&c);
        switch(c)
          {
            case 1:
              printf("\n\tEnter the Data : ");
              scanf("%d", &n);
              rbInsert(n);
              break;
            case 2:
              printf("\n\tInorder : ");
              inOrder(root);
              printf("\n\tPreorder : ");
              preOrder(root);
              printf("\n\tPostorder : ");
              postOrder(root);
              break;
            case 3:
              printf("\tEnter a Number to Search : ");
              scanf("%d", &n);
              printf((Search(n) == Ptr) ? "\t%d is not present" : "\t%d is found it is
%s: ",n,(Search(n))->Color==0?"Red":"Black");
              col=Ptr->Color;
```

```
                    break;
                case 4:
                    printf("\tEnter Data to delete: ");
                    scanf("%d", &n);
                    if((Search(n) == Ptr))
                        {
                            printf( "\t%d  is not present ",n);
                        }
                    else
                        {
                            printf( "\t%d is Deleted ",n);
                            rbDel(Search(n));
                        }
                    break;
                case 5:
                    printf("\tMinumum: %d\n", (findMin(root))->Data);
                    break;
                case 6:
                    printf("\tMaximum: %d\n", (findMax(root))->Data);
                    break;
            }
        }while(c!=7);
        return 0;
    }
```

Output

1. Insert	Enter a Choice : 3
2. Traversal	Enter a Number to Search : 8
3. Search	8 is found it is Black:
4. Delete	
5. Minimum	Enter a Choice : 3
6. Maximum	Enter a Number to Search : 45
7.Exit	45 is found it is Red:
Enter a Choice : 1	Enter a Choice : 3
Enter the Data : 8	Enter a Number to Search :
Enter the Data : 2	456
Enter the Data : 43	456 is not present
Enter the Data : 12	
Enter the Data : 45	Enter a Choice : 4
	Enter Data to delete: 123
Enter a Choice : 2	123 is not present
Inorder : 2 - B, 8 - B, 12 - R, 43 - B, 45 - R,	Enter a Choice : 4
Preorder : 8 - B, 2 - B, 43 - B, 12 - R, 45 - R,	Enter Data to delete: 45

Postorder : 2 - B, 12 - R, 45 - R, 43 - B, 8 - B,	45 Number is Deleted
	Enter a Choice : 5 Minumum: 2
	Enter a Choice : 6 Maximum: 43

Multi-way Tree

A tree that can have more than two children is known as a multi-way tree. A multi-way tree allows each node to have up to **M** children. B-Trees and B+ Trees are extensions of multi-way trees.

B Tree
A B-Tree is a self-balancing multi-way tree. It is used to store, organize, and manage large datasets efficiently.

B+ Tree
A B+ Tree is an improved version of a B-Tree. Like a B-Tree, the B+ Tree is a balanced tree that can have more than two children. Each node in a B+ Tree can contain at most **N key fields** and **N+1 pointer fields**. The keys in every node are arranged in **ascending sorted order**.

1. Insert the new node as a leaf node (at root)
2. After inserting a value if the leaf doesn't have required space, split the node and shift the middle node.

Difference between B Tree and B+ Tree

B tree	B+ tree
In B Tree every internal nodes and as well as the Leaf node have data pointers	In B+ Tree only the Leaf nodes have data pointers.
It is a balancing tree that helps in maintaining and sorting data, and also allows searching, inserting and deletions. However	B+ tree is modified from B tree. Insertion, Deletion is mother than B Tree

Insertion may take longer than B+ Tree.	
Often search is difficult due to unavailability of the key in Leaf.	In the case of B+ tree, only the leaf nodes include data pointers. The Presence of Keys in Leaf made the searching faster.
The insertion takes a longer time.	Insertion is faster than the B tree.

The **B-Tree** and **B+ Trees** are used to index the data mainly in large databases, because accessing the data that is stored in databases on disks is slow

B+Tree - Insertion and Deletion

Insertion

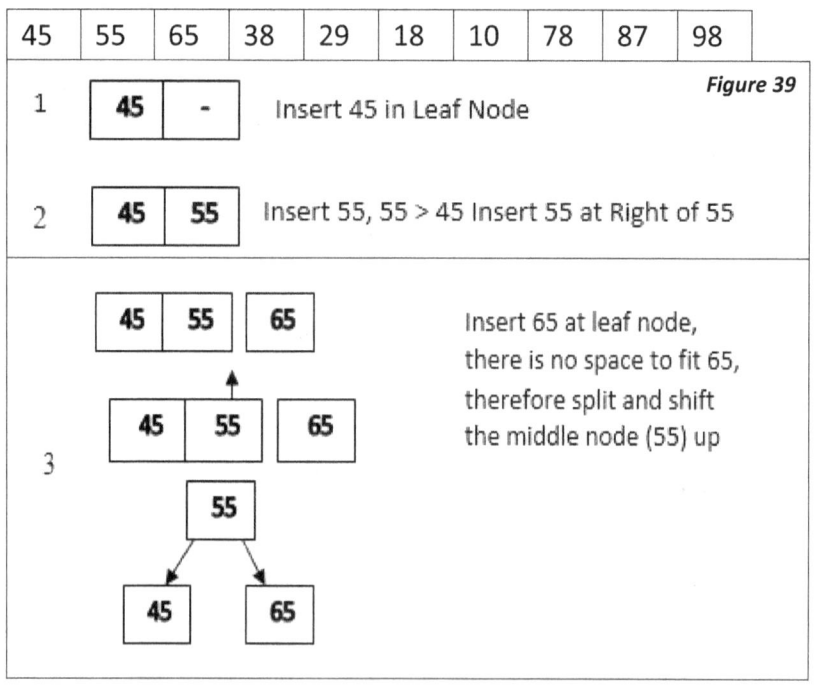

Figure 39

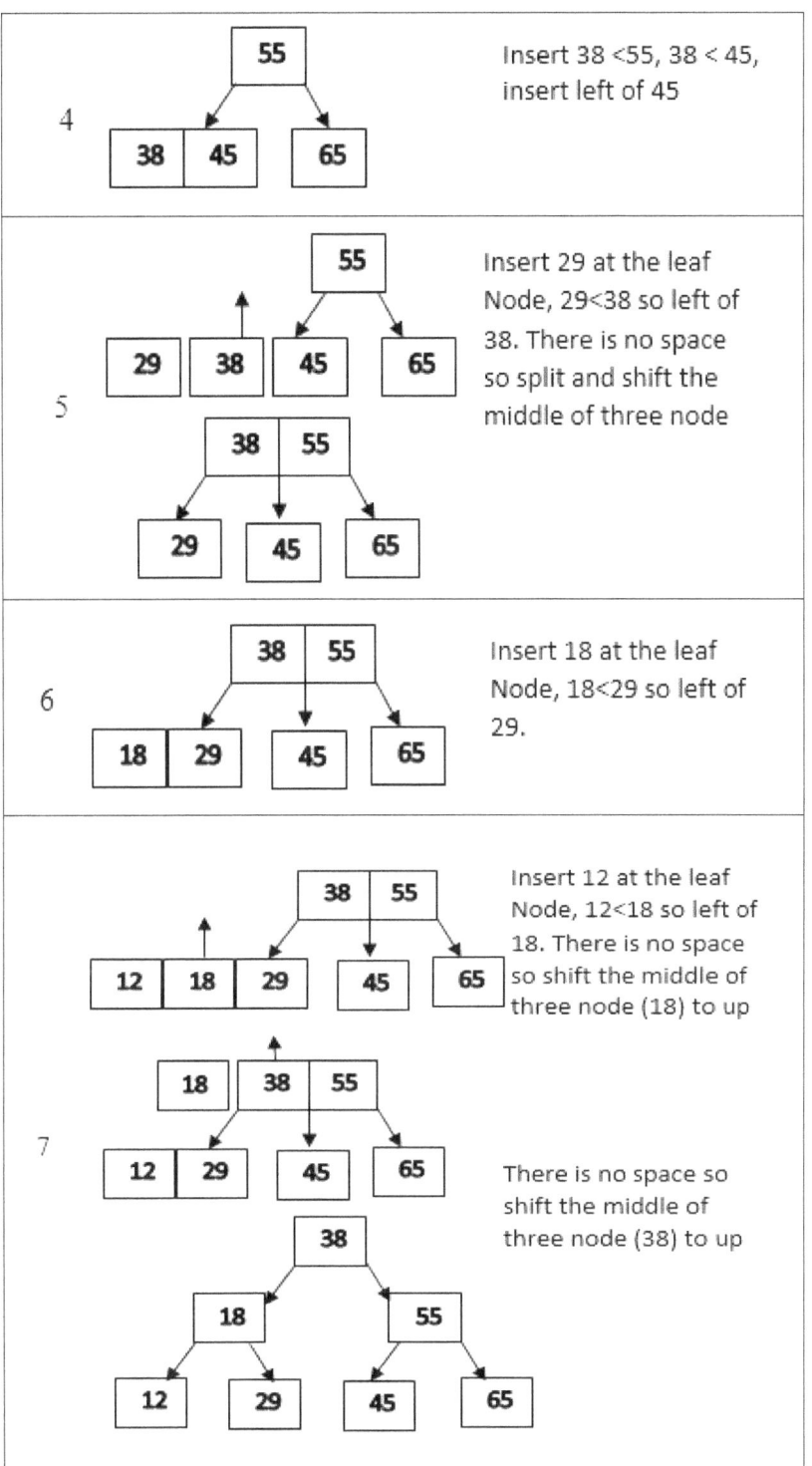

4	Insert 38 <55, 38 < 45, insert left of 45
5	Insert 29 at the leaf Node, 29<38 so left of 38. There is no space so split and shift the middle of three node
6	Insert 18 at the leaf Node, 18<29 so left of 29.
7	Insert 12 at the leaf Node, 12<18 so left of 18. There is no space so shift the middle of three node (18) to up
	There is no space so shift the middle of three node (38) to up

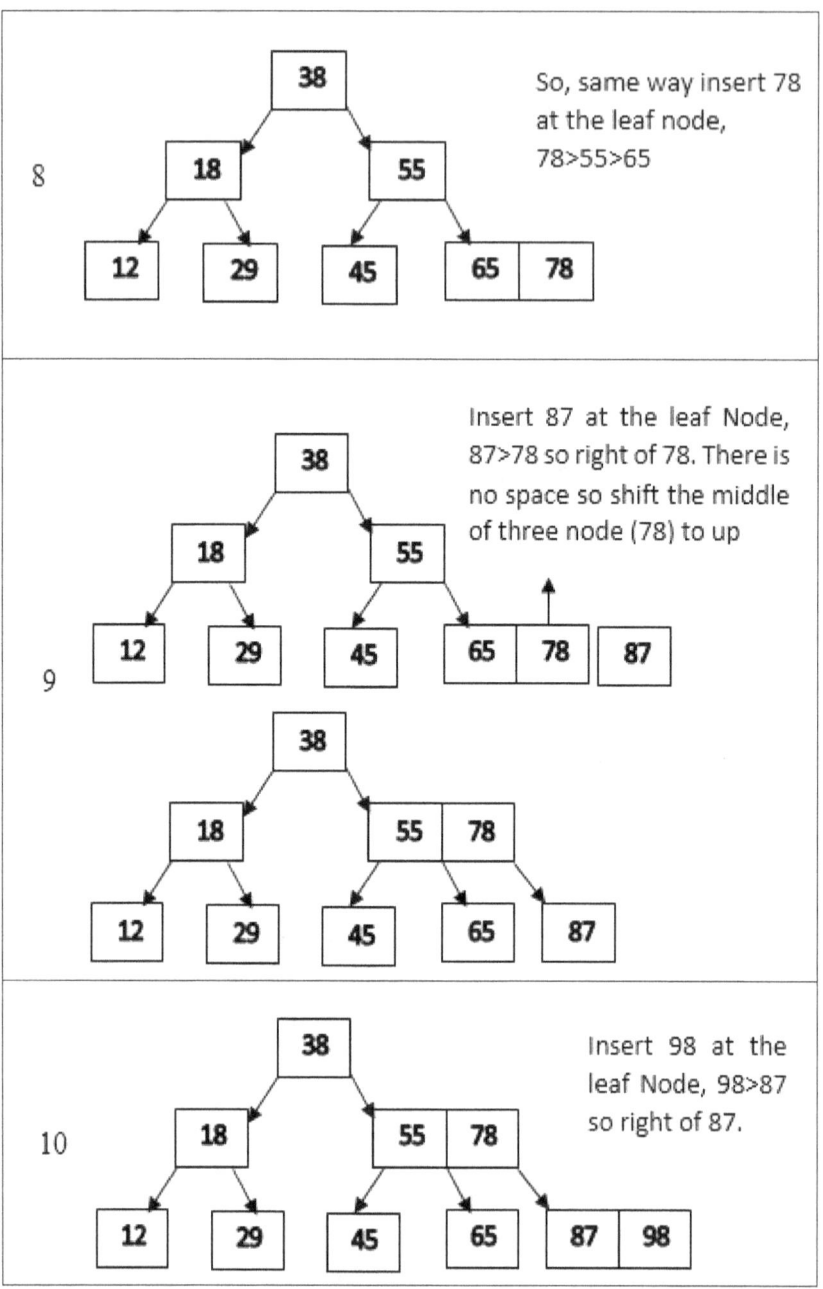

8

So, same way insert 78 at the leaf node,
78>55>65

9

Insert 87 at the leaf Node, 87>78 so right of 78. There is no space so shift the middle of three node (78) to up

10

Insert 98 at the leaf Node, 98>87 so right of 87.

Deletion

1. Begin at the root and look for leaf L for key entry.
2. Search and Delete the entry.

3. If L (Leaf) is at least half-full then stop.
4. If L has only n-1 entries re-distributed by borrowing from a sibling, it can be a neighbouring node with the same parent as L.
5. If re-distribution fails, combine L and sibling.
6. If merge happened, must delete entry (pointing to L or sibling) from parent of L.
7. Merge could spread to root, lessening height.

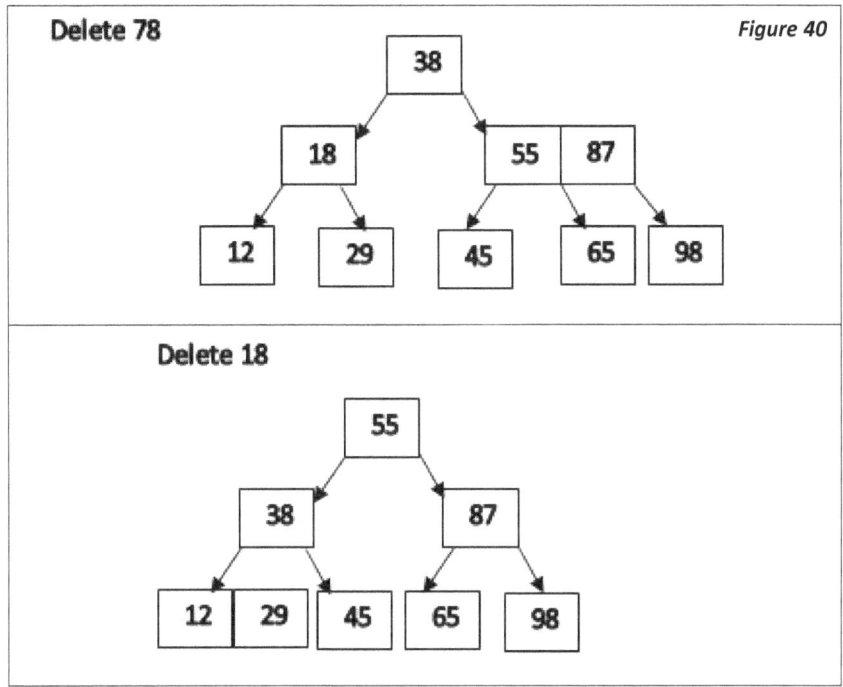

Delete 78

Figure 40

Delete 18

Hash Table

A hash table is a data structure used to store key-value pairs. A hash function processes the key and performs mathematical operations on it. The resulting value, often referred to as the **hash value** or **hash**, determines the index of the key-value pair in the hash table.

A simple hash table contains two components:

Hash Function: Given a set of inputs of any size, a hash function can map them into a table or other data structure with fixed-size elements.

An Array: All of the table's key-value elements are stored in the array. The array's size should be determined based on the anticipated amount of data to be stored.

Collisions:

When two keys are assigned to the same index, a collision occurs.

There are various approaches to handling collisions.

1. Linear probing: If a key-value pair is hashed to an already-occupied slot, it looks for the next available space in the table sequentially.
2. Chaining: An array of linked lists will make up the hash table. All keys that map to the same index are stored in a linked list at that index.
3. Double hashing: Double hashing is among the best open addressing techniques currently in use, as the resulting permutations share many properties with randomly selected permutations.

Pros and Cons:

Hash tables are a quick and effective way to find, add, and remove stored data. Hash tables, in particular, often perform value lookups more quickly than binary search trees. Hash tables typically have a consistent time complexity regardless of the input size.	Hashing can lose its effectiveness if there are too many collisions. When the number of collisions grows, each storage holds more tuples, the bucket size increases, and the time complexity becomes more linear, O(n).

There is more than one way a hash function can be implemented to find the proper key:

Remainder Methods

The process is taking the remainder of a key, k, after dividing it by m, as shown in the hash function. Mapping it into one of m slots.

$$h(k) = k \bmod m \text{ (m is the table size)}$$

Using Prime:

All prime numbers are distinct. Because a prime number is used, the product of a prime with any other number will be unique. A hashing function leverages this characteristic. The idea is to make the length of your hash table a prime number to reduce collisions. When the array size is a prime number, it cannot be evenly divided by any other number, ensuring that the probe sequence will eventually check every cell.

The multiplication method

The multiplication method involves multiplying the key K by a constant C, where 0<C<10<C<1, to derive the fractional part of KC. This value is then multiplied by m, and the floor of the result is calculated to determine the hash value.

$$h(k) = floor (m * frac (k * c)) (m \text{ is the table size})$$

String Hashing: Cast each character in the input stream into an integer. This integer represents the character's ascii code. Transform this integer value to hexadecimal, then add it to the final hex string.

Example: Abcd : A = 65, b = 123, c = 124, d = 125

Total of ASCII of Abcd = 437 and Hexa(417B7C7D)

Hash table with collisions example

Take the value to be hashed mod 5 and enter it in that cell of the hash table using the Remainder Method.

Numbers to hash: 21, 12, 10, 15, 52 (**Table Size = 5**)

H[k] = 21%5 = 1, 12%5 = 2, 10%5 = 0, 15%5 = 0, 52%5 = 2

Index	Value		H[k]
0	21		1
1	12		2
2	10		0
3	15	Collision with index 2	0
4	52	Collision with index 1	2

Prog-40. Simple Hashing using Modulo Method

```c
#include<stdio.h>
#include<stdlib.h>
   void Insert(int val,int *arr,int n)
     {
     int hk = val % n;
     if(arr[hk] == -1)
       {
```

```c
        arr[hk] = val;
        printf("\n\t%d Inserted @ arr[%d]", val,hk);
        }
    else
        {
        printf("\n\tCollision : arr[%d] an element %d already inserted",hk,arr[hk]);
        printf("\n\tNot Inserting %d\n",val);
        }
    }
void Disp(int *arr,int n)
    {
    int i;
    for(i = 0; i<n; i++)
        {
            if(arr[i]!=-1)
                {
                printf("arr[%d] @ %d\n",i,arr[i]);
                }
        }
    }
void Del(int val, int *arr,int n)
    {
    int hk = val % n;
    if(arr[hk] == val)
        {
        arr[hk] = -1;
            }
    else
        {
        printf("\n\t%d is Not present",val);
            }
    }
void Search(int val, int *arr,int n)
    {
    int hk = val % n;
    if(arr[hk] == val)
            {
        printf("\n\t%d is Present");
            }
        else
            {
                printf("\n\t%d is Not Present");
            }
```

```c
}
int main()
{
    int *arr,n,i,ch=0,item;
    printf("\n\tEnter Array size ; ");
    scanf("%d",&n);
    arr=(int *)malloc(n*sizeof(int));
    for(i = 0; i< n; i++) //Iniatilize the Array
{
    arr[i] = -1;
    }
    do
      {
        printf("\n\t1. Insert\n\t2. Delete\n\t.3 Search\n\t4. Display\n\t5. Exit");
        printf("\n\t\tChoice? ");
        scanf("%d",&ch);
        switch(ch)
          {
            case 1:
              printf("\n\tEnter a Value : ");
              scanf("%d",&item);
              Insert(item,arr,n);
              break;
            case 2:
              printf("\n\tEnter Item to Delete : ");
              scanf("%d",&item);
              Del(item,arr,n);
              break;
            case 3:
              printf("\n\tEnter Item to Search : ");
              scanf("%d",&item);
              Search(item,arr,n);
              break;
            case 4:
              printf("\n\tHash Table : ");
              Disp(arr,n);
              break;
        }
      }while(ch!=5);
    return 0;
    }
```

Output

Enter Array size : 5	Choice? 4
1. Insert	Hash Table :
2. Delete	arr[0] @ 45
3. Search	arr[2] @ 12
4. Display	arr[3] @ 23
5. Exit	
Choice? 1	Choice? 2
Enter a Value : 12	Enter Item to Delete : 12
12 Inserted @ arr[2]	
Choice? 1	Choice? 4
Enter a Value : 23	Hash Table :
23 Inserted @ arr[3]	arr[0] @ 45
Choice? 1	arr[3] @ 23
Enter a Value : 45	Choice? 3
45 Inserted @ arr[0]	Enter Item to Search : 23
	23 is Present

Graph Theory

A graph is a non-linear data structure that represents relationships between points and lines. The points are called vertices, and the lines are known as edges.

A graph can be described as a collection of vertices and edges. Graph theory primarily involves the study of networks based on the precise concept of a graph. An edge connects exactly two vertices.

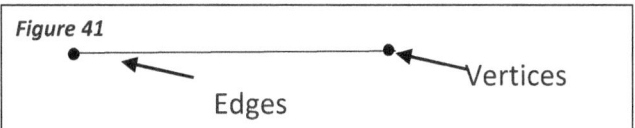

Figure 41

Edges   Vertices

Graph Terminologies

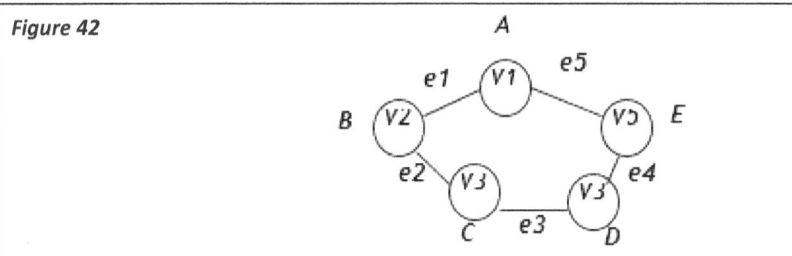

Figure 42

Graph Representation: Generally, a graph is symbolized as a pair, Vertex and an Edge (V, E).

V = { A, B, C, D, E }

E = { AB, BC, CD, DE, EA}

1. **Vertex:** The vertices or nodes are the components of a graph. The vertices are connected by edges (V1, V2, etc.).
2. **Edge :** An edge (e1, e2, etc.) is a line that connects two vertex points.
3. **Path:** Path is a sequence of edges between two nodes.
4. **Adjacent Nodes:** Two nodes are called adjacent if they are connected by an edge.

Degree of a Vertex : Number of times the edges connected with a Vertex.

Types of Graph:

There are many types of graphs, but here we will discuss only directed and undirected graphs.

Some types of graphs include: Null Graph, Connected Graph, Disconnected Graph, Directed Graph, Undirected Graph, Complete Graph, Cycle Graph, Cyclic Graph, Bipartite Graph, Finite Graph, Infinite Graph, Regular Graph, Hamiltonian Graph, Euler Graph, Simple Graph, and others.

Directed and undirected graphs are two fundamental types of graphs.

Directed Graph:Error! Reference source not found.

Directed graphs contain ordered pairs of vertices. Each edge in a directed graph has a direction associated with it. A directed graph is also known as a digraph.

V={A,B,C,D,E}

E={{A,B},{B,C},{C,D},{D,E},{E,A}}

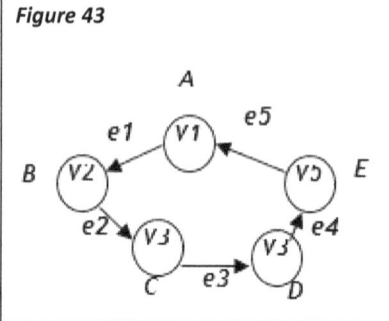

Figure 43

Un-Directed Graph

An undirected graph has unordered pairs of vertices. The edge can be traversed in either direction.

V={A,B,C,D,E}

E={{A,B},{B,A},{B,C},{C,B},{C,D},{D,E},{E,D},{E,A},{A,E}}

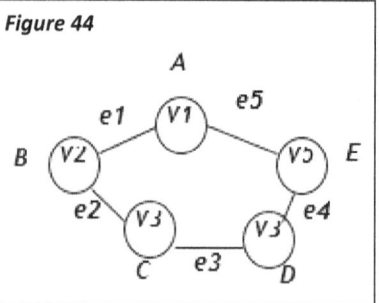

Figure 44

Loop: A loop in a graph is an edge that connects a vertex to itself.

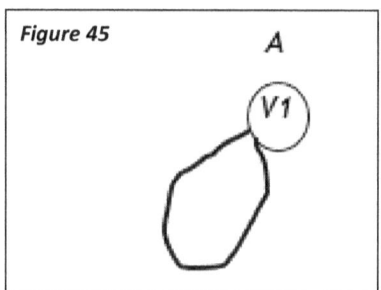

Figure 45

Adjacency Matrix:

An adjacency matrix is a 2-D array that represents the vertices of a graph and their adjacency to other vertices. It is a way of representing a graph as a matrix of values, typically 0 and 1 (boolean values). An adjacency matrix is a square matrix with V×V rows and columns, where V is the number of vertices.

Adjacency Matrix for Undirected Graph

	A	B	C	D
A	0	1	0	1
B	1	0	1	0
C	0	1	0	1
D	1	0	1	0

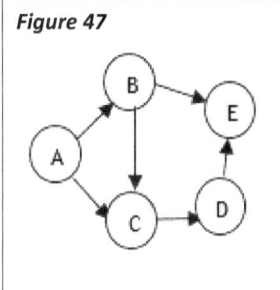

Figure 46

Adjacency Matrix for Directed Graph

	A	B	C	D	E
A	0	1	1	0	0
B	0	0	1	0	1
C	0	0	0	1	0
D	0	0	0	0	1
E	0	0	0	0	0

Figure 47

Adjacency List

An adjacency list is an array of linked lists. Each array index represents a vertex, and each element of the linked list represents the other vertices connected by an edge to that vertex.

Directed Graph

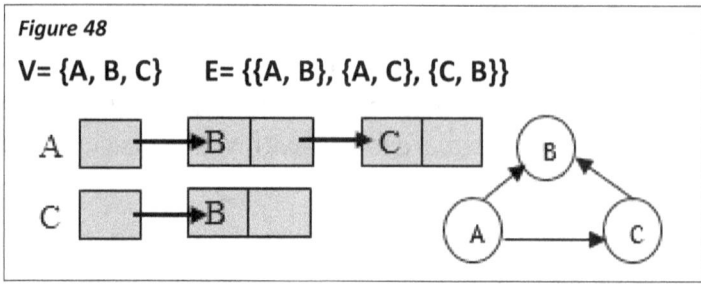

Figure 48

V= {A, B, C}   E= {{A, B}, {A, C}, {C, B}}

Undirected Graph.

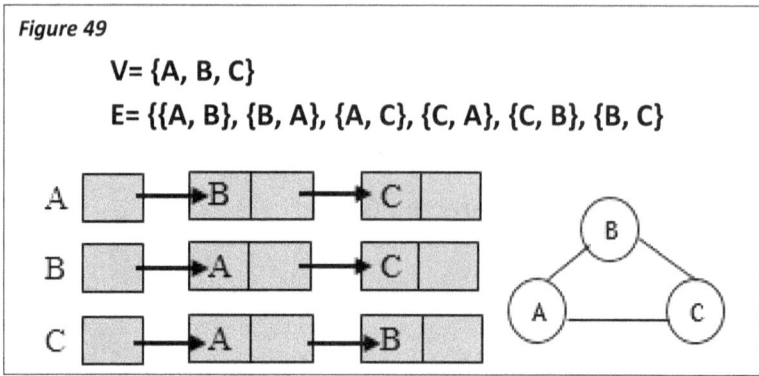

Figure 49

V= {A, B, C}
E= {{A, B}, {B, A}, {A, C}, {C, A}, {C, B}, {B, C}

Graph Traversal

Like tree traversal, graph traversal is the process of visiting all the vertices of a graph. Graph traversal involves visiting all the vertices, excluding looping paths. Unlike trees, where traversal typically starts from the 'root', in graph traversal, it starts from a given starting vertex. There are two types of graph traversal.

1. DFS (Depth First Search)
2. BFS (Breadth First Search)

BFS (Breadth First Search)

In BFS (Breadth-First Search), traversal starts from a given starting node (vertex) and explores the graph. In this technique, vertices are visited level by level, with sibling vertices visited before their child vertices. Generally, a queue is used in BFS traversal to keep track of the vertices to be visited next.

Here's a general overview of how BFS works:

1. **Initialization:**

- Start with the root node (or an arbitrary node if it's a graph).
- Use a queue to keep track of nodes to visit.
- Mark the starting node as visited.

2. **Explore neighbours**:
   - Dequeue a node from the front of the queue.
   - Visit all unvisited neighbouring nodes and enqueue them.

3. **Repeat**:
   - Continue until the queue is empty, meaning all reachable nodes have been visited.

Time Complexity:

- **O(V + E)**, where:
- V is the number of vertices (nodes).
- E is the number of edges in the graph.

DFS (Depth First Search)

DFS (Depth-First Search) is a graph traversal algorithm that uses a stack data structure. In DFS, traversal occurs in a depth-first direction, exploring as far down a branch of the graph as possible before backtracking. Unlike BFS, which traverses level by level, DFS typically follows a pre-order traversal pattern.

Here's a general overview of how BFS works. Unlike BFS, which explores all neighbours at the present depth level first, DFS explores as far as possible along a branch before backtracking.

How DFS works:

1. **Initialization**:
   - Start at the root node (or an arbitrary node for a graph).
   - Use a stack (or recursion) to explore nodes.
   - Mark the starting node as visited.

2. **Explore deeper**:
   - Visit the unvisited neighbours of the current node, and explore the neighbors of each one.
   - If there are no unvisited neighbours, backtrack to the previous node and continue exploring other unvisited neighbours.

3. **Repeat**: Continue until all nodes have been visited or the graph/tree has been fully traversed.

Types of DFS:

- **Recursive DFS**: Uses the call stack for backtracking.
- **Iterative DFS**: Uses an explicit stack to manage backtracking.

Time Complexity:

- **O(V + E)**, where:
- **V** is the number of vertices (nodes).
- **E** is the number of edges.

Starting Vertex is A

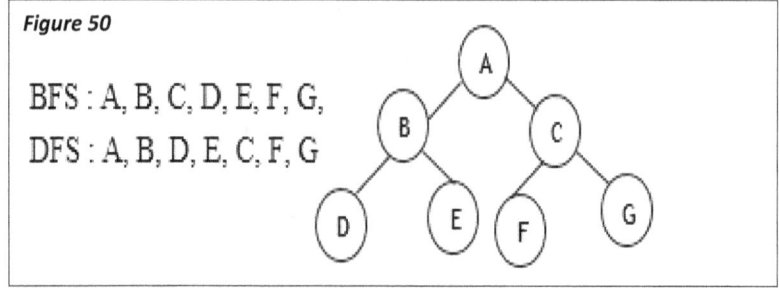

Figure 50

BFS : A, B, C, D, E, F, G,

DFS : A, B, D, E, C, F, G

Starting Vertex is A

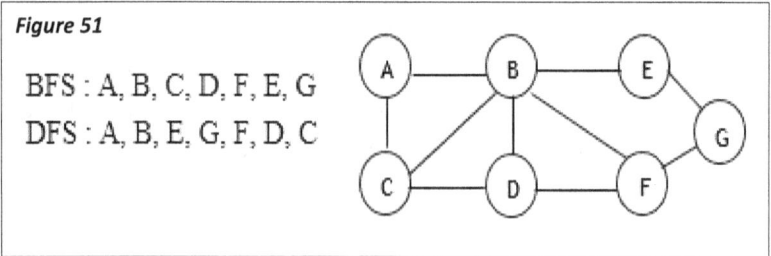

Figure 51

BFS : A, B, C, D, F, E, G

DFS : A, B, E, G, F, D, C

Weighted Graph

A weighted graph is a graph in which each edge has a numerical value called a weight. These types of graphs are commonly used to calculate the shortest path between vertices.

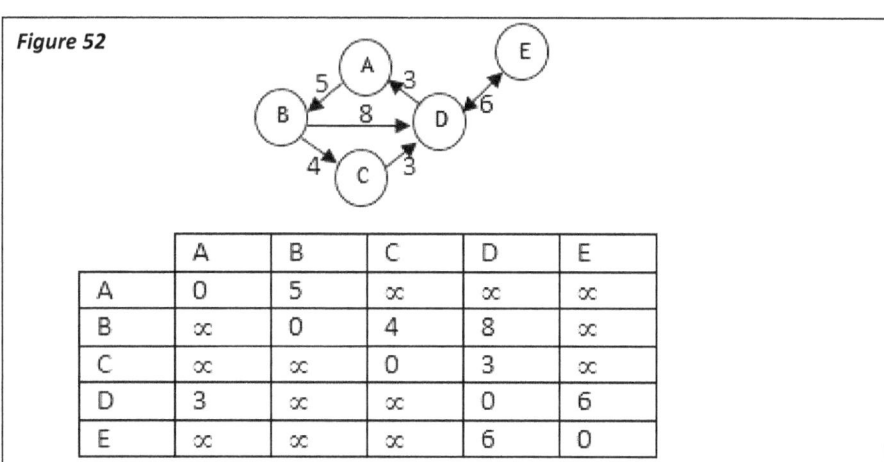

Figure 52

	A	B	C	D	E
A	0	5	∞	∞	∞
B	∞	0	4	8	∞
C	∞	∞	0	3	∞
D	3	∞	∞	0	6
E	∞	∞	∞	6	0

Figure 53

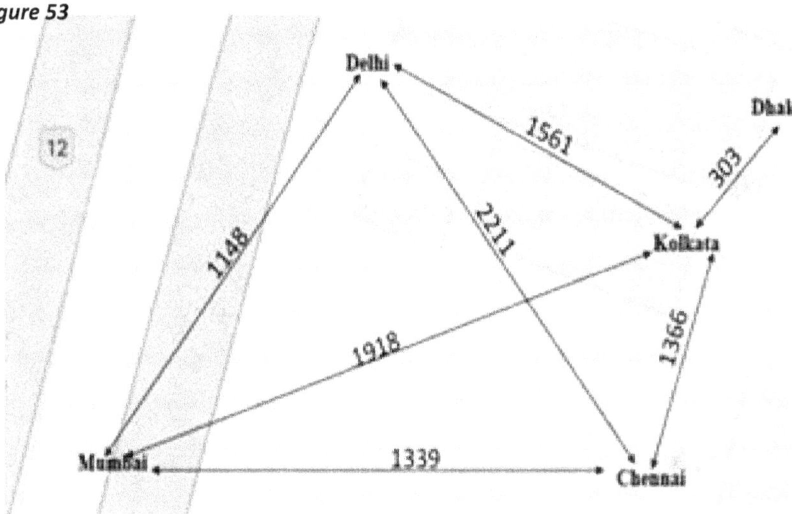

	Delhi	Mumbai	Chennai	Kolkata	Dhaka
Delhi	0	1148	2211	1561	∞
Mumbai	1148	0	1399	1918	∞
Chennai	2211	1339	0	1366	∞
Kolkata	1561	1918	1366	0	303
Dhaka	∞	∞	∞	303	0

Prog-41. Adjancency Matrix

```
#include<stdio.h>
#include<stdlib.h>
int **adm; //Adjacency matrix
int v; // nodes in the graph
```

```c
void main()
 {
    int edg,vn,i,j,x,y;
    char grtype;

    while(1)
      {
        printf("\n\tEnter Graph type, (d)irected or (u)ndirected : ");
        fflush(stdin);
        grtype=getche();
        if(grtype=='d' || grtype=='D' || grtype=='u' || grtype=='U')
          break;
      }
    printf("\n\tNumber of nodes : ");
    scanf("%d",&v);
    vn=v+1;
    adm=(int **)malloc(vn*sizeof(int *));
    for(i=0;i<vn;i++)
      {
        adm[i]=(int *)malloc(vn*sizeof(int *));
      }
    for(i=0;i<vn;i++)
      {
        for(j=0;j<vn;j++)
        {
            adm[i][j]=0; //Initializing the Matrix
          }
      }
    fflush(stdin);
    if(grtype=='u') //Nos. of Edges
        edg=v*(v-1)/2;
    else
        edg=v*(v-1);
    for(i=1;i<=edg;i++)
      {
        printf("\n\tEnter edge for Vertex %d( 0 0 to quit ) : ",i);
        printf("\t");
        scanf("%d",&x);
        printf("\t\t\t\t\t\t\t");
        scanf("%d",&y);
        if( (x==0) && (y==0) )
          break;
        if( x > v || y > v || x<=0 || y<=0 || x==y)
```

```
            {
                printf("\n\tInvalid edges for %d vertex edges, Renter");
                i--;
            }
            else
            {
                adm[x][y]=1;
                if( grtype=='u')
                    adm[y][x]=1;
            }
        }
    printf("\n\tAdjacency matrix :\n      ");
    for(i=1;i<=v;i++)
        printf("%c      ",(char)(64+i));
    printf("\n =================================\n");

    for(i=1;i<=v;i++)
    {
        printf(" %c  |",(char)(64+i));
        for(j=1;j<=v;j++)
        {
            printf(" %3d   ",adm[i][j]);
        }
        printf("\n");
    }
    getch();
}
```

Output

Enter Graph type, (d)irected or (u)ndirected : d		For Directed Graph
Number of nodes : 4		
Enter edge for Vertex 1(0 0 to quit) : 1 2		
Enter edge for Vertex 2(0 0 to quit) : 1 3		
Enter edge for Vertex 3(0 0 to quit) : 2 3		
Enter edge for Vertex 4(0 0 to quit) : 2 4		
Enter edge for Vertex 5(0 0 to quit) : 3 1		
Enter edge for Vertex 6(0 0 to quit) : 3 4		
Enter edge for Vertex 7(0 0 to quit) : 4 1		
Enter edge for Vertex 8(0 0 to quit) : 0 0		

For Directed Graph

```
        A   B   C   D
  ====================
A |     0   1   1   0
B |     0   0   1   1
C |     1   0   0   1
D |     1   0   0   0
```

For Un-Directed Graph

```
        A   B   C   D
  ====================
A |     0   1   1   0
B |     1   0   1   1
C |     1   1   0   1
D |     0   1   1   0
```

Prog-42. Adjanency List

```c
#include<stdio.h>
#include<stdlib.h>
 struct AList
   {
     int val;
     struct AList *Next;
   };
   int **adm; //Adjacency matrix
   int v; // No nodes in the graph
   typedef struct AList aNode;
   aNode *Pptr=NULL;

   aNode *Insert(int n)
     {
     aNode *Ptr;
     Ptr=(aNode *)malloc(sizeof(aNode));
     Ptr->val=n;
     Ptr->Next=NULL;
     return(Ptr);
     }
   void display(aNode **hD,int v)
     {
       aNode *Ptr;
       int i;
       for(i=0;i<v;i++)
         {
           printf("\n\t v%d ",i+1);
           Ptr=hD[i];
           if(Ptr==NULL)
             printf("\tNUL");
           while(Ptr!=NULL)
             {
               printf(" ->v%d",Ptr->val);
               Ptr=Ptr->Next;
             }
           printf("\n");
         }
     }
 aNode *Search(aNode *hd)
   {
     aNode *Ptr;
```

```c
      Ptr=hd;
      while(Ptr->Next!=NULL)
        {
          Ptr=Ptr->Next;
        }
      return(Ptr);
}

int main()
  {
     aNode *Ptr,*Pptr,**Head;
     int edg,vn,i,j,x,y;
       char grtype;
       printf("\n\tNumber of nodes : ");
       scanf("%d",&v);
       vn=v+1;
       adm=(int **)malloc(vn*sizeof(int *));
       for(i=0;i<vn;i++)
         {
            adm[i]=(int *)malloc(vn*sizeof(int *));
         }
       Head=(aNode **)malloc(vn*sizeof(aNode *));
       for(i=0;i<vn;i++)
         {
            for(j=0;j<vn;j++)
            {
               adm[i][j]=0; //Initializing the Matrix
            }
         }
       for(i=0;i<v;i++)
       {
         for(j=0;j<v;j++)
           {
              printf("\tEnter Matrix[%d][%d] : ",i+1,j+1);
              scanf("%d",&adm[i][j]);
              if(i==j)
                adm[i][j]=0;
           }
       }
       printf("\n\t Adjacency Matrix :\n \t      ");
       for(i=0;i<v;i++)
         printf(" %c    ",(char)(65+i));
```

```c
printf("\n\t =================================\n");

for(i=0;i<v;i++)
  {
    printf("\t %c  |",(char)(65+i));
    for(j=0;j<v;j++)
      {
        printf(" %3d   ",adm[i][j]);
      }
    printf("\n");
  }
for(i=0;i<v;i++)
  {
    Head[i]=NULL;
  }
for(i=0;i<v;i++)
  {
    for(j=0;j<v;j++)
      {
        if(adm[i][j]==1)
          {
            Pptr=Insert(j+1);
            if(Head[i]==NULL)
            Head[i]=Pptr;
          else
            {
              Ptr=Search(Head[i]);
              Ptr->Next=Pptr;
            }
      }
    }
  }
printf("\n\tAdjacency list : \n");
display(Head,v);
}
```

Output

Number of nodes : 4 Enter Matrix[1][1] : 0 Enter Matrix[1][2] : 1 Enter Matrix[1][3] : 1 Enter Matrix[1][4] : 1 Enter Matrix[2][1] : 1 Enter Matrix[2][2] : 0 Enter Matrix[2][3] : 0 Enter Matrix[2][4] : 1 Enter Matrix[3][1] : 1 Enter Matrix[3][2] : 1 Enter Matrix[3][3] : 0 Enter Matrix[3][4] : 0 Enter Matrix[4][1] : 1 Enter Matrix[4][2] : 0 Enter Matrix[4][3] : 1 Enter Matrix[4][4] : 0	Adjacency Matrix : A B C D ===================== A | 0 1 1 1 B | 1 0 0 1 C | 1 1 0 0 D | 1 0 1 0 Adjacency list : v1 ->v2 ->v3 ->v4 v2 ->v1 ->v4 v3 ->v1 ->v2 v4 ->v1 ->v3

Prog-43. BFS DFS from Adjanency Matrix

```c
#include <stdio.h>
#include <stdlib.h>
int **adm; //Adjacency matrix
int v; // nodes in the graph
int *Q, *Visited,front=0,rear=-1,i,j;
char grtype;
void adj_Mat()
    {
    int edg,x,y;
    for(i=0;i<=v;i++)
      {
        for(j=0;j<=v;j++)
        {
            adm[i][j]=0; //Initializing the Matrix
          }
       }
    fflush(stdin);
    if(grtype=='u') //Nos. of Edges
        edg=v*(v-1)/2;
    else
        edg=v*(v-1);
    for(i=1;i<=edg;i++)
```

```c
      {
        printf("\n\tEnter edge for Vertex %d( 0 0 to quit ) : ",i);
        printf("\t");
        scanf("%d",&x);
        printf("\t\t\t\t\t\t\t");
        scanf("%d",&y);
        if( (x==0) && (y==0) )
          break;
        if( x > v || y > v || x<=0 || y<=0 || x==y)
          {
            printf("\n\tInvalid edges for %d vertex edges, Renter");
            i--;
          }
        else
          {
            adm[x][y]=1;
            if( grtype=='u')
              adm[y][x]=1;
          }
      }
    printf("\n\tAdjacency matrix :\n      ");
    for(i=1;i<=v;i++)
      printf("%c     ",(char)(64+i));
    printf("\n =====================================\n");

    for(i=1;i<=v;i++)
      {
        printf(" %c  |",(char)(64+i));
        for(j=1;j<=v;j++)
          {
            printf(" %3d   ",adm[i][j]);
          }
        printf("\n");
      }
  }
void BFS(int sv)
  {
    for(i = 1; i <= v; i++)
    {
      if(adm[sv][i] && !Visited[i])
      Q[++rear] = i;
    }
    if(front <= rear)
```

```c
        {
            Visited[Q[front]] = 1;
            BFS(Q[front++]);
        }
    }
void DFS(int sv)
  {
     int i;
     printf(" %d ",sv);
     Visited[sv]=1;
     for (i=1;i<=v;i++)
        {
        if(adm[sv][i] && !Visited[i])
           {

               DFS(i);
           }
        }
    }
int main()
  {
     int ch=0,sv;
     while(1)
        {
           printf("\n\tEnter Graph type, (d)irected or (u)ndirected : ");
           fflush(stdin);
           grtype=getche();
           if(grtype=='d' || grtype=='D' || grtype=='u' || grtype=='U')
              break;
        }
     printf("\n\tNumber of nodes : ");
     scanf("%d",&v);
     sv=v+2;
     adm=(int **)malloc(sv*sizeof(int *));
     Q=(int *)malloc(sv*sizeof(int *));
     Visited=(int *)malloc(sv*sizeof(int *));
     for(i=0;i<=v;i++)
        {
           Visited[i]=0;
           Q[i]=0;
           adm[i]=(int *)malloc(v*sizeof(int *));
        }
```

```
        do
         {
            printf("\n\t1. Adjancenacy Matrix\n\t2. BFS\n\t3. DFS\n\t4. Exit");
            printf("\n\tEnter your Choice : ");
            scanf("%d",&ch);
            switch(ch)
              {
                case 1: adj_Mat();break;
                    case 2:        printf("\n\tEnter Starting Vertex (integer) :");
                                   scanf("%d",&sv);
                                   if(sv<1 || sv>v)
                                        {
                                                        printf("\n\t\tInvalid Input!!!");
                                                        break;
                                        }
                                   BFS(sv);
                                   printf("\n\tBreadth First Traversal :\n\t\t");
                                   for (i=1;i<=v;i++)
                                        {
                                                        if(Visited[i])
                                                                printf("%d\t",i);
                                        }
                                   break;
                    case 3: printf("\n\tEnter Starting Vertex (integer) :");
                                   scanf("%d",&sv);
                                   if(sv<1 || sv>v)
                                        {
                                                        printf("\n\t\tInvalid Input!!!");
                                                        break;
                                        }
                                   for(i=0;i<=v;i++)
                                                Visited[i]=0;
                                   printf("\n\tDepth First Traversal :\n");
                                   DFS(sv);
                                   break;
              }
         }while(ch!=4);
      }
```

Output

Enter Graph type, (d)irected or (u)ndirected : d Number of nodes : 6	Adjacency matrix : A B C D E F ===========================

```
1. Adjancenacy Matrix                       A |  0   1   1   0   0   1
2. BFS                                      B |  1   0   0   1   1   0
3. DFS                                      C |  0   1   0   1   0   1
4. Exit                                     D |  0   1   0   1   0   1
Enter your Choice : 1                       E |  0   1   1   0   0   0
                                            F |  0   1   0   1   0   0
Enter edge for Vertex 1( 0 0 to quit ) : 1 2
Enter edge for Vertex 2( 0 0 to quit ) : 1 3    Enter your Choice : 2
Enter edge for Vertex 3( 0 0 to quit ) : 1 6
Enter edge for Vertex 4( 0 0 to quit ) : 2 1
Enter edge for Vertex 5( 0 0 to quit ) : 2 5
Enter edge for Vertex 6( 0 0 to quit ) : 2 4
Enter edge for Vertex 7( 0 0 to quit ) : 3 2

Enter edge for Vertex 8( 0 0 to quit ) : 3 4    Enter Starting Vertex (integer) :1
Enter edge for Vertex 9( 0 0 to quit ) : 3 6
Enter edge for Vertex 10( 0 0 to quit ) : 4 6   Breadth First Traversal :
Enter edge for Vertex 11( 0 0 to quit ) : 5 3     1    2    3    4    5    6
Enter edge for Vertex 12( 0 0 to quit ) : 5 2   Enter your Choice : 3
Enter edge for Vertex 13( 0 0 to quit ) : 0 0   Enter Starting Vertex (integer) :1
                                                Depth First Traversal :
                                                  1    2    4    6    5    3
```

What is Optimization?

An optimization problem is one that seeks to find the maximum or minimum value in order to maximize or minimize the result.

The greedy algorithm, dynamic programming, and branch-and-bound techniques are commonly used to solve optimization problems.

Some of the algorithms used to solve graph theory and networking problems:

Greedy Algorithm.

What is a Greedy Algorithm?

A greedy algorithm is an algorithmic model that follows a problem-solving approach by making the locally best choice at each stage, with the hope of finding a global optimum.

In computer networking, such as in a large Local Area Network (LAN) that requires many switches, calculating a Minimum Spanning Tree (MST) is crucial. With the MST, the minimum number of packets will be transmitted through the network.

Advantages and Dis-advantages of Greedy Algorithm

Advantages	Dis-Advantages
1. Greedy algorithms are generally simple to understand, and their solutions may be more easily formulated; however, the proving process may be difficult. 2. Dynamic programming (DP) solutions assess all potential options at each step, whereas greedy algorithms just consider the best option at each step.	1. You can't solve every issue with a greedy algorithm. People frequently assume that a greedy strategy will succeed when, in reality, Dynamic Programming is used. 2. Dynamic programming can be used to address the greedy problem, but not the other way around.

The greedy algorithm is used to solve many problems, some of it:

1. Selection Sort.
2. Minimal Spanning Tree Algorithm.
   a. Prim's Algorithm.
   b. Kruskal's Algorithm.
3. Dijkstra's Algorithm, Shortest Path.
4. Fractional Knapsack Problem.

Spanning Tree

A spanning tree is a tree that contains the least possible edges from a graph, and each vertex is connected once Way back in 1926, the algorithm was invented by Cczech scientist Otakar Borůvka.

Generally, it can be said that in a graph G with N numbers of vertices, one can have a spanning tree with a maximum of N – 1, edges.

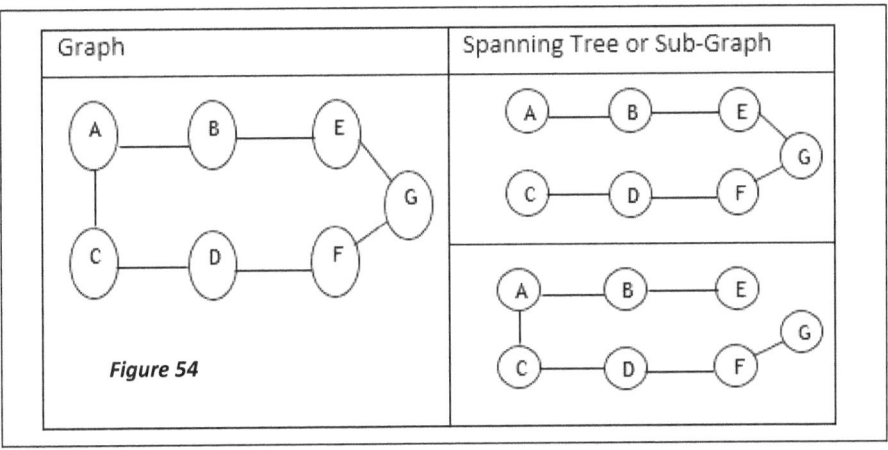

| | Graph | Spanning Tree or Sub-Graph |

Figure 54

Minimum Spanning Tree (MST)

A minimum spanning tree (MST) is a type of spanning tree that includes the minimum total weight. Applications of MSTs are used in communication networks (internet connection). In other words, a spanning tree means a subgraph of a graph.

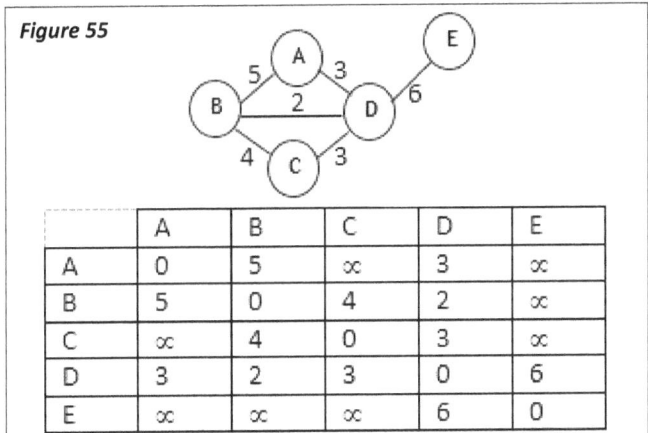

Figure 55

	A	B	C	D	E
A	0	5	∞	3	∞
B	5	0	4	2	∞
C	∞	4	0	3	∞
D	3	2	3	0	6
E	∞	∞	∞	6	0

The total Edge weight: 5 + 4 + 3 + 6 + 3 + 2 = 23 (Figure 55)

It is difficult to determine the minimum cost of a tree by generating all possible spanning trees. Constructing all possible spanning trees to check the minimum cost is only feasible for smaller graphs. Therefore, Prim's and Kruskal's algorithms are used to find the minimum spanning tree. The following algorithms are commonly used:

1. Kruskal's Algorithm
2. Prim's Algorithm

Kruskal's Algorithm:

Kruskal's algorithm is a greedy algorithm used to find the Minimum Spanning Tree (MST). By applying Kruskal's algorithm, we can find the MST for each connected component. The steps for Kruskal's algorithm are as follows:

1. All loops in the graphs should be removed.
2. Form a table of edges and their respective weights.
3. Sort all of the edges in ascending order by weight.
4. Select the smallest edge and if a cycle is not formed by the selected edge, include this edge, otherwise discard it.

Edges	AB	AD	BC	BD	CD	DE
Weight	5	3	4	2	3	6

Now Sort in Ascending order on Weight:

Edges	BD	AD	CD	BC	AB	DE
	2	3	3	4	5	6

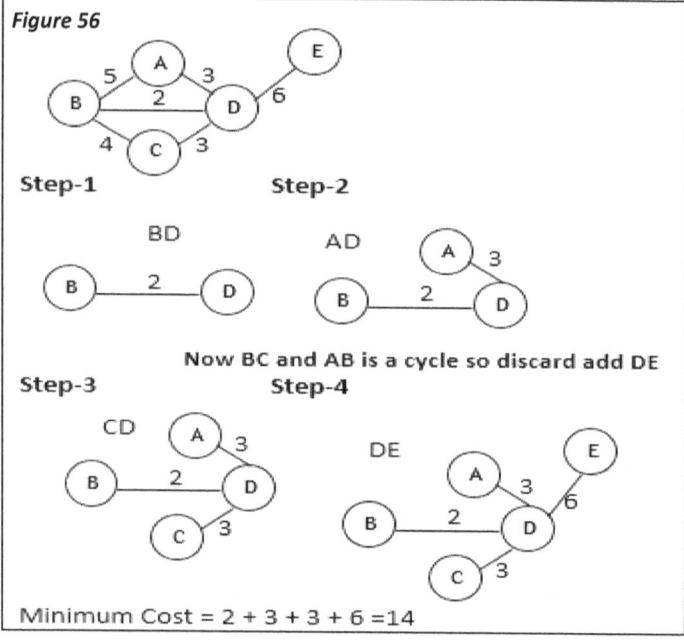

Figure 56

Step-1

Step-2

Step-3

Step-4

Now BC and AB is a cycle so discard add DE

Minimum Cost = 2 + 3 + 3 + 6 = 14

Prog-44. Kruskal Algorithm

//Instead of 999 one can use INT_MAX from <limits.h>

```c
#include<stdio.h>
#define V 6
   int parent[V]={0};
   //Find Source Edge
   int Find(int a)
     {
     while(parent[a]!=0)
        {
           a=parent[a];
        }
     return a;
     }
     //Checking a Cycle is created or not
   int Union(int a ,int b)
     {
     if(a!=b)
        {
        parent[b]=a;
        return 1;
        }
     return 0;
     }
   int main()
     {
        int mincost=0,min,edge=1;
        int i,j,u,v,x,y,chk;
     int n=V-1;
     int weight[V][V];int ab[V][V]={{0,5,0,3,0},
                                    {5,0,4,2,0},
                                    {0,4,0,3,0},
                                    {3,2,3,0,6},
                                    {0,0,0,6,0}};
        printf("\n\t\t** Calculate Minimum Cost (Kr Algorithm)  **\n");
       printf("\n\t\tThe Cost Adjacency Matrix:\n\t\t");
      for(j=1;j<=n;j++)
        printf("  %c ",(char)(j+64));
      for(i=1;i<=n;i++)
        {
        printf("\n\t %c\t",(char)(i+64));
        for(j=1;j<=n;j++)
          {
          weight[i][j]=ab[i-1][j-1];
          if(weight[i][j]==0)
```

```
        weight[i][j]=999;
        printf("%4d ",weight[i][j]);
     }  }
//kruskal's Algorithm
printf("\n");
while(edge<n)
 {
  min=999;
  // finding Minimum weight in adjacency matrix
  for(i=1;i<=n;i++)
    {
    for(j=1;j<=n;j++)
      {
        if(weight[i][j]<min)
        {
          min=weight[i][j];
          x=u=i;
          y=v=j;
        } } }
 // finding Source of the vertex
  u=Find(u);
  v=Find(v);
 // Checking for cycle
  chk=Union(u,v);
  if(chk==1)
    {
    printf("\n\tEdge (%c , %c) = %d",(char)(x+64),(char)(y+64),min);
    edge++;
    mincost+=min;
    }
  weight[x][y]=weight[y][x]=999;
}
printf("\n\n\tMinimum Cost of the Spanning Tree is = %d ",mincost);
return 0;    }
```

Output

```
          ** Calculate Minimum Cost (Kr Algorithm)  **
             The Cost Adjacency Matrix:
             A    B    C    D    E
       A    999    5  999    3  999
       B      5  999    4    2  999
       C    999    4  999    3  999
       D      3    2    3  999    6
```

E   999   999   999   6   999

Edge (B , D) = 2
Edge (A , D) = 3
Edge (C , D) = 3
Edge (D , E) = 6

Minimum Cost of the Spanning Tree is = 14

Prim's Algorithm

Prim's algorithm is also a greedy algorithm used to find the minimum spanning tree. Each vertex is visited once, and the sum of the weights of the edges is minimized. Prim's algorithm starts from a node known as the starting node, which can be any arbitrary node in the graph. From the starting node, the algorithm explores all adjacent nodes and their connecting edges at each step. The edges with the minimal weights are selected, ensuring that no cycles are formed in the graph.

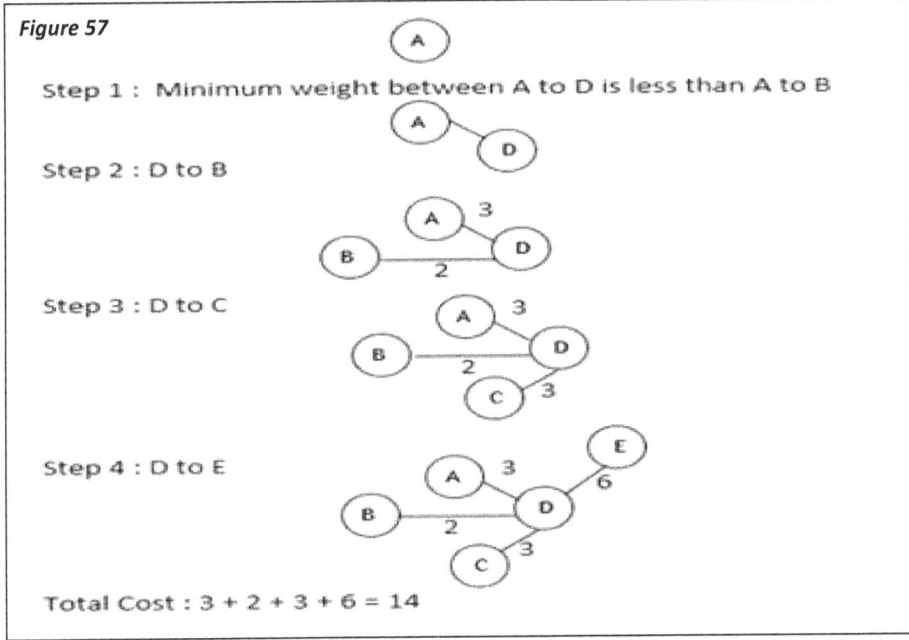

Figure 57

Step 1 : Minimum weight between A to D is less than A to B

Step 2 : D to B

Step 3 : D to C

Step 4 : D to E

Total Cost : 3 + 2 + 3 + 6 = 14

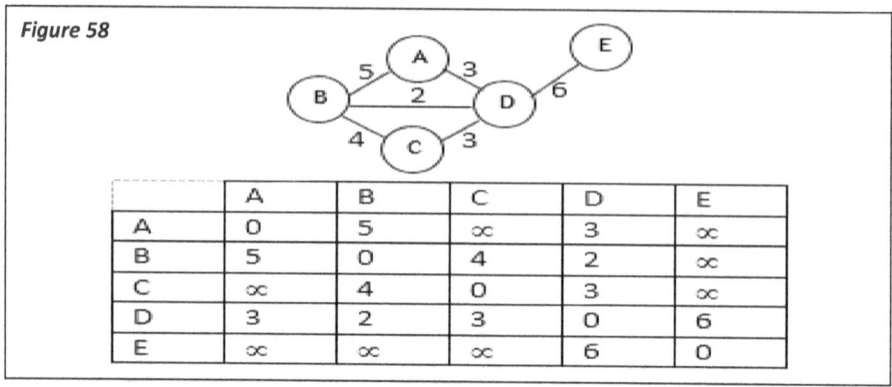

Figure 58

	A	B	C	D	E
A	0	5	∞	3	∞
B	5	0	4	2	∞
C	∞	4	0	3	∞
D	3	2	3	0	6
E	∞	∞	∞	6	0

Let **A** is the starting node

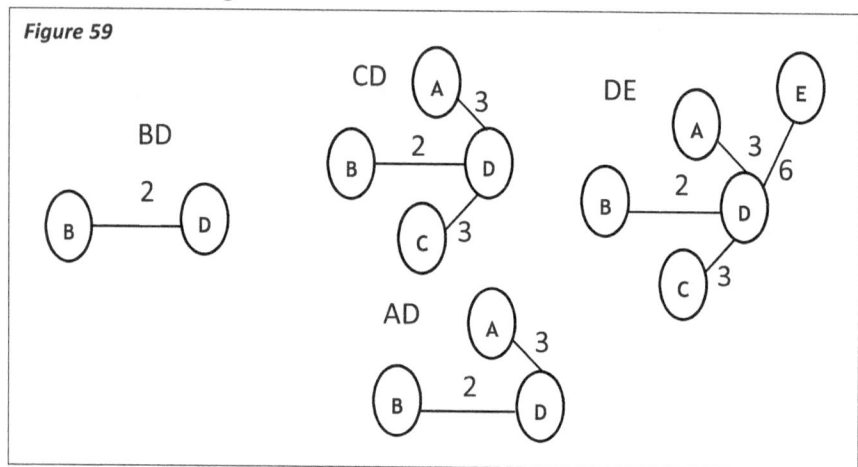

Figure 59

Prog-45. Prim's Algorithm

```
#include <stdio.h>
#define V 5

int main()
{
    int adm[V][V]={{0,5,0,3,0},
                   {5,0,4,2,0},
                   {0,4,0,3,0},
                   {3,2,3,0,6},
                   {0,0,0,6,0}};
    int x,y,u,n,i,j,v,ne=1;
    int visited[V]={0},min,min_cost=0,cost[V][V];
    n=V;
    printf("\n\t\t** Calculate Minimum Cost (Prim's Algorithm) **\n");
    printf("\n\t\tThe Cost Adjacency Matrix:\n\t\t");
```

```c
for(j=1;j<=n;j++)
 printf("  %c ",(char)(j+64));
  for(i=1;i<=n;i++)
   {
     printf("\n\t  %c \t",(char)(i+64));
     for(j=1;j<=n;j++)
       {
         cost[i][j]=adm[i-1][j-1];
         if(cost[i][j]==0)
           cost[i][j]=999;
         printf(" %4d ",cost[i][j]);
       }
   }
 printf("\n");
// finding minimum
visited[1]=0;
while(ne<n)
 {
  min=999;
  for(i=1;i<=n;i++)
   {
     for(j=1;j<=n;j++)
       {
       if(cost[i][j]<min)
         {
         if(visited[i]!=0)
           {
             min=cost[i][j];
           x=i;
           y=j;
           }
       } } }
  //When not visited
  if(visited[y]==0)
   {
     printf("\n\t(%c , %c)  cost = %d",(char)(x+64),(char)(y+64),min);
     min_cost=min_cost+min;
     ne++;
   }
  visited[y]=1;
  // The Matrix initialize with maximum value
  cost[x][y]=cost[y][x]=999;
 }
```

```
        printf("\n\n\tMinimum Cost is = %d",min_cost);
        return 0;
    }
```

Output

            ** Calculate Minimum Cost (Prim's Algorithm) **
            The Cost Adjacency Matrix:
                A   B   C   D   E
            A   999 5 999   3 999
            B   5 999   4   2 999
            C   999 4 999   3 999
            D   3   2   3 999   6
            E   999 999 999   6 999

            (B , D) cost = 2
            (D , A) cost = 3
            (D , C) cost = 3
            (D , E) cost = 6

            Minimum Cost is = 14

Dijsktra Algorithm

Finding the Single Source shortest path from a starting node to a target node in a weighted graph is Dijkstra's algorithm. Developed in 1956 by Edsger W. Dijsktra. The objective is to find the shortest path from a given source vertex to all other vertices of G.

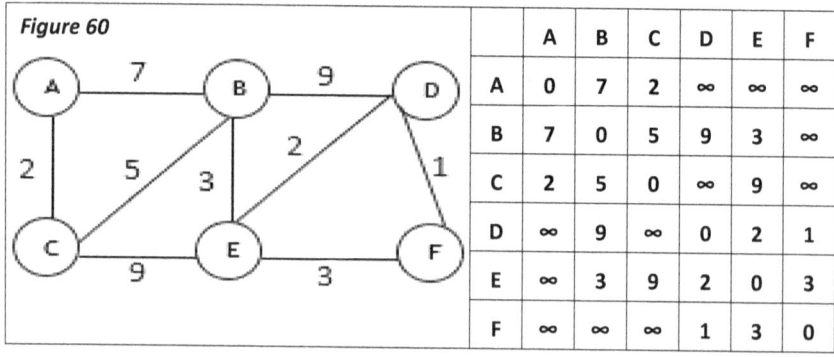

Figure 60

	A	B	C	D	E	F
A	0	7	2	∞	∞	∞
B	7	0	5	9	3	∞
C	2	5	0	∞	9	∞
D	∞	9	∞	0	2	1
E	∞	3	9	2	0	3
F	∞	∞	∞	1	3	0

** Formula Min (destination, weight / cost + current marked value)

Starting Node: A

Step	V	C	D(A)	D(B)	D(C)	D(D)	D(E)	D(F)	Path to F
0	-	{A, B, C, D, E, F}	0	∞	∞	∞	∞	∞	-
1	A	{B, C, D, E, F}	0	7	2	∞	∞	∞	-
2	C	{B, D, E, F}	0	7	2	∞	∞	∞	-
3	B	{D, E, F}	0	7	2	16	10	∞	-
4	E	{D, F}	0	7	2	16	10	13	E -> F
5	F	{D}	0	7	2	16	10	13	E -> F
6	D	{}	0	7	2	16	10	13	E -> F

Figure 61

Marked	A	B	C	D	E	F
A	0	∞	∞	∞	∞	∞
A	0	Min(∞,0+7) 7	Min(∞,0+2) 2	∞	∞	∞
A, C	0	Min(7,2+5) 7	2	∞	Min(∞,2+9) 11	∞
A, C, B	0	7	2	Min(∞,7+9) 16	Min(11,7+3) 10	∞
A, C, B, E	0	7	2	Min(16,7+3+2) 12	10	Min(∞,7+3+3) 13
A, C, B, E, D	0	7	2	12	10	Min(13,7+9+1) 13
A, C, B, E, D, F	0	7	2	12	10	13

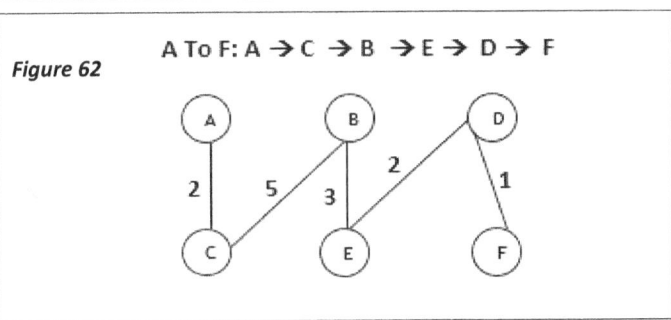

A To F: A → C → B → E → D → F

Figure 62

Shortest Path: A -> C -> B -> E -> F

Explanation:

- We follow the same Dijkstra's algorithm steps as before, but now we track the path to node F as we update the distances.
- At step 4, when node E is selected, we see that its distance to F is 3. Since this is the first time we have a finite distance to F, we record the path as "E -> F".
- In subsequent steps, the distance to F does not change, so the path remains "E -> F".

Therefore, the shortest path from A to F is A -> C -> B -> E -> F with a total distance of 13.

Prog-46. Dijkstra Algorithm

```c
#include <stdio.h>
#define N 6
  int minDist(int distance[], int visited[])
    {
    int min = 999, index;
    int v;
    for (v = 0; v < N; v++)
      {
        if (visited[v] == 0 && distance[v] <= min)
          {
            min = distance[v], index = v;
            }
      }
    return index;
    }

  void Disp(int distance[], int n)
    {
    printf("\tThe Distane of each Vertex from Source\n");
    int i;
    for (i = 0; i < N; i++)
    {
      printf("\t%c \t\t %d\n", (char)(i+65), distance[i]);
        }
    }

  void dijkstra(int graph[N][N], int source)
    {
    int distance[N]; //Distance from Source
```

```c
    int visited[N];
    int i, c, v;
    for (i = 0; i < N; i++)
      {
         distance[i] = 999, visited[i] = 0;
         }
  distance[source] = 0;
  for (c = 0; c < N - 1; c++)
      {
    int u = minDist(distance, visited);
    visited[u] = 1;
    for (v = 0; v < N; v++)
      {
         if (!visited[v] && graph[u][v] && distance[u] != 999 && distance[u]+
graph[u][v] < distance[v])
            {
            distance[v] = distance[u] + graph[u][v];
               }
         }
      }
  Disp(distance, N);
      }
  int main()
    {
      int i,j;
      int adm[N][N]={{0,7,2,999,999,999},
                        {7,0,5,9,3,999},
                        {2,5,0,999,9,999},
                        {999,9,999,07,1},
                        {999,3,9,0,999,3},
                        {999,999,999,1,3,0}}; //Cost Array
      printf(""\n\t\tThe Cost Matrix\n\t\t "");
      for(j=1;j<=N;j++)
    printf("  %c ",(char)(j+64));
    printf("\n");
      for(i=1;i<=N;i++)
        {
          printf("\t %c \t",(char)(i+64));
          for(j=1;j<=N;j++)
            {
              printf(" %4d ",adm[i-1][j-1]);
            }
          printf("\n");
```

```
    }
    printf("\n\t Source is A and Distance from Source\n\n");
    dijkstra(adm, 0);
    return 0;
}
```

Output

The Cost Matrix

	A	B	C	D	E	F
A	0	7	2	999	999	999
B	7	0	5	9	3	999
C	2	5	0	999	9	999
D	999	9	999	7	1	0
E	999	3	9	0	999	3
F	999	999	999	1	3	0

Source is A and Distance from Source

The Distane/Cost of each Vertex from Source

A	0
B	7
C	2
D	14
E	10
F	13

Fractional Knapsack Problem

A challenge in complementary or integrative optimization is known as the knapsack problem. In this type of problem, a set of items is provided, each with a specific weight and value. The task is to determine the quantity of each item to include in the collection, ensuring that the total weight is as close as possible to a specified limit while maximizing the total value. The algorithm may use a fraction of an item, but this option is only applicable to the last item selected.

In Fractional Knapsack, for instance, by using a greedy approach in which maximum value, M =25kg.

Item No	Weight	Profit	X (P/W)
1	10	40	4
2	6	15	2.5
3	5	32	6.4
4	8	35	4.375
5	4	6	1.5

After sorting the table in decreasing order of X (p/w).

Item No	Weight	Profit	X (P/W)
3	5	32	6.4
4	8	35	4.375
1	10	40	4
2	6	15	2.5
5	4	6	1.5

Fill the sack with the weights and the sack will be filled, considering the maximum profit: weight ratio.

Calculation:

  Item 3: Weight = 5, Profit = 32

  Take the whole item.

Remaining capacity = 25−5=20, Total profit = 32.

Item 4: Weight = 8, Profit = 35

Take the whole item.

Remaining capacity = 20−8=12, Total profit = 32+35=67

Item 1: Weight = 10, Profit = 40

Take the whole item.

Remaining capacity = 12−10=2, Total profit = 67+40=107.

Item 2: Weight = 6, Profit = 15

Only 2 units can be taken. Fractional profit = 15×(2/6)=5.

Remaining capacity = 0, Total profit = 107+5=112.

Prog-47. Fractional Knapsack

```
#include <stdio.h>
#define N 5
```

```c
typedef struct Product
 {
   char Itemid[8];
   int weight;
   int profit;
   float ratio;
 }Prod;
 Prod Items[5] = {{"Item-1",10,40,0},
                  {"Item-2", 6,15,0},
                  {"Item-3", 5,32,0},
                  {"Item-4", 8,35,0},
                  {"Item-5", 4, 6,0},
                  };
 void fKsack(Prod items[], int Cap)
   {
   float val;
     int i, w;
   float tW = 0, tProfit = 0;
     printf("\nItem In Sack:\n");
   for(i = 0; i < N; i++)
       {
       if(items[i].weight + tW <= Cap)
           {
           tW = tW + items[i].weight;
           tProfit = tProfit + items[i].profit;
           printf(" %-8s  Weight : %3d  Profit: %6.2f  Ratio: %6.2f Total Profit:
%6.2f\n", items[i].Itemid, items[i].weight, items[i].profit, tW, tProfit);
           }
       else
           {
           w = Cap - tW;
           val = w * (float)((items[i].profit) / items[i].weight);
           tW = tW + w;
           tProfit = tProfit + val;
           printf(" %-8s  Weight : %3d  Profit: %6.2f  Ratio: %6.2f Total Profit:
%6.2f\n", items[i].Itemid, w, val, tW, tProfit);
           break;
           }
       }
     printf("\nTotal Weight : %f\n", tW);
     printf("\nTotal Profit: %f\n", tProfit);
     }
```

```c
int main(void)
    {
      Prod temp;
    int i, j;
    //maximum limit of the knapsack
    int Cap = 25;
    for(i = 0; i < N; i++)
        {
        Items[i].ratio = (float)(Items[i].profit) / (float)(Items[i].weight);
        }
      printf("\n\tOriginal Data:\n");
    for(j = 0; j < N; j++)
        {
          printf("%-10s %3d %3d
%5.2f\n",Items[j].Itemid,Items[j].weight,Items[j].profit,Items[j].ratio);
        }
  //sorting decreasing order by ratio
    for(i = 0; i < N; i++)
        {
        for(j = 0; j < N - i-1; j++)
            {
            if(Items[j].ratio < Items[j+1].ratio)
                {
                temp = Items[j+1];
                Items[j+1] = Items[j];
                Items[j] = temp;
              }
            }
        }
      printf("\n\tData After Sorting :\n");
    for(j = 0; j < N; j++)
        {
          printf("%-10s %3d %3d
%5.2f\n",Items[j].Itemid,Items[j].weight,Items[j].profit,Items[j].ratio);
        }
      fKsack(Items,Cap);
    return 0;
    }
```

Output

```
        Original Data:
Item-1   10 40 4.00
Item-2    6 15 2.50
Item-3    5 32 6.40
Item-4    8 35 4.38
Item-5    4  6 1.50

        Data After Sorting :
Item-3    5 32 6.40
Item-4    8 35 4.38
Item-1   10 40 4.00
Item-2    6 15 2.50
Item-5    4  6 1.50

Item In Sack:
Item-3  Weight :  5 Profit:  0.00 Ratio:  5.00 Total Profit: 32.00
Item-4  Weight :  8 Profit:  0.00 Ratio: 13.00 Total Profit: 67.00
Item-1  Weight : 10 Profit:  0.00 Ratio: 23.00 Total Profit: 107.00
Item-2  Weight :  2 Profit:  4.00 Ratio: 25.00 Total Profit: 111.00

Total Weight : 25.000000

Total Profit: 111.000000
```

Dynamic Programming

What is Dynamic Programing?

Dynamic Programming, invented by Richard Bellman, is a technique used to solve problems by breaking them down into smaller sub-problems, solving these sub-problems independently, and combining their solutions. The key idea is to store the results of solved sub-problems to avoid redundant computations, making the approach both efficient and systematic.

Advantages	Dis-Advantages
1. Processing is sped up by dynamic programming because it uses references that have already been calculated	1. Each sub-calculated program's result must be saved in a large amount of memory without any

2. It decreases the number of lines of code in the programme since it uses recursive programming.	guarantee that it will be used or not.
	2. The output value is saved and never used during the execution of the subsequent sub-program. As a result, unnecessary memory is used.
	3. Functions are called recursively in dynamic programming, due to this, the stack memory keeps growing.

There are unaccounted problems that can be solved using DP, but here are a few that will be discussed:

1. Floyd Warshall Algorithm
2. Bellman–Ford Algorithm
3. 0-1 Knapsack Problem

Diference between Greedy and Dynamic programming

Greedy Method	Dynamic programming
1. A single decision sequence is produced.	1. Numerous decision sequences could be produced.
2. It contains a particular set of feasible solutions.	2. More dependable.
3. Top-to-bottom approach.	3. There is no special set of feasible solutions.
4. It is unmanageable.	4. Bottom-to-up approach.
5. Shortest path, Fractional knapsack.	5. It chooses the optimal solution to the sub-problem.
	6. 0/1 Knapsack

Floyd-Warshall Algorithm

Dynamic Programming, in its modern form, was recognized by Robert Floyd and Stephen Warshall in 1962, although it closely resembles algorithms published earlier by Bernard Roy in 1959.

Dijkstra's Algorithm is an example of a single-source shortest path algorithm. Given a source vertex, it calculates the shortest paths from the source to all other vertices in a graph. On the other hand, the **Floyd-Warshall Algorithm** is designed to compute the shortest paths between all pairs of nodes in a graph.

The **Floyd-Warshall Algorithm** exemplifies the principles of dynamic programming by dividing the problem into smaller subproblems, solving each independently, and then combining their solutions to address the main problem.

In the following graph, if A is the source, then find the shortest path from: A → B, A → C, when B considered as the source then B → A, B → C, with C, C → A or C→ B.

Figure 63

A directed graph of four vertex presented below with the cost matrix, K=0.

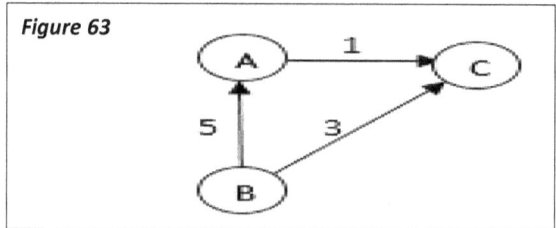

D[0]	A	B	C	D
A	0	∞	1	∞
B	5	0	3	∞
C	∞	∞	0	4
D	∞	2	∞	0

Figure 64

Copy only the first column and first row of D0 to D1 as it is and then fill up the remaining spaces using the following formula.

$D_K[I,J]=min(D_{K-1}[I,J],D_{K-1}[I,k]+D_{K-1}[K,J])$ place the minimum value in D_K [I,j] else leave the original as it is.

Where K is the iteration, I and J are the cell locations. K = 0 when D[0] and it will increase by 1 for the next matrix.

I=2, J=3, K=1	D1(2,3)=MIN(D0[2,3]>D0[2,1]+D0[1,3]) =MIN(3,5+1) = 3
I=2, J=4, K=1	D1(2,4)=MIN(D0[2,4],D0[2,1]+D0[1,4]) =MIN(∞,∞+5) = ∞
I=3, J=2, K=1	D1 [3, 2]=MIN(D0 [3, 2] > D0 [3, 1] + D0 [1 , 2])=MIN(∞,∞+∞)=∞
I=3, J=4, K=1	D1 [3, 4] =MIN(D0 [3, 4] , D0 [3, 1] + D0 [1 , 4])=MIN(4, ∞+∞)=4
I=4 J=2 K=1	D1[4,2]=MIN(D1[4,2],D1[4,1]+D1[1,2])=MIN(2,∞+∞)=2
I=4 J=3 K=1	D1[4,3]=MIN(D0[4,3],D0[4,1]+D0[1,3]) =MIN(∞,1+∞)=∞

D1	A	B	C	D
A	0	∞	1	∞
B	5	0		
C	∞		0	
D	∞			0

D1	A	B	C	D
A	0	∞	1	∞
B	5	0	3	∞
C	∞	∞	0	4
D	∞	2	∞	0

Copy the second row and second coloumn from D1 to D2 and then proceed with same formula for K=2

I=1 J=3 K=2	D2[1,3]>= MIN(D1[1,3],D1[1,2]+D1[2,3]) = MIN(1,∞+3)=1
I=1 J=4 K=2	D2[1,4]=MIN(D1[1,4],D1[1,2]+D1[2,4])MIN(∞,∞+∞)=∞
I=3 J=1 K=2	D2[3,1]=MIN(D1[3,1],D1[3,2]+D1[2,1])=MIN(∞,5 + ∞)= ∞
I=3, J=4, K=2	D2[3,4]=MIN(D1[3,4],D1[3,2]+D1[2,4])=MIN(4, 5 + ∞)=4
I=4 J=1 K=2	D2[4,1]=MIN(D1[4,1],D1[4,2]+D1[2,1])=MIN(∞,2+5)= 7
I=4 J=3 K=2	D2[4,3]=MIN(D1[4,3],D1[4,2]+D1[2,3])=MIN(∞,2+3)=5

D2	A	B	C	D
A	0	∞		
B	5	0	3	∞
C		∞	0	
D		2		0

D2	A	B	C	D
A	0	∞	1	∞
B	5	0	3	∞
C	∞	∞	0	4
D	7	2	5	0

Copy the third column of D2 to D3

I=1 J=2 K=3	D3[1,2]=MIN(D2[1,2],D2[1,3]+D2[3,2])=MIN(∞,1+∞) =∞
I=1 J=4 K=3	D3[1,4]=MIN(D2[1,4],D2[1,3]+D2[3,4])=MIN(∞,1+4)=5
I=2 J=1 K=3	D3[2,1]=MIN(D2[2,1],D2[2,3]+D2[3,1])=MIN(5,3+∞)=5
I=2 J=4 K=3	D3[2,4]= MIN(D2[2,4],D2[2,3]+D2[3,4])=MIN(∞,3+4)=7
I=4 J=1 K=3	D3[4,1]=MIN(D2[4,1],D2[4,3]+D2[3,1])=MIN(7,∞+5)= 7
I=4 J=2 K=3	D3[4,2]=MIN(D2[4,2],D2[4,3]+D2[3,2])=MIN(2,∞+5)=2

D3	A	B	C	D
A	0		1	
B		0	3	
C	∞	∞	0	4
D			2	0

D3	A	B	C	D
A	0	∞	1	5
B	5	0	3	7
C	∞	∞	0	4
D	7	2	5	0

Copy the fourth column of D3 to D4

I=1 J=2 K=4	D4[1,2]=MIN(D3[1,2],D2[1,4]+D2[4,2])=MIN(∞,5+2)=7
I=1 J=3 K=4	D4[1,3]=MIN(D3[1,3]>D2[1,4]+D2[4,3]=MIN(1,5+5)=1
I=2 J=1 K=4	D4[2,1]=MIN(D3[2,1],D2[2,4]+D2[4,1])=MIN(5,7+7)=5
I=2 J=3 K=4	D4[2,3]=MIN(D3[2,3],D2[2,4]+D2[4,3])=MIN(3,7+5)=3
I=3 J=1 K=4	D4[3,1]>=MIN(D3[3,1],D3[3,4]+D3[4,1])=MIN(∞,4+7)=11
I=3 J=2 K=4	D4[3,2]>=MIN(D3[3,2],D3[3,4]+D3[4,2])=MIN(∞,4+2)=6

D4	A	B	C	D
A	0			5
B		0		7
C			0	4
D	7	2	5	0

D4	A	B	C	D
A	0	7	1	5
B	5	0	3	7
C	11	6	0	4
D	7	2	5	0

Prog-48. Floyd Warshall Algorithm

```
#include<stdio.h>
#define V 4
  void flW (int dist[][V])
    {
      int i,j,k;
      for (k = 0; k < V; k++)
        {
        for (i = 0; i < V; i++)
```

```c
        {
          for (j = 0; j < V; j++)
            {
              if (dist[i][j]>dist[i][k] + dist[k][j])
                {
                            dist[i][j] = dist[i][k] + dist[k][j];
                }
            }
        }
    }
  }
int main()
 {
    int i,j;
    int dist[V][V]= {{0,999,1,999},
                     {5,0,3,999},
                     {999,999,0,4},
                     {999,2,999,0}};
    printf("\n\t\tThe Cost Matrix\n\t\t ");
    for(j=0;j<V;j++)
 printf("  %c ",(char)(j+65));
 printf("\n");
    for(i=0;i<V;i++)
     {
        printf("\t  %c \t",(char)(i+65));
        for(j=0;j<V;j++)
          {
            printf(" %4d ",dist[i][j]);
          }
        printf("\n");
      }

    flW(dist);
    printf("\n\n\tShortest distances between every pair of vertices :\n\t\t ");
    for(j=0;j<V;j++)
 printf("  %c ",(char)(j+65));
 printf("\n");
    for(i=0;i<V;i++)
     {
        printf("\t  %c \t",(char)(i+65));
        for(j=0;j<V;j++)
          {
            printf(" %4d ",dist[i][j]);
```

```
        }
        printf("\n");
    }
    return 0;
}
```

Output

The Cost Matrix

	A	B	C	D
A	0	999	1	999
B	5	0	3	999
C	999	999	0	4
D	999	2	999	0

Shortest distances between every pair of vertices :

	A	B	C	D
A	0	7	1	5
B	5	0	3	7
C	11	6	0	4
D	7	2	5	0

Bellman-Ford algorithm

What Is a Cycle?

In graph theory, a **cycle** is a path that starts and ends at the same vertex, without visiting any vertex more than once (except for the start/end vertex). This means that a cycle forms a loop within the graph.

What is meant by negative weight cycle?

A **negative weight cycle** refers to a cycle in a weighted graph where the sum of the weights of the edges in that cycle is negative. In other words, if you traverse the cycle and sum up the weights of the edges, the total will be negative.

The method was first developed by Alfonso Shimbel in 1955, but it was Richard Bellman and Lester Ford Jr. who published it in 1958 and 1956, respectively, and it is named after them.

The **Bellman-Ford** technique propagates precise distance estimates to all nodes in a graph in N− 1 steps, unless there is a negative weight cycle (where N stands for the total number of vertices). While the Dijkstra algorithm is designed for finding single-source shortest paths from a starting node to a target node, the Bellman-Ford algorithm computes the shortest path for all vertices connected to the source node.

It tracks the weight distance from the origin and the previous node in the shortest path while iterating over edges and connections N times, where N is the total number of nodes. While slower than Dijkstra's algorithm, it can handle negative edge weights and detect negative weight cycles, making it less efficient but more versatile.

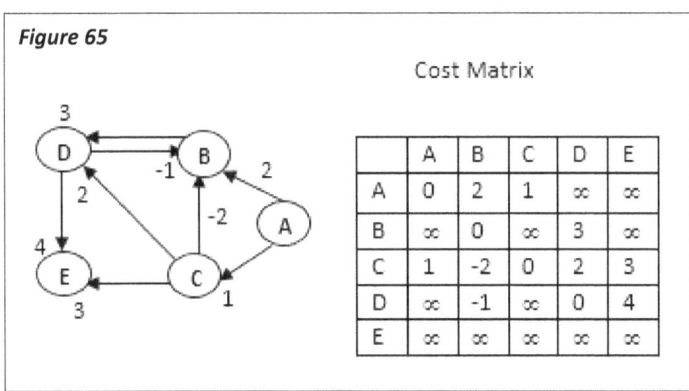

Figure 65

Cost Matrix

	A	B	C	D	E
A	0	2	1	∞	∞
B	∞	0	∞	3	∞
C	1	-2	0	2	3
D	∞	-1	∞	0	4
E	∞	∞	∞	∞	∞

Apart from A, fill the remaining table with ∞

Vertex	A	B	C	D	E
Distance	0	∞	∞	∞	∞

Edge U → V, D = Distance, W IS Weight

Relax D (U, V) = MIN(D(U)+D(U, V),D(V))

Source Vertex: A	**Iteration 1:** A→B: Distance(B)=min(∞,0+2)=2 A→C: Distance(C)=min(∞,0+1)=1	**Updated distances:** | Vertex	A	B	C	D	E
Distance	0	2	1	∞	∞	
	Iteration 2: From B: B→D: Distance(D)=min(∞,2+3)=5 From C: C→A: Distance(A) =min(0,1+1)=0 (No change) C→B: Distance(B)=min(2,1+(−2)=−1	

Updated distances:

Vertex	A	B	C	D	E
Distance	0	-1	1	3	4

C→D : Distance(D)=min(5,1+2)=3 C→E : Distance(E)=min(∞,1+3)=4	

Iteration 3 and 4:

No further updates, as all shortest distances are already computed.

Final Distances from A:		A	B	C	D	E
	A	0	-1	1	3	4

Source Vertex: B

Initialization:	**Updated distances:**					
	Vertex	A	B	C	D	E
	Distance	∞	0	∞	∞	∞

Iteration 1:	**Updated distances:**					
B→D : Distance(D)=min(∞,0+3)=3	Vertex	A	B	C	D	E
	Distance	∞	0	∞	3	∞

Source Vertex: B

Iteration 2:	**Updated distances:**					
From D:	Vertex	A	B	C	D	E
D→B : Distance(B)=min(0,3+(−1))=0 (No change)	Distance	∞	0	∞	3	7
D→E : Distance(E)=min(∞,3+4)=7						

Iteration 3 and 4: No further updates.

Final Distances from B Will be same as above table shown after Iteration 2.

Source Vertex: C

Initialization:	**Updated distances:**					
Iteration 1:						
C→A: Distance(A)=min(∞,0+1)=1						
C→B: Distance(B)=min(∞,0+(−2))=−2	Vertex	A	B	C	D	E
C→D: Distance(D)=min(∞,0+2)=2	Distance	1	-2	0	2	3
C→E: Distance(E)=min(∞,0+3)=3						

Final Distances from C:

Vertex	A	B	C	D	E
Distance	1	-2	0	2	3

Final Results

From/To	A	B	C	D	E
A	0	-1	1	3	4
B	∞	0	∞	3	7
C	1	-2	0	2	3
D	∞	-1	∞	0	4
E	∞	∞	∞	∞	0

Prog-49. Bellman-Ford Algorithm

```c
#include <stdio.h>
#include <stdlib.h>
#define INF 999
#define N 5
int i,j,k;
  int BF(int cost[5][5], int e, int ed[5][2])
    {
    int u,v,k,dist[20],P[20],source,f=1,c=0;
    for(i=0;i<N;i++)
      {
          dist[i] = INF , P[i] = -1 ;
    }
      source=1;
    dist[source-1]=0 ;
     for(i=0;i<N-1;i++)
      {
      for(j=0;j<e;j++)
        {
            u = ed[j][0] ;
              v = ed[j][1] ;

        if(dist[u]+cost[u][v] < dist[v])
        {

          dist[v] = dist[u] + cost[u][v] , P[v]=u ;
```

```c
            }
          }
        }
        for(j=0;j<e;j++)
          {
              u = ed[j][0] , v = ed[j][1] ;
              if(dist[u]+cost[u][v] < dist[v])
                 f = 0 ;
          }
        if(f==1)
                for(i=0;i<N;i++)
            {
            if(P[i]<0)
                {
                      c=0;
                    }
                else
                    {
                      c=P[i];
                    }
             printf("\n\tSource Vertex %c -> cost = %3d Parent Vertex =
%c",(char)(64+i+1),dist[i],(char)(c+1+64));
                }
        return f;
        }
      int main()
        {
        int ed[20][2],cost[5][5]={{0,2,1,0,0},{0,0,0,3,0},{0,-2,0,2,3},{0,-
1,0,0,4},{0,0,0,0,0}};
        k=0;
          for(i=0;i<N;i++)
          {
             for(j=0;j<N;j++)
            {
            if(cost[i][j]!=0)
              {
              ed[k][0]=i,ed[k++][1]=j;
                }
            }
          }
          for(i=0;i<N;i++)
            {
              printf("    %c ",(char)(65+i));
```

```c
    }
    printf("\n =====================================\n");

    for(i=0;i<N;i++)
      {
        printf(" %c  |",(char)(65+i));
        for(j=0;j<N;j++)
          {
            printf(" %3d  ",cost[i][j]);
          }
        printf("\n");
      }
  if(BF(cost,k,ed))
  {
    printf("\n\tNot a negative weight cycle\n");
  }
  else
    {
      printf("\n\tA negative cycle of weight exists. \n");
    }
  return 0;
}
```

Output

```
        A   B   C   D   E
    =========================
    A | 0   2   1   0   0
    B | 0   0   0   3   0
    C | 0  -2   0   2   3
    D | 0  -1   0   0   4
    E | 0   0   0   0   0

        Source Vertex A -> cost =  0 Parent Vertex = A
        Source Vertex B -> cost = -1 Parent Vertex = C
        Source Vertex C -> cost =  1 Parent Vertex = A
        Source Vertex D -> cost =  2 Parent Vertex = B
        Source Vertex E -> cost =  4 Parent Vertex = C
        Not a negative weight cycle
```

NP-Hard (Non-deterministic Polynomial Hard):

- **Definition**: A problem is NP-hard if any problem in NP can be transformed into it in polynomial time. This means that NP-hard problems are at least as hard as any NP-problem, and may even be harder. Examples of NP-hard problems include circuit-satisfactory and halting problems.
- **Key Characteristics**:
1. It may or may not belong to NP (i.e., it is not required to have a solution that can be verified in polynomial time).
2. NP-Hard problems are not necessarily decision problems; they can be optimization problems.
3. Example: The **Halting Problem** is NP-Hard but not in NP.

NP-Complete:

- **Definition**: A problem is NP-complete if it is both in NP and NP-hard. NP-complete problems are the most difficult problems in NP. Examples of NP-complete problems include determining the Hamiltonian cycle in a graph and determining the
- **Key Characteristics**:
1. A problem is in NP if its solution can be verified in polynomial time.
2. Being NP-Hard means it is as hard as the hardest problems in NP.
3. Solving an NP-Complete problem efficiently (in polynomial time) would mean all NP problems can also be solved efficiently.
4. Example: **Traveling Salesman Problem** (decision version), **3-SAT Problem**.

Summary:

- All NP-Complete problems are NP-Hard, but not all NP-Hard problems are NP-Complete.
- NP-Hard includes problems outside NP, while NP-Complete is a subset of NP.

Tavelling Salesman Problem Algorithm

The Traveling Salesman Problem (TSP) is a well-known optimization challenge in the field of operations research. It is also one of the most extensively studied problems in this domain. The TSP was first explored in the 1930s by a group of applied mathematicians.

The problem involves a scenario where a salesperson must travel to nnn cities, visiting each city exactly once before returning to the starting location. While the order in which the cities are visited is not predetermined, the objective is to minimize the total travel distance or time. The problem can be modeled as a network, where the cities are represented as nodes connected by edges, with each edge assigned a weight corresponding to the travel time or distance between the two cities.

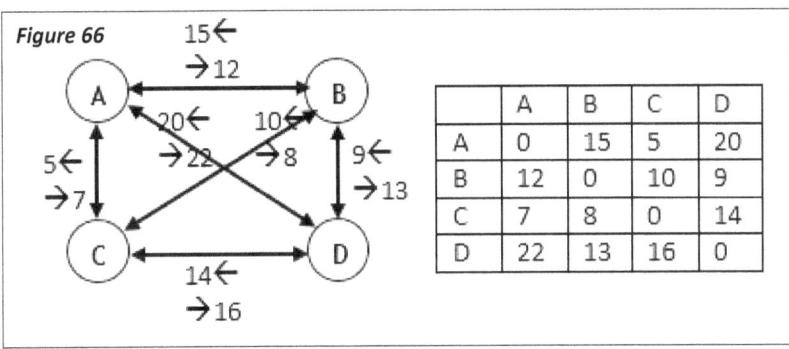

Beginning with a bottom-to-top approach, starting from the last node (also assuming the starting point), **Figure 66** depicts all possible routes the salesman can take. The minimal time is determined using the provided time as it moves up in all possible directions. The minimum time is then found and taken into consideration. Refer to the **Figure 67**.

DA	22
CA	7
BA	12
CDA	14 + 22 =36
DCA	16 + 7 = 23
BDA	8 + 22 = 30
DBA	13 + 12 =25
BCA	10 + 7 = 17

CBA	8 + 12 = 20
BCDA BDCA	MIN(10+36,8+23)=31
CBDA CDBA	MIN(8+30,, 14+25) =38
DBCA DCBA	MIN(13+17,16+20)=30
ABCDA, ABDCA, ACBDA, ACDBA, ADBCA, ADCBA	MIN(31+15,,5+38,30+20)=43

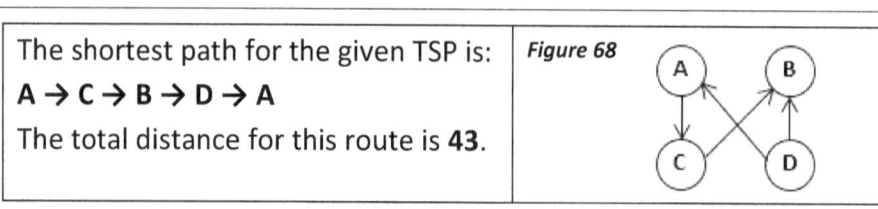

Figure 67

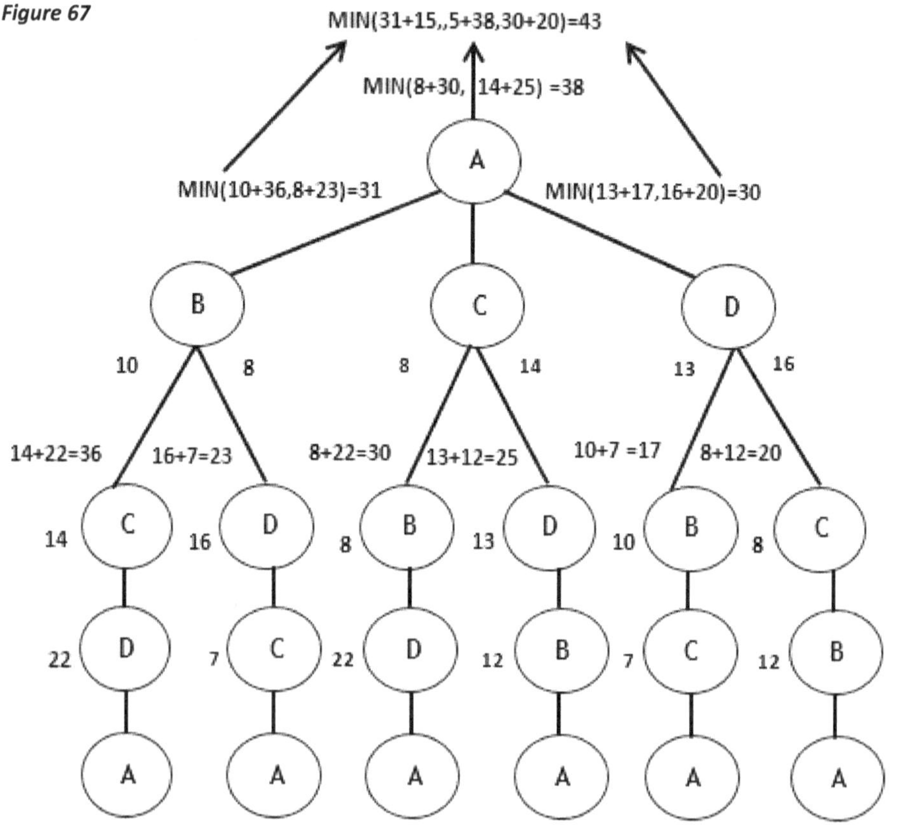

MIN(31+15,,5+38,30+20)=43

MIN(8+30, 14+25) =38

MIN(10+36,8+23)=31   A   MIN(13+17,16+20)=30

B   C   D

10   8   8   14   13   16

14+22=36 / 16+7=23   8+22=30 / 13+12=25   10+7 =17 / 8+12=20

14 C   16 D   8 B   13 D   10 B   8 C

22 D   7 C   22 D   12 B   7 C   12 B

A   A   A   A   A   A

The shortest path for the given TSP is: **A → C → B → D → A** The total distance for this route is **43**.	*Figure 68*

Prog-50. Tavelling Salesman Problem Algorithm

```c
#include<stdio.h>
#define N 4
int
Data[4][4]={{0,15,5,20},{12,0,10,8},{7,8,0,14},{22,13,16,0}},Visited[10],n=4,cost=0;
  void Disp()
   {
       int i,j;
       printf("\t\nThe Cost Matrix:\n   ");
       for(i=0;i<N;i++)
         printf("   %c",(char)(65+i));
       printf("\n ====================================\n");

       for(i=0;i<N;i++)
         {
         printf(" %c  |",(char)(65+i));
           for( j=0;j < N;j++)
             {
                printf("%3d ",Data[i][j]);
             }
           printf("\n");
           Visited[i]=0;
         }

   }
  void minimumcost(int Cities)
    {
      int i,nc;
      Visited[Cities]=1;
      printf("%c->",(char)(Cities+1+64));
      nc=smallest(Cities);
      if(nc==999)
        {
          nc=0;
          printf("%c",(char)(nc+1+64));
          cost+=Data[Cities][nc];
          return;
        }
      minimumcost(nc);
    }
int smallest(int c)
    {
      int i,ct=999;
```

```
    int minimum=999,min;
    for(i=0;i < N;i++)
      {
        if((Data[c][i]!=0)&&(Visited[i]==0))
          {
            if(Data[c][i]+Data[i][c] < minimum)
              {
                minimum=Data[i][0]+Data[c][i];
                min=Data[c][i];
                ct=i;
              }
          }
      }
    if(minimum!=999)
      {
        cost+=min;
      }
    return ct;
  }
int main()
  {
    Disp();
    printf("\n\nThe Most Economical Path is: \n");
    minimumcost(0); //starting vertex
    printf("\n\nMinimum cost is %d\n ",cost);
    return 0;
  }
```

Output

The Cost Matrix:
```
    A  B  C  D
  =================
A | 0 15  5 20
B | 12 0 10  8
C | 7  8  0 14
D | 22 13 16  0
```

The Most Economical Path is:
A->C->B->D->A

Minimum cost is 43

0/1 Knapsack Algorithm

The Fractional Knapsack problem has already been discussed under the greedy algorithm. For an optimal solution to the Fractional Knapsack problem, the given sack can be filled with fractions of items. However, in the 0/1 Knapsack problem, items can only be included or excluded as a whole. This means that items cannot be broken into smaller parts, you either take the entire item or leave it. This characteristic is the reason behind calling it the 0/1 Knapsack problem.

Assume the Weight Limit W = 5, there are four items, the weights and the profits are given in Table-T[][]:

Item i	1	2	3	4
Weight[i]	3	2	4	1
Profit[i]	10	2	6	4

item = 4

Fill the first column w with 0 weight 0 with items 0

T[w]	w=0	1	2	3	4	5
i=0	0	0	0	0	0	0
1	0					
2	0					
3	0					
4	0					

Apply the the following formula to fill remaining cell or Table t[][] to find the maximum profit with given weight limits.

```
if wt[i]>w then
        T[I,w]=T[i-1,w]
else
        wt[i]<=w then
                T[i,w]=max(T[i-1,w],p[i]+T[i-1,w-wt[i]])
        i = 1 w = 1
                fill table T[1,1] wt[i]> w , 3>1 yes T[I,w]=T[i-1,w]
        w=2
                wt[i]> w , 3>2 yes T[I,w]=T[i-1,w]
        w=3
                wt[i]> w , 3>3 no T[i,w]=max(T[i-1,w],p[i]+T[i-1,w-wt[i]])
                T[I,w] =max(0,10+0) =10
        w=4
```

```
                    wt[i]> w , 3>4 no
                    T[i,w]=max(T[i-1,w],p[i]+T[i-1,w-wt[i]])
        w=5
                    wt[i]> w , 3>5 no
                    T[i,w]=max(T[i-1,w],p[i]+T[i-1,w-wt[i]])
```

Fill remaining table with same formula when i=2 and so on

T[w]	W=0	1	2	3	4	5
i=0	0	0	0	0	0	0
1	0	0	0	10	10	10
2	0					
3	0					
4	0					

After all iteration the table will look like.

T[w]	W=0	1	2	3	4	5
i=0	0	0	0	0	0	0
1	0	0	0	10	10	10
2	0	0	2	10	10	12
3	0	0	2	10	10	12
4	0	4	4	10	14	14

Item i	1	2	3	4
Weight	3	2	4	1
Profit	10	2	6	4

Maximum Value (Last Row and Last Column) = 14

To mark the weight from the table, use folloing algorithm :

i=item w = W

T[I,w]!=T[1-1,w] Mark the wt[i] and set the value of w=w-wt[i]

Move above, repeat the above algorithm until by decreasing i and w>0,

Above calculation will give the following cell, thos are ticked. Maximum weight in the sack is = 4 and Profit =14.

Item i	1✓	2	3	4✓
Weight	3	2	4	1
Profit	10	2	6	4

Prog-51. 0/1 Knapsack (Dynamic Programming)

```c
#include<stdio.h>
  int i,j;
  int max(int a, int b)
   {
      return (a > b)? a : b;
   }
  int knapsack(int W, int w[], int P[], int item)
    {
      if (item == 0 || W == 0)
        {
           return 0;
        }
      if (w[item-1] > W) //Check the weight in table and Total Weight(W)
        {
          return knapsack(W, w, P, item-1);
        }
      else
        {
           return max( P[item-1] + knapsack(W-w[item-1], w, P, item-1),
knapsack(W, w, P, item-1) );
        }
    }

  int main()
    {
      int w[] = {3,2,4,1};
      int P[] = {10, 2, 6, 4};
      int  W = 5;
      int item = 4;
      int Max;
      printf("\n\t Data Table: \n");
      printf("\n\tItem\t");
      for (i = 0; i < item; i++)
        {
          printf("%3d ",i+1);
        }
```

```
printf("\n\tWeight\t");
for (i = 0; i < item; i++)
  {
    printf("%3d ",w[i]);
  }
printf("\n\tProfit\t");
for (i = 0; i < item; i++)
  {
    printf("%3d ",P[i]);
  }
printf("\n");
Max = knapsack(W, w, P, item);
printf("\n\tMaximum profit = %d", Max);
return 0;
}
```

Output

Data Table:

```
Item    1 2 3 4
Weight  3 2 4 1
Profit  10 2 6 4
```

Maximum profit = 14

Branch and Bound Algorithm

Branch and Bound is an organized method for solving optimization problems. It is a useful optimization technique when the greedy algorithm and dynamic programming fall short. However, this algorithm is slower compared to the other two.

Branch and Bound to solve the 0/1 Knapsack problem.

The Fractional Knapsack with the Greedy Algorithm and the 0/1 Knapsack with Dynamic Programming have already been covered in the previous topics. Here is an example of using the Branch and Bound approach to solve the 0/1 Knapsack problem. The LC (Least Cost) method will be utilized. The data table will include the number of items (n), their weights (w), and their respective profits (p), similar to dynamic programming.

Item	1	2	3	4
Profit	10	10	12	18
Weight	2	4	6	9

Upper Bound UB = ΣProfit[i] <=W

Cost = ΣProfit[i](included Fraction of Profit[i])

As it is discussed that in 0/1 Knapsack no fraction is considered, so, in final consideration, no profit fraction will be considered. In 0/1 Knapsack, it must be 0 or 1.

Total Items n = 4   Total Weight (W) = 15

Initial UB = ∝

Upper Bound	Cost
10 + 10 + 12 =32 2 4 6	10+10+12 + 6 =38 2 4 6 18/9*3
2+4+6=12 ΣProfit[i] <=W	2+4+6=12<15 = 15=12, needed 3. Fraction of profit of fourth item will be calculated as 18/9*3 = 6. ΣProfit[i](included Fraction of Profit[i])
To convert this into a minimization problem by taking negative of the given values <div align="center">UB = ∝ = -32</div><div align="center">COST = -38</div>	

The algorithm is followed with following pattern:

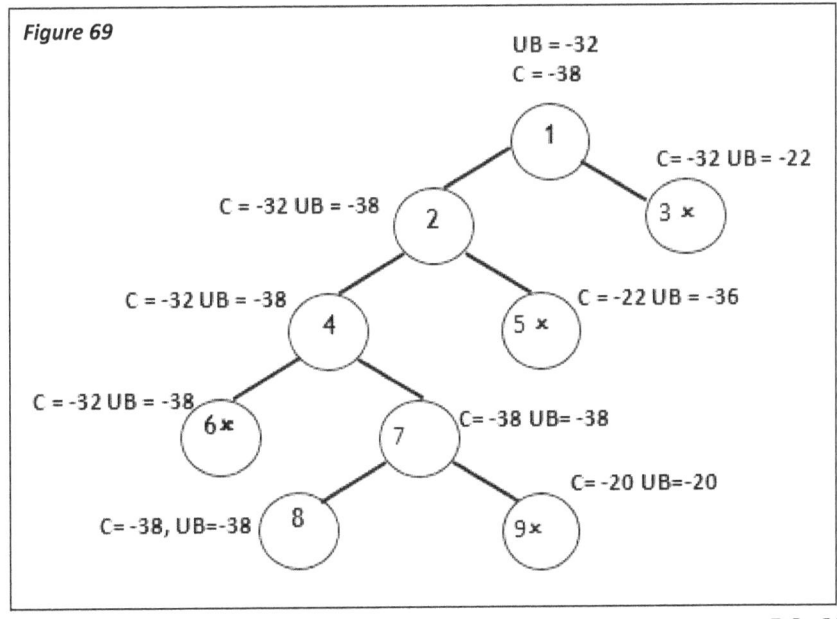

Figure 69

The steps are as it is:.

Problem Statement: Given the items in above table:

Weight Capacity (W): Assume W for this example.

Steps in the Branch and Bound Approach:
1. **Initialization**:
    - Sort items by **profit-to-weight ratio** (Pi/Wi):
    - Item 1: 10/2=5
    - Item 2: 10/4=2.5
    - Item 3: 12/6=2

    Item 4: 18/9=2

After sorting, the order is **Item 1, Item 2, Item 3, Item 4**.
2. **Branching:**
    - Represent the solution space as a tree. At each node, decide whether to include (1) or exclude (0) the current item.
3. **Bounding:**
    - Use a bounding function to calculate the **upper bound** of profit at each node. This helps prune branches that cannot lead to an optimal solution.
    - Upper Bound Calculation:
    - Bound=Profit of included items + Profit of fractions of remaining items (if possible).
4. **LC (Least Cost) Search**:
    - Use a priority queue to explore nodes with the highest bound first (most promising nodes).

Example Walkthrough:

Initial Node:

- Start with no items included (x1,x2,x3,x4=0x1,x2,x3,x4=0).
- **Weight = 0, Profit = 0**.
- Compute the upper bound:
- Bound=0+10+10+12+18=50..

Branch 1 (Include Item 1):
　　Include Item 1 (x1=1).
　　Weight = 2, Profit = 10.
　　Compute the bound:
　　Bound=10+10+12+18=50.
Branch 2 (Exclude Item 1):
　　Exclude Item 1 (x1=0x1=0).
　　Weight = 0, Profit = 0.
Bound = 50 (same as initial since no items are included).Continue Exploring:

Repeat this process by including/excluding subsequent items while computing the bound for each branch. Use the bound to prune branches that exceed the capacity or cannot surpass the current maximum profit.

Optimal Solution:

Using Branch and Bound with W=15:

- Optimal selection: Include Items 1, 2, and 4.
- Weight = 2 + 4 + 9 = 15.
- Profit = 10 + 10 + 18 = 38.

Prog-52. 0/1 Knapsack (Branch and Bound).

```
//0/1 Knapsac (Branch and Bound)
#include <string.h>
#include <stdio.h>
#include <stdlib.h>
#define N 4

int TWeight = 0;
int minPr = 0;
//Add Wt, Profit
void AddedWP (int P[],int W[],int included[N], int *wt, int *profit)
{
  int i, Tw = 0, Tprofit = 0;
  for (i = 0; i < N; ++i) {
    if (included[i]) {
      Tw += W[i];
      Tprofit += P[i];
    }
  }
}
```

```c
    *wt = Tw;
    *profit = Tprofit;
}

    void Disp (int P[],int W[],int included[N])
      {
        int i,Tprofit = 0;
        printf("\tAdded in the Sack = [ ");
        for (i = 0; i < N; ++i)
          {
            if (included[i])
              {
                  printf("%d ", W[i]);
                  Tprofit += P[i];
              }
          }
        printf("]; Total  = %d\n", Tprofit);
}
//Calculating the UB/Cost Checking
    void KnapsackBB (int P[],int W[],int included[N], int v)
      {
        int ChkWt, Chkval;
        AddedWP(P,W,included, &ChkWt, &Chkval);
        if (ChkWt <= TWeight)
          {
            if (Chkval > minPr)
            {
                Disp(P,W,included);
                minPr = Chkval;
            }
          }
        if (v == N || ChkWt >= TWeight)
          {
            return;
          }
        int x = W[v];
        int Taken[N], ignore[N];
        memcpy(Taken, included, sizeof(Taken));
        memcpy(ignore, included, sizeof(ignore));
        Taken[v] = 1;
        ignore[v] = 0;
        KnapsackBB(P,W,Taken, v+1);
        KnapsackBB(P,W,ignore, v+1);
```

```
        }
int main() //Main
  {
    int Pr[N]={10,10,12,18};
    int Wt[N]={2,4,6,9};
    int included[N], i;
    printf("\n\t  The Data Table\n\tItem\tWeight\tProfit\n\t");
    for (i = 0; i < N; ++i)
      {
        printf("%3d\t%3d\t%3d\n\t",i+1,Wt[i],Pr[i]);
        included[i] = 0;
      }
    printf("\n");
    TWeight=15;
    KnapsackBB(Pr,Wt,included, 0);
    return 0;
  }
```

Output

```
        The Data Table
    Item   Weight  Profit
     1       2       10
     2       4       10
     3       6       12
     4       9       18

    Added in the Sack = [ 2 ]; Total      = 10
    Added in the Sack = [ 2 4 ]; Total    = 20
    Added in the Sack = [ 2 4 6 ]; Total  = 32
    Added in the Sack = [ 2 4 9 ]; Total  = 38
```

Backtracking

Backtracking is an algorithmic strategy designed to uncover every possible solution to a problem using brute force. It involves constructing a list of potential solutions incrementally, piece by piece. Solutions that fail to meet the problem's constraints are discarded. Backtracking is a general technique for recursively exploring and testing all possible answers to a problem.

Backtracking: It addresses problems that are not related to optimization. Branch and Bound methods are exclusively used for optimization problems. Some searches are optimized using specific techniques, but these are generally applied to highly complex problems. Depth-First Search (DFS) is used in backtracking. In contrast, Branch and Bound typically relies on Breadth-First Search (BFS).

Key Characteristics of Backtracking:

1. **Exploratory Approach:** The algorithm systematically tests all possible solutions, ensuring that every potential path is explored.

2. **Early Stopping:** If a path is found to be invalid or unproductive, the algorithm abandons it immediately (backtracks) and tries a different option.

3. **Step-by-Step Solution Building:** Solutions are constructed incrementally, with each decision informed by previous choices.

Common Applications of Backtracking:

- **Solving puzzles** (e.g., Sudoku, N-Queens problem)
- **Generating permutations and combinations**
- **Pathfinding** (e.g., maze-solving)
- **Graph coloring**
- **Subset sum problems**

N-Queen

Backtracking can be used to solve N-Queens problems, for example. The N-Queens problem is provided by the following rules:

Place a queen in the first legitimate position (column) of each row before moving on to the next row.

1. One goes back to the previous row and tries the next position if there isn't a valid position.

2. If a queen can be correctly positioned on the last row, a solution has been found.

3. In order to discover the answer, go back.

4. The N-Queens Problem: Backtracking with a Stack.

State Space Tree for 4 - Queens

Figure 70

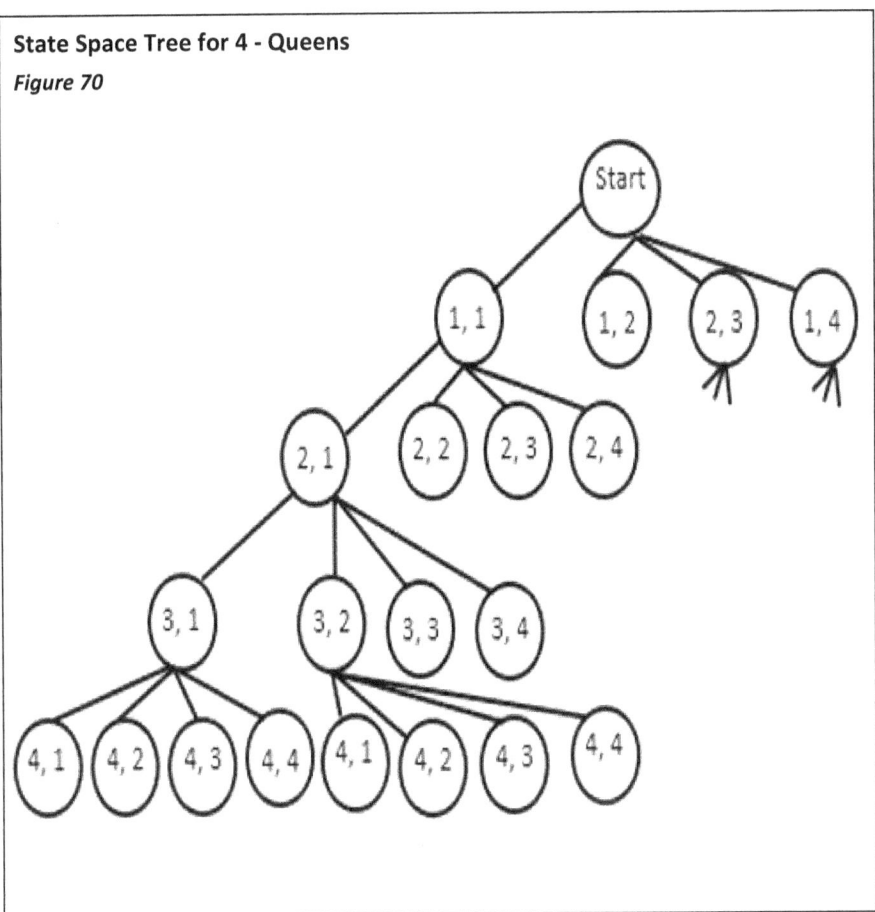

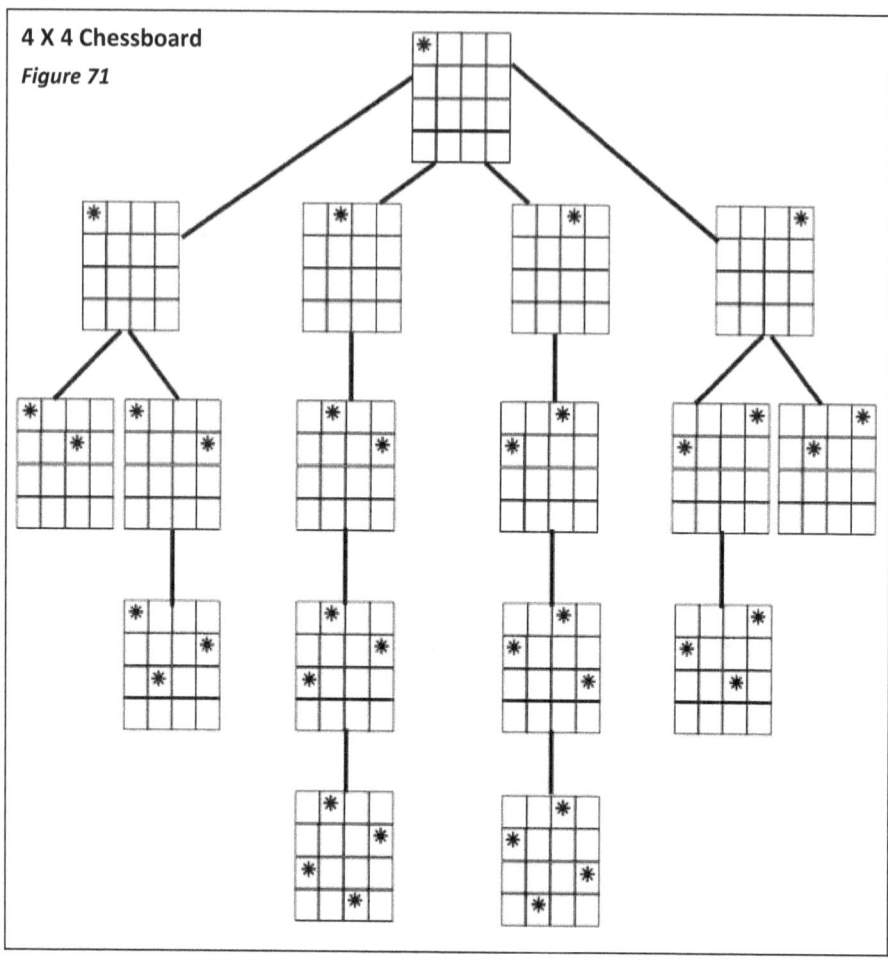

4 X 4 Chessboard

Figure 71

Prog-53. N-Queens

```
#include<stdio.h>
#include<math.h>

  int term=0;

  void DispBoard(int n,int CB[])
    {
      int i,j;
      printf("\n\n\tSol. No . %d:\n\t",++term);
    for(i=1;i<=n;++i)
        {
        printf("\t%d",i);
        }
```

```c
    for(i=1;i<=n;++i)
        {
        printf("\n\n\t%d",i);
        for(j=1;j<=n;++j)
          {
            if(CB[i]==j)
              {
                  printf("\tQ");
              }
            else
              {
                  printf("\t. ");
              }
          }
        }
    }
//Checking Row/Colum/Diagonal Clashing
    int place(int R,int C,int CB[])
      {
        int i;
        for(i=1;i<=R-1;++i)
          {
          if(CB[i]==C)
            {
              return 0;
            }
          else
            {
              if(abs(CB[i]-C)==abs(i-R))
                {
                    return 0;
                }
            }
          }
        return 1;
      }
    void Nqueen(int R,int n,int CB[])
      {
        int C;
        for(C=1;C<=n;++C)
          {
          if(place(R,C,CB))
```

```c
        {
          CB[R]=C;
          if(R==n)
              {
                DispBoard(n,CB);
              }
        else
          {
            Nqueen(R+1,n,CB);
          }
        }
        }
      }
    }
  int main()
    {
      int Q,i,j;
      int CB[20];
      printf("\n\tNumber of Queens: ");
      scanf("%d",&Q);
      printf("\n\tOn the chessboard, the N-Queen problem provides ");
      printf("\n\tmany more possibilities than just one, only when the input is > =
4. : ");
      printf("\n\n\tN Queens Soving Using Backtracking for %d x %d board :
",Q,Q);
      Nqueen(1,Q,CB);
      return 0;
    }
```

Output

Number of Queens: 4
On the chessboard, the N-Queen problem provides
many more possibilities than just one, only when the input is > = 4. :
N Queens Soving Using Backtracking for 4 x 4 board :

SOL - 1

	1	2	3	4
1	-	Q	-	-
2	-	-	-	Q
3	Q	-	-	-
4	-	-	Q	-

SOL – 2

	1	2	3	4
1	-	-	Q	-
2	Q	-	-	-
3	-	-	-	Q
4	-	Q	-	-

Complexity Cheatsheet:

Search	Worst Case	Best Case	
Linear Search	O(n)	O(1)	
Binary Search	O(log 2 N)	O(1)	
Interpolation Search	O(log2(log2 n))	O(1)	

Sort			
	Best	Average	Worst
Bubble sort	$O(n)$	$O(n^2)$	$O(n^2)$
Insertion sort	$O(n)$	$O(n^2)$	$O(n^2)$
Selection sort	$O(n^2)$	$O(n^2)$	$O(n^2)$
Quick sort	$O(n \log(n))$	$O(n \log(n))$	$O(n^2)$
Merge sort	$O(n \log(n))$	$O(n \log(n))$	$O(n \log(n))$
Heap sort	$O(n \log(n))$	$O(n \log(n))$	$O(n \log(n))$
Radix Sort	$\Omega(nk)$	$\theta(nk)$	$O(nk)$

Binary Tree			
Process	Worst Case	Average Case	Best Case
Insert	O(N)	$O(N^{0.5})$	O(logN)
Search	O(N)	$O(N^{0.5})$	O(1)
Delete	O(N)	$O(N^{0.5})$	O(logN)

Graph		
Algorithm	Time Complexity	
BFS	O(V + E)	
DFS	O(V + E)	
Kruskal	O(E log V)	
Prims	(|E| log |V|)	
Dijkstra's	O(|E| log |V|)	
Fractional Knapsack	O(NlogN)	
Bellman-Ford	O(|E| · |V|)	
Flyod-Warshall	O(|V|^3)	
Travelling Salesman	Greedy : O(N^2LogN)	DP: O(N^22^N)
0/1 Knapsack	O(N*W)	

About Author (*BeeeBeees*)

After two decades of working across various IT disciplines, I began to feel a sense of ennui. During my career, I contributed to numerous website and software development projects. However, exhaustion led me to seek a new direction, ultimately stepping away and making slow progress on a project that had initially sparked great enthusiasm. My true passion, academia, holds a special place in my heart. This book, primarily designed for engineering students, focuses on "Data Structures."

As both an educator and a computer programmer, I approach classes with a mindset of learning rather than just teaching. While my primary goal is to teach and share knowledge.

 beeebose@gmail.com

https://x.com/BeeeBeees

 http://www.facebook.com/beeesbose

https://www.instagram.com/beeesbose/

https://www.linkedin.com/in/beee-beees-13910025b/

 http://beeebeees.blogspot.com/
http://open-sesames.blogspot.com/

www.ingramcontent.com/pod-product-compliance
Lightning Source LLC
Chambersburg PA
CBHW072356290526
45794CB00001B/88